D1263853

THE PRICE OF SILVER

The Story of the
Sunshine Silver Mine Disaster

JAMES M. DAY

ISBN 1-893157-21-0
ISBN 13 digit 978-1-893157-21-7

Published by

Bridger House Publishers

P.O. Box 2208, Carson City, NV 89702, USA

1-800-729-4131

Cover Design / Layout: therighttype.com

Cover photo credit: Shauna Hillman, 2001
Sunshine Mine Memorial statue created by Kenneth Lonn, 1974

Printed in the United States of America
10 9 8 7 6 5 4 3 2 1

~~~

To the miners who in the past and future
toil underground for our minerals
and the career employees of the
Mine Safety and Health Administration
who are dedicated to their safety.

~~~

TABLE OF CONTENTS

Figures

Maps

Sidebars

Appendix

PREFACE

I should have written this account thirty years ago. The 1972 Sunshine Mine fire in Kellogg, Idaho, resulted in the deaths of ninety-one miners and became a pivotal point in improving mine health and safety. It was also a turning point in my life and ingrained the suffering of the victims' families in my memory forever. Writing the story of a mine disaster forces one to live through it minute-by-minute.

I was assigned to conduct a public hearing to determine the cause of the disaster, whether the Sunshine Mine was in compliance with the safety standards under the Federal Metal and Nonmetallic Mine Safety Act of 1966, and what action should be taken to prevent similar disasters in the future. It was the second worst non-coal mine disaster in United States history. Congress and the mining unions were justifiably dissatisfied with the weak 1966 Act and the Interior Department's Bureau of Mines enforcement of the 1966 Act and the pervasive Federal Coal Mine Health and Safety Act of 1969. A clamor arose for the transfer of mine health and safety enforcement to the Department of Labor that was administering the recently enacted Occupational Safety and Health Act of 1970.

A Democrat-controlled Congress faulted President Richard Nixon's Republican administration, notwithstanding the 1966 Act was passed when the Democrats controlled Congress during Lyndon Johnson's Democrat administration. The meager excuse for the pathetic 1966 Act was that non-coal mines were safer than coal mines with their highly flammable and explosive coal dust and methane gas. The conventional misinformation was that there was nothing to burn in a "hard rock" mine was proven wrong. The Sunshine Mine, like many large non-coal mines, had millions of board feet of old timber underground.

The idea of an independent public hearing into the cause of a mine disaster was a new concept. Secretary of the Interior Rogers C.B. Morton and Assistant Secretary for Mineral Resources Hollis M. Dole insisted someone independent of the Bureau of Mines conduct the hearing to avoid the stigma of the Bureau's report on the disaster being labeled a "whitewash." Neither trusted the Bureau's Director and his deputy assigned to conduct the Bureau's investigation. Dole put it simply: "The Bureau cannot be permitted to investigate itself and determine if it is properly enforcing the law." As Director of the Office of Hearings and Appeals (OHA) charged with independently adjudicating the Department's administrative hearings and appeals, I was selected to hold the hearing and write my findings, including a review of the Bureau's enforcement. Inside the Department I had the autonomy by virtue of reporting directly to the Secretary. While such authority proved the OHA's independence within the Department, I was a political appointee and could be viewed with a jaundiced eye by outsiders.

Congress scheduled oversight hearings to take place before and after my hearings while the mine was still on fire. The Congressional hearings ended while the mine was still burning. I recessed my hearing until after the fire had been extinguished and the Bureau completed its investigation and issued a final report. Nevertheless, there was pressure to issue an interim report, which was well-received by the press and labor unions and showed there would be no whitewash. The *Washington Post* quoted part of my summary:

> ". . . it is evident that a large number of deaths and the magnitude of the disaster are a direct result of inadequate safety standards, industry-wide poor safety practices, the lack of training of miners in the event of a disaster... Further, not only are some standards inadequate, but have been diluted and rendered ineffective by interpretation."

One of my recommendations was left unwritten, but made verbally to Secretary Morton and Assistant Secretary Dole. I reported that the Bureau had a built-in conflict of interest in its twofold responsibility to promote the mining industry and enforce mine health and safety. I confirmed what they already knew. Dole's deputy, John B. Rigg, Sr., was charged with the responsibility of separating the divisions and selecting a head of the new agency. The move caused a battle over the appointment of the head of the new agency, the Mine Enforcement and Safety Administration (MESA). The Democrats demanded it be headed by a labor official and the Republican Nixon administration insisted appointing a mining industry executive. After a stalemate of eight months, I was named MESA Administrator.

Accepting the appointment presented an enigma. As the head of an agency managed by the career civil servants charged with mine safety enforcement during the disaster, my report could be labeled a "coverup." And as a lawyer and political outsider managing an organization consisting of mining engineers and inspectors, who were former miners, it could prove difficult to gain their loyalty, if I criticized their enforcement. It was decided that the report could wait until I left MESA. The two-year delay was warranted. I gained the confidence of the MESA employees and MESA eventually evolved into an effective enforcement agency as proven by lower fatality and injury rates, although not without many bumps in the road. Within weeks, I learned that it was impossible to please both industry and labor. It was like warding off two pit bulls who could never be satisfied with anyone's enforcement policies. Things have not changed in over three decades.

After thirty-odd years, I realized that my 171-page report, like most government reports, contained little cognizance of politics or people. Nor did it include the difficulties promulgating safety regulations opposed by a powerful mining industry lobby claiming they were too stringent and unions believing they were too weak. I also failed to adequately cover the actions of the individuals and underlying factors that contributed to the deaths of ninety-one miners or the heroic actions of the men who helped save lives. Such omissions had to be remedied, if for no other reason than to explain how and why men died or risked their lives to save their fellow miners and record it for their families and descendants. It will also permit me to empty four file drawers of documents from my study that have been calling me to tell the story for three decades.

Hopefully, the years of experience added a scintilla of wisdom, mellowness, and independence. The biggest advantage was the advent of computers to establish the timing of events that caused conjecture and disagreement with the Bureau's report by industry, labor, and me. For whatever reason, I admit to changing parts of my analysis in my official report.

MESA was transferred to the Department of Labor in 1977 and its name was changed to the Mine Safety and Health Administration. It is the most effective mine health and safety agency in the world. In 2003 at the Black Wolf coal mine in Que Creek, Pennsylvania, the mine was inundated with 50 million gallons of water. After being trapped 240 feet below the surface for three days, nine miners were rescued in a wire cage 36 inches in diameter and eight and one-half feet in length. The press heralded the rescue as a miracle. But such a capsule was first used at the Sunshine Mine on May 9, 1972, by Bureau and Sunshine Mine volunteers to rescue two miners trapped 4,800 feet below the surface for eight days.

This is not only the story of miners, but of the federal mining engineers and inspectors whose job is to save miners' lives. It also involves the press, the miners' families, politicians, the mining industry… and the price of silver.

Describing a hard rock mine to anyone who has not ridden a rattling cage thousands of feet down into the black depths of a mine, walked the winding miles of levels or climbed 200 feet up the raises is like depicting an alien world. To afford an understanding of the size of the mine and distances, they are reported according to Sunshine maps or as paced by the author while facing the blasts of thousands of cubic feet a minute of cold grimy air on the levels or in the ninety-plus-degree stopes as would a miner. When known, precise times are given to set the time frames of the many events occurring in various locations throughout the mine simultaneously. Time is of the essence during a mine disaster because of the limited short life of self-rescuers to protect the miners from deadly carbon monoxide before the fire cuts off all avenues of escape.

Technical language was avoided to the extent feasible to make descriptions readable for those not familiar with mining terminology, but common mining terms had to be used to maintain credibility and the essence of a miner's underground world. (A Glossary is provided.) For readers who have never ventured in a deep hard rock mine, picture your viewpoint from the light of a miner's cap lamp. Without the single light it is blacker than a starless night except in the workshops and shaft stations. The walls (ribs), back (roof), and sill (floor) are rock and you are several thousand feet below the surface. Each numbered level denotes the depth in feet. Be careful of the ribs and back, they can fall and crush you under the pressure of millions of tons of rock above. When entering a drift (tunnel), look for the ways out. In the Sunshine Mine, there was only one effective escape route during a fire. Today hard rock mines are required to have two escapeways to the surface. *The second escapeway is part of the Price of Silver paid for by the Sunshine Mine miners.*

James M. Day
Arlington, Virginia
2007

PART ONE

_____ **SILVER**

CHAPTER 1

GOLD'S POOR STEPSISTER

History and Politics

In March 2006, the price of silver hit over $10.00 a troy ounce for the first time in twenty-two years. The price of gold was around $550. A gold to silver price ratio of 55 to 1 is a far cry from William Jennings Bryan's historic "Cross of Gold" speech at the Democratic national convention in 1896 and campaign pledge: "We will answer their demand for a gold standard by saying to them: You shall not press down upon the brow of labor this crown of thorns, you shall not crucify mankind upon a cross of gold." Bryan lost the election and his quest for free and unlimited coinage of silver and a gold to silver ratio of 16 to 1.

Silver was first mined for jewelry and ornaments during the fourth millennium B.C. in Cappadocia, now part of Turkey. Between 500 and 200 B.C., the Greeks used silver in preference to gold because of is economic and utilitarian value. In 269 B.C., Rome adopted silver as part of its monetary system. Silver was an ideal because of its intrinsic value and malleability to mint coins. Coinage classes became distinct: gold for governments, royalty, and the extremely wealthy; silver for merchants and trade; and copper, brass, and bronze for ordinary citizens. Silver was weighed in ingots or "pieces of silver." Christ was betrayed for thirty pieces of silver. Early monetary silver units included the Phoenician talent, Hebrew shekel, and English pound sterling. Today sterling silver is 92.5 percent silver.

Spain's vast silver discoveries in Mexico, Bolivia, and Peru gave it control over the world's silver in the sixteenth century that lasted until its colonies revolted in 1820. The Spanish dollar became the basis of currency in the Americas, including the fledgling United States. Readers of Robert Louis Stevenson's *Treasure Island* will recall the parrot on Long John Silver's shoulder squawking: "Pieces of eight." A Spanish dollar or piece of eight was valued at eight reals and often cut in half (four reals, a half-dollar or four bits) and quarters (two reals, a quarter-dollar or two bits). Americans still refer to a quarter as "two bits."

The revolt of the Spanish colonies and Spain's loss of its silver mines caused a temporary world silver shortage. The famous Comstock Lode in the Sierra Nevada mountains in the late 1850s blessed the United States with its first major silver source. Until 1900, the United States was the world's largest silver producer. But after the reopening of the mines in South America and Mexico and discoveries around the world there was never a world shortage of silver.

The United States first coined silver in 1794 under the Coinage Act of April 2, 1792, which also dictated minting copper half cents and cents and nickel five-cent pieces, hence its name. Half dimes, dimes, quarters, half dollars, and dollars were minted according to the silver content. Silver dollars were required to contain 416 grains of silver and be .8924 fine.[1] The minting of silver dollars ended in 1804 due to the high price of silver and use of paper tender. Between 1801 and 1804, less than 200,000 silver dollars were minted. Silver dollars returned in 1840 as a result of silver discoveries in the West and ceased in 1873, except for "Trade Dollars" minted with 420 grains until 1885 for use in the Orient to compete with foreign trade silver currencies.

The demand for cheap money and the remonetization of silver became a major political issue. The Bland-Allison Act of 1878 required the minting of silver dollars of 412.5 grains and the Secretary of the Treasury to purchase $2 to $4 million worth of silver monthly. Under pressure of the powerful silver lobby and Free Silver movement, the Sherman Silver Purchase Act of 1893 was passed, requiring the Treasury to purchase 4.5 million ounces of silver every

---

1 Fine or fineness refers to the proportion of pure silver in the alloy. In 1837 the weight was changed to 412.5 grains and a fineness of .900 (90%).

month. In the meantime, Europe was gradually adopting a gold standard. By 1916, only China remained on the silver standard. The United States lobbied the world trading powers to accept a silver standard without success. During the Depression, Congress remonetized silver in 1934 and mandated the Treasury to purchase silver until it represented one-fourth of the nation's bullion reserve and cease minting silver dollars in 1935.

During the 1930s science began to discover that silver had uses as an industrial metal. Long used for silverware, jewelry, and in dentistry, it found a demand by the chemical industry. Until recently, photography accounted for between 35 to 50 percent of the silver demand, but the advent of digital photography drastically lowered the use. The modern electronics and computer industries are now a major consumer because of silver's excellent thermal and electrical conductivity. The silver industry has had no choice but to look for uses other than coins since the passage of the Coinage Act of 1965, mandating a copper-nickel-clad alloy be used in all coins except the dollar. In 1970 the Coinage Act was amended to require the dollar be made from the alloy for minting the Eisenhower dollar.

Silver is now a mere commodity traded on the New York Mercantile Exchange, like copper, corn, and pork bellies. The United States produces approximately one-eighth of the world's silver, but has one of the highest mining costs because of our more stringent and costly mine health and safety standards . . . which is part of the price of silver.

The Silver Valley

Early prospectors thought only of gold. And they knew gold when they saw it, although greenhorns were often fooled by iron pyrite or "fool's gold." Gold was also easy to look for. All a prospector needed was a pick, shovel, and a pan to wash the tiny flecks of gold from a stream bed. Gold freely disassociates with other elements and can be found loose in nuggets and glimmering in a quartz vein. Silver readily combines with other minerals and is difficult to recognize because of its various colorations and forms. In the Comstock Lode, for years it was a slimy blue muck that stuck to a gold prospector's boots before they discovered it was a silver bonanza. Colorado's biggest silver find was as black as tar. In other areas silver ore might be red from iron or yellow from sulfur. Prospectors looking for gold often passed the silver ores off as worthless unless they had the ore sample assayed.

Gold was first discovered in Idaho in 1860 by an Indian trader on the Nez perce Lapwai Reservation. As usual, the Indian lands were promptly stolen by the white men. The United States Army was sent in to drive the Indians off their lands protected only by easily broken treaties. Several small gold deposits were discovered in Idaho over the next two decades, including placer gold along the tributaries of the Coeur d'Alene River in the Northern Idaho panhandle in 1882. In less than a year the gold rush was over except for a few stubborn prospectors around the town of Murray.

Noah Kellogg, a part-time carpenter and wannabe full-time gold prospector, left one of the greatest and saddest mining legends. In 1885, Kellogg obtained a $17.85 grubstake worth of supplies (roughly $370.00 in 2006) and a jackass from Cooper and Peck, general store owners. One night the jackass wandered off from their camp in Milo Gulch, forcing Kellogg and others to look for it in the morning. The tale was told by a promoter, Jim Wardner, who muscled in on the famous mining claims, in his immodest memoir, *Jim Wardner of Wardner, Idaho, by Himself:*

> Looking across the creek we saw the jack standing upon the side of the hill, and apparently gazing intently across the canyon at some object which attracted his attention. We went up the slope after him, expecting that, as usual, he would give us a hard chase; but he never moved as we approached. His ears were set forward, his eyes fixed upon some object, and he seemed wholly absorbed. Reaching his side, we were astonished to find the jackass standing upon a great outcropping of mineralized vein-matter and looking in apparent amazement at the marvelous ore-shoot across the canyon, which by then, as you now see it, was reflecting the sun's rays like a mirror. We lost no time in making our locations, and where the Jack stood we called the Bunker Hill, and the big chute we named the Sullivan (after a companion prospector).

Swarms of prospectors rushed to the area and named the new nearby town Kellogg. The Bunker Hill and the Sullivan Mines evolved into two of America's richest silver-lead-zinc mines. Thomas A. Rickard, a mining engineer, wrote in *A History of American Mining:* "The talk of a glittering mass of silvery ore sticking out of a mountain-side so brilliantly to mesmerize the ass, and others not the wiser, is pure moonshine." He pointed out that galena ore exposed to the atmosphere is dull in color, a matte black or, if oxidized by iron pyrite, a rusty red. Rickard didn't have to tell housewives that silver tarnishes, loses its brightness, and turns a drab gray and when exposed to air.

Kellogg used up his grubstake supplies and returned to Murray to show his discovery to Cooper and Peck, but they were unimpressed with the gray galena ore. Believing the grubstake agreement was terminated, Kellogg and others returned and perfected their claims. When Cooper and Peck learned of the value, they sued and were awarded a one-forth in the Bunker Hill claim. Kellogg sold his interest in the mines for a pittance to a large mining syndicate. But Kellogg is a hard man to feel sorry for. Another tale is that he became irritated at having to constantly search for his wandering jackass and tied dynamite to its back and drove it off. Later, he heard a distant explosion that told him he never had to search for the jackass again. But that might also be a tall tale.

Mining Claims

Until after the Civil War, prospectors, including California's "Fortyniners," were trespassers on the nation's public lands. It was impossible for the Army to patrol the millions of square miles of public lands to eject the trespassers or force them to pay the Treasury royalties. In 1865, the federal government desperately needed revenue to pay its war debts. This allowed Western mining interests to lobby through Congress the Lode Law of 1866 that opened the public lands to lode mining claims for gold, silver, cinnabar, and copper at $5.00 an acre. The Placer Act of 1870 followed, which allowed the purchase of placer claims at $2.50 an acre. The theory was based on what we call today "trickle-down economics." Gold and other valuable mineral production would increase the value of the public lands for sale to homesteaders and indirectly pay the national debt.

The laws were unusual in that they permitted the rules of the many mining camps to govern the location of the claims if they did not conflict with federal laws. They also had a major impact on the development of the West by recognizing the prior appropriation of water necessary for mining. The first to use the water had the right to take it as long as he didn't waste the precious resource in the arid West. The 1866 and 1870 Acts were succeeded by the General Mining Law of 1872 that permitted claims for "other valuable minerals" by "citizens of the United States and those who have declared their intention to become such." In the wild West everything was wide open to everyone. The General Mining Law of 1872 is still on the books. Except for public lands withdrawn for use, such as National Parks, Wildlife Refuges, and military bases, the open rangelands and National Forests are open to mining claims by purchase at $2.50 or $5.00 an acre . . . certainly something to write your Congressman and Senator and complain about.

Placer claims are limited to 20 acres per individual and 160 acres to an association of persons. The claims are far more generous than the small lots allowed in most mining camps that in some areas were limited to a 100 by 100-foot square. Lode claims followed the general laws of the mining camps, but were extended to a maximum of 1,500 feet in length along the vein or lode and 300 feet on each side of the vein (20.66 acres). The claims added something unique to the English common law of real property that violated the doctrine: "To whomsoever the soil belongs, he also owns to the sky and to the depths," which law professors call the "Heaven to Hell" doctrine. In mining on federal lands, it was extended outside the boundary and called "extralateral rights." The claimant has the exclusive right:

> "to all the surface within their lines of their locations, and of all veins, lodes, and ledges throughout the entire depth, *the top or apex of which lies inside of such surface lines extended down vertically, although such veins, lodes, or ledges may depart from the perpendicular in their course as to extend outside the vertical side lines of such surface location.* But their right of possession to such outside parts of such veins or ledges shall be confined to such portions described, through the end lines of

their locations, so continued in their own direction
that such planes will intersect such exterior parts of
such veins or ledges." *(Emphasis added.)*

Extralateral rights awarded the claimant the right to follow the
apex of the vein, often an outcrop, to wherever it dipped on federal
lands that were in the public domain when he located the claim,
assuming he staked the claim with perpendicular end lines (many
were not) and satisfied the location requirements that varied from
state to state and in the territories. The law has many complications
that still require lawyers specializing in the field. In the early days,
lawyers specialized in stealing the claims from poor prospectors and
small mining companies who had to prove an underground apex
where there was no apex outcrop, called a "blind apex." The semi-
nal law school textbook case analyzing extralateral rights involved
the Sunshine Mining Company. Sunshine claimed extra lateral
rights it did not own and was required to pay the Silver Surprize for
the value of the silver ore it illegally took from under its claim.[2]

The Sunshine Mine

The Silver Valley of the Coeur d'Alene district has mined more silver than the famous Potosi, Bolivia, mines, and the Sunshine Mine
alone produced more silver than the celebrated Comstock Lode.
Deep hard rock mines require major capital investments, making
small or inadequately capitalized mines constant takeover targets by
large mining corporations. The original Sunshine lode mining claim
filed by Dennis Blake and his brother in 1884 and mined for over 30
years was surrounded by mining claims the Sunshine Mining Company later acquired or shared under production agreements until it covered over ten square miles in 1978. *(See Figure No. 1.)* In 1972,
Sunshine was the nation's largest silver mine and produced 20 percent
of the nation's silver. But the Sunshine Mining Company only owned
57 percent of the mine. The Hecla Mining Co. (owner of the nearby
Consolidated Silver, Lucky Friday and Star-Morning Mines) owned 33
percent and the Silver Dollar Mining Co. owned 10 percent.

---

2 *Silver Surprize, Inc. v. Sunshine Mining Co.,* 15 Wash. App. 1, 547 P.2d
1240 (1976).

The Sunshine Mining Company had many other interests. In the 1960s it turned into a small conglomerate. Its most profitable subsidiary was Anchor Post Products, Inc., a major producer of chain-link fences. Other subsidiaries included the manufacturing of radio crystals and metal cabinets and a small Canadian oil and gas producing company. Its mining interests encompassed copper in Alaska, silver in Nevada, and gold in Montana, all of which were unprofitable.

Following a hostile takeover in 1965 by a New York group led by Louis Beryl, an insurance executive, and Irwin P. Underweiser, a corporate lawyer specializing in banking and insurance, the new board of directors used the company as a base in the takeover and merger game. In 1969, Sunshine borrowed $20 million, twenty times the small company's debt over the last decade, to acquire a failing electronics firm. The acquisition proved a poor investment and resulted in a stockholders suit against Sunshine's chairman and president Irwin Underweiser, a director of the electronics company, and other Sunshine directors, who personally benefited from the deal. Other lawsuits sprang up against the directors and officers for diverting funds for their personal benefit and exorbitant salary increases.

At the May 2, 1972, shareholders meeting, Underweiser was forced to explain the company's $1.1 million loss on a poor investment and the wasted $1 million in annual interest payments to fund ill-conceived takeover investments. Although the corporation paid a 26¢ dividend early in 1971, by the end of the year it had a 22¢ per share loss for the year, even though the Sunshine Mine, Anchor Post, and the oil and gas operation showed profits. The small western mining company had a history of paying dividends at the end of each year and angry voices were raised at the meeting. The shareholders didn't believe Underweiser's attempt to blame the price of silver, down from an average of $1.77 an ounce in 1970 to $1.545 in 1971, and cringed when he promised "growth through internal expansion and *acquisitions*."

Before the shareholders meeting ended, many thought it was the end of the company. The mining personnel were called out because of a fire at the mine. The shareholders were told that all the miners had been evacuated. Later they would learn that it was the second worst hard rock mine disaster in the nation's history and *ninety-one miners were killed.*

Figure No. 1.

SUNSHINE MINING COMPANY INTERESTS
1978

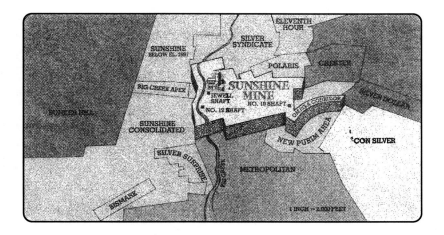

The Sunshine Mining Company interest in the Sunshine Mine was 57 percent. Interests in the Bunker Hill, Chester, and Silver Dollar were up to 84 percent. The Con Silver interest was less than 50 percent. All other interests shown were over 50 percent. *(Supplement to the Sunshine Mining Company 1978 Annual Report.)*

PART TWO

FIRE

CHAPTER 2

TUESDAY, MAY 2, 1972

The Miners

It was like any other day at the Sunshine Mine, except no one was in charge. Sunshine's management was attending the annual stockholders meeting in Coeur d'Alene, 45 miles from the mine.

The day shift hours were 7 a.m. to 3 p.m., but the underground crews arrived a half-hour early to begin their daily ritual of donning their T-shirts, slickers or denim jackets, steel-toed boots, and hard hats in the change room. Next they picked up their cap lamps and batteries in the lamp room that had been recharging since their last shift. The last step was to check in with their shifters (shift bosses) at the shifters shack before walking to the mine portal. Hard rock "gypo" or contract miners are paid by the amount of rock mined and work with a partner. It is a two-man job and the hazardous conditions out of sight and earshot of their shifter and fellow miners require that no miner work alone in case of injury. The shifters checked that every gypo miner's partner and the "day's pay" men paid by the hour, such as the motor and grizzly men, reported to work and jockeyed around replacements for missing or additional men needed on their levels. Mechanics, electricians, repairmen, and other day's pay men reported to their supervisors on the 3700 level.

Another check-in and check-out system employed by the Sunshine Mine and most hard rock mines to keep track of men underground was their designated numbered battery cap lamps in the lamp room. An empty numbered battery charger meant the man was underground. It was a practice that would prove ineffective.

About the time the day shift was driving up Big Creek Canyon leading to the mine, the 11 p.m. to 7:00 a.m. graveyard shift was riding the man train towards the Jewell shaft station, 3,700 feet below on the "3700 level." Shaft repairmen Ben Sheppard and Glen Shoop had been cutting steel on the 3100 No. 10 shaft station to bring down to the 5000 level before going off shift. Shoop, the senior man, had toiled twenty-two years at the Sunshine and his twenty-five-year-old partner had worked at the mine since he was seventeen. As the train passed the Strand electric substation near the 910 raise, a sealed opening extending up to the 3550 and 3400 levels, both smelled smoke, but did not see any in the dark drift lit only by cap lamps. Sheppard passed it off as emanating from a hot electric motor or someone smoking on the man coach. Shoop agreed, "It's probably someone smoking in the front of the train." Smoking was prohibited on the trains, but many men enjoyed a cigarette at the end of a shift. Neither mentioned smelling smoke to their shifter, Raymond Rudd, who had just lit a cigarette, nor to Laverne Melton, shaft repairman and president of the United Steelworkers of America Local Union 5087, riding in the man train a few feet ahead of them.

The first leg of the 173-man day shift's trip was down the Jewell shaft to the 3700 level on the chippy hoist, a four-deck cage designed to carry twelve men on each deck at a wind-swept 800 to 1,000 feet per minute that jerked their entire bodies when it stopped. At the 3700 Jewell shaft station they boarded a man train for the one-mile ride to the 3700 No. 10 shaft station. Conversation was limited by 41,000 cubic feet per minute of air whistling past their ears. There was little to see in the dark tunnel except flickering shadows cast by the cap lamps dancing on the gray rock ribs (walls) and back (roof). Unlike the surface, where even the blackest night might have a few stars or a cloudy moonlit haze, mine passages (drifts) are pitch-black, denying the sight of one's hand in front of his face without a cap lamp. The drift height and width depended on the size of the equipment traversing the drift and left little room to spare, so arms and legs are kept inside the man cars. The ribs and back were supported by 10- and 12-inch square timbers or rockbolts drilled four to six feet into the country rock that held steel mats in place. Strung along the upper corners and ribs were wires and cables for electricity and pipes carrying water and compressed air. The only landmarks were an air door, the old No. 4 and 5 shafts, crosscuts leading

to areas mined-out years ago, and the humming Strand electric substation transforming 13,800 volts into 2,300 volts and sending power
throughout the mine. The train dropped the men off at the 3700 No.
10 shaft station switch siding. There the man cars fitted with seats
were uncoupled and ore cars were hooked up for hauling ore to the
Jewell shaft, where it was hoisted to the surface.

Figure 2

SCHEMATIC OF SUNSHINE MINE LEVELS AND SHAFTS

1972

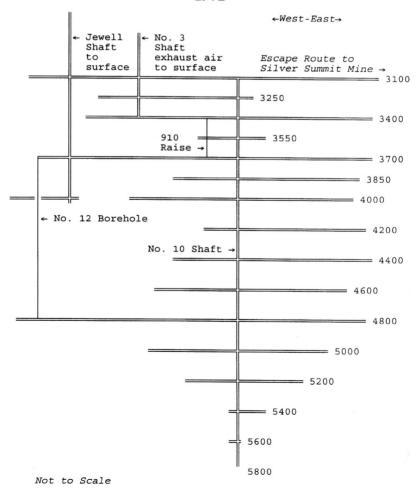

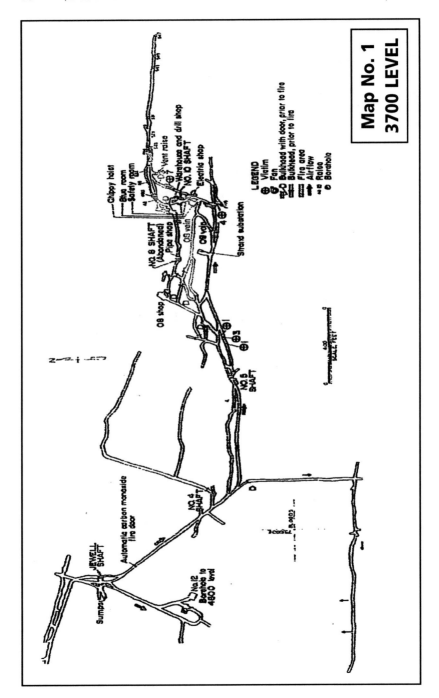

Map No. 1
3700 LEVEL

Most of the shift boarded another four-deck chippy cage for the trip down the No. 10 shaft in the order of their assigned levels, starting with the men sinking the shaft on the 5800 level and the 5600 development level, over one mile beneath the surface. Next followed 5400, 5200, 5000, 4800, 4600, 4400 and last the 4200 level. As the four-deck cages only held 48 men, multiple trips were required. From the shaft stations the men walked or rode battery-operated vehicles called "motors" to their work places along the miles of drifts. *(See Figure No. 2.)*

Men walked to their work places on the 3700 level. The 3700 No. 10 shaft station area was an underground street of shops mined from the rock. The 750-foot tunnel branched out and followed mined-out veins that extended like meandering country lanes. *(See Map No. 1.)*

Adjacent to the 3700 No. 10 shaft station was the wide warehouse entrance to facilitate the delivery of tools and equipment. The rear of the warehouse connected to the drill shop. There mechanics reported to pick up their work assignments throughout the mine and repaired drills, tools, and machines. The drill shop's second entrance was 150 feet north of the shaft station next to an air door that opened to the mined-out Chester vein drift and led to the pipe and 08 machine shops.

Across from the shaft, the safety room containing first-aid supplies, stretchers, blankets, and self-rescuers sat in a cavity in the rock. Sixty feet south of the safety room the blue room was carved out of the rock. Here the foremen met to plan and schedule work with the mine superintendent and eat lunch. The blue room earned its name after its walls were painted pastel blue to reflect its dim and dusty lights for the foremen to handle their paperwork.

Adjacent to the blue room sat the huge chippy hoist room, where the hoist raised and lowered men and materials in the No. 10 shaft between the 3700 level and lower levels on a four-deck cage. The twenty-foot wide entrance opened on the drift 120 feet to the south of the blue room. An opening in the cavernous roof angled up to the 3550 level, where the headframe dropped the steel hoist rope over a sheave and vertically down the east compartment of the shaft. "Chippy" is a local term to distinguish it from the double-drum hoist, a one thousand-horsepower giant located on the 3100 level capable of raising eight tons of ore or muck (waste rock) 1,500 feet per minute up the No. 10 shaft. The new double-drum hoist was in a room 40 feet wide, 60 feet long, and 42 feet high. A tunnel extended diagonally to the shaft headframe on the 2950 level. Ore was hoisted to the 3700 level and loaded on a train through chutes for haulage to the Jewell shaft station, where it was hoisted to the surface on another double-drum hoist. Muck was hoisted to the 3100 level and hauled to the Jewell shaft station, for hoisting to the surface. A single nine-man cage was suspended below both skips (buckets) on the double-drum hoist that raised one skip as it lowered the other in counterbalance in the north and south shaft compartments.

The electric shop was located 75 feet diagonally across from the blue room near a fork in the drift leading to the No. 10 shaft station on the left and a railroad switch for loading the ore train on the right. The shop was a 30 by 75-foot hollow that held benches where the electricians repaired electric motors and equipment under florescent lights.

The pipe shop sat in the bottom of the abandoned No. 8 shaft. The pipe fitters spent little time in the shop except to pick up tools and supplies for the installation of water and compressed air pipes wherever men worked. It was reached through the air door next to the drill shop entrance and travelling west 600 feet on the old Chester vein drift. The 08 machine shop for the repair of heavy machines and equipment was 100 feet behind a metal door 450 feet west of the pipe shop in the bottom of an abandoned raise leading up to the 08 vein. The "08 shop" was a noisy 30 by 60-foot room furnished with drill presses, metal saws, welding equipment, and three work benches.

After finishing his coffee in the drill shop, essential to jump-start his day, Leslie Mossburgh, a mechanic with thirty-seven years in the mines, asked lead mechanic Delbert "Dusty" Rhoads to assign him a partner to help him repair a jumbo drill on the 5400 level. Dusty paired him with William "Bill" Bennett, a mechanic born the year Mossburgh started in the mines. The mechanics lugged their tool boxes to the chippy hoist and rode down to the 5400. They completed the minor repairs and were back at the drill shop at 10:50. Their timing was good. Lunch time was from 11:00 to 11:30 a.m.

Special projects foreman Harvey Dionne assigned mechanic Homer Benson to cut rock bolts out of the 3400 drift's rib and back with an oxygen-acetylene torch for repairmen Custer Keough and William Walty. The repairmen were enlarging the drift to decrease the resistance to 95,000 cubic feet per minute of exhaust air roaring through the drift and vented up and out the Sunshine tunnel and Big Hole. His cutting torch and acetylene and oxygen tanks were hoisted up the No. 10 shaft in the double-drum hoist cage to the 3400 level. Before the heavy tanks could be transported to the job site on a Mancha Midget, a small battery-powered vehicle, Keough and Walty spent an hour clearing a path through the rock debris left from their blasting and barring down loose rock the previous day.

Benson sat on the motor and watched the repairmen. Wasting time didn't bother Benson, a veteran of over thirty years in the mines as a contract miner and shift boss now enjoying the less strenuous job of a mechanic. Few men over fifty worked as "gypo" contract miners paid by the number of feet of rock they mine. Their pay was almost double what the days pay men earned, but risky shortcuts taken to earn the big bucks caused injuries and three or four deaths in the Silver Valley every year. By middle age they were often "stoked out" by the 100°F heat in the stopes and broken bones, and many welcomed less pay for a steady job.

The three men rode the motor 1,400 feet west of the No. 10 station. About 1,100 along the drift they passed through a curve lined with a smooth coating of rigid polyurethane foam to aid coursing the enormous volume of exhaust air crossing the abandoned 09 vein drift. Originally constructed in 1964, plywood nailed to heavy timbers was covered with an asphaltic mastic and sprayed with a rigid foam. *(See Appendix A.)* Behind the air-tight seal stood old wooden bulkheads, constructed no one could recall when, to seal off the intersecting 09 vein on both sides of the drift. Hidden in back of the east bulkhead were the openings to the abandoned 909 raise to the 3250 level, 910 raise to the 3550 and 3700 levels, and the 911 raise to the 3250 and 3550 levels.

The 3400 drift was bald, miners' slang for not supported by timbers. Nevertheless, the repairmen followed foreman Dionne's orders and sprayed the floor and ribs with water before using an acetylene torch. Keough drove the Mancha Midget while Benson stood on the top with the acetylene torch and cut off the ends of the roof bolts dangling from the back, which had held steel mats to support the country rock. Walty walked behind the motor and picked up the hot bolts with pliers and dropped them in a bucket. Benson had all he could do to hang on to his hat and keep the dirt and dust out of his eyes in the gale-like wind churned by two 150 horsepower fans installed near the station.

Keough drove Benson back to the station then returned to drill holes in preparation to install new rockbolts and steel mats. Benson arrived at the drill shop around 10:35 a.m., too late to start another job and too early for lunch that started at 11:00. Benson and Dusty Rhoads sat at a bench and discussed what jobs had to be done that afternoon and shot the breeze until lunchtime.

Shaft Repairman Harvey "Hap" Fowler had toiled forty-four years in the mines and had held almost every job there was underground. Hap started mining at seventeen in the California "Mother Lode" country during the Depression. That week he was temporarily assigned the soft job of replacing the warehouseman who had fallen and broken his hip. He started the morning by going underground at 6:00 a.m. to open the Warehouse for men needing materials to start their day. It was a slow morning with few requisitions to fill. His bench by the warehouse entrance faced the No. 10 shaft and allowed him to see and gab with everyone on the shaft station.

Hap waved at Robert Launhardt, the safety engineer, as he got off the chippy cage at 10:00 after inspecting the 5400 and 5600 levels. Launhardt went to the blue room and safety room to complete his paperwork and left around 10:30. As was his practice, Launhardt walked to the Jewell shaft. He didn't smell or see any smoke when he passed the Strand electric substation and 910 raise during the one-mile hike.

Kenneth Ross, a geologist, went underground at 7:15 to survey the stopes on the 4200, 4400, and 4600 levels. He caught the chippy hoist in time to arrive at the 3700 No. 10 station and catch the man train scheduled to leave around 11:30 for the Jewell station so he could eat lunch on the surface. Larry Hawkins, a twenty-eight-year old geology department sampler, took the Jewell chippy hoist down with the production level crews at 7:00 to take measurements and samples for assaying the ore in the stopes on the 4600 and 4800 levels. Hawkins rode the chippy cage to the 3700 level with Ross.

Floyd Strand, the electrical foreman, spent the morning in the electric shop. A minute or so before 11:30 a.m., he checked with Gene Johnson, shaft foreman, in the blue room to determine if the train was leaving at 11:30. Gene told him it could wait another five minutes. Strand hurried back to the electric shop to give a few last minute instructions and ran to catch the train. On board were Ross, Hawkins, and John Reardon, a mechanic. Reardon had been repairing a pump on the 5400 level and was scheduled to work in the surface mechanic's shop that afternoon. The riders estimated they left between 11:35 and 11:40 and that the trip took between eight to twelve minutes.[3] None of passengers reported seeing or smelling smoke as they passed the Strand station and under the 910 raise.

As was their custom, the foremen returned from their morning rounds to eat lunch in the blue room. It was a typical lunch, except that the mine superintendent, Albert Walkup, was attending the Sunshine Mining Company stockholders meeting instead of spending the morning in the mine. Special projects foreman Harvey Dionne, a wiry man with an eye to detail and a determination for doing things properly, normally ate lunch after work, but joined the others for coffee as they sat and gabbed about work and nothing in particular. Jim and Bob Bush, rugged brothers and production foremen, and Jim Salyer, drift miner foreman, had come up from the production levels. That morning shaft foreman Fred "Gene" Johnson had inspected the 3700 Jewell shaft repairs and the No. 10 shaft station expansion work on the 5400 and 5600 levels. The foremen were experienced miners and looked the part, rough-hewn and soft-spoken, but with voices of unquestionable authority.

Where there's smoke, there's fire
Mechanics Richard Breazeal and Wilber "Jack" Harris worked at the 3700 Jewell station during the morning installing new shoes (metal guides) on the chippy hoist. They rode the flatbed timber truck past

---

3   The passengers gave varying times when the train left and how long it took to travel the one mile between the No. 10 station and the Jewell shaft. The author timed the train ride after the mine reopened at eight minutes and forty seconds.

the Strand electric substation to the No. 10 station around 10:50 and ate lunch in the drill shop with the other mechanics. After lunch, they wheeled acetylene and oxygen tanks out of the drill shop and onto the chippy cage needed to weld broken ore car couplings on the 4800 level. They waited while two cagers, George "Randy" Peterson and Roger Findley, loaded fan line pipe on the cage for Dusty Rhoads. Nineteen-year-old Findley had only worked in the mines for eights months. The cage left the 3700 level No. 10 station around 11:40.

As the cagers unloaded the fan line on the 4400 level, Peterson said he smelled something burning. Breazeal and Harris stepped off the cage and smelled smoke, but could not see any on the station. Rhoads called a shaft repairman in the 4400 pocket approximately seventy feet below, who had been working in the area that morning. The repairman told Dusty that he and his partner had been welding on the 4500 timber station, a small area off the shaft used to store timbers, and it was possible they might have ignited some wood. Dusty told Findley, Breazeal, and Harris to go the 4500 and look for the source of the smoke while he and Peterson checked around the 4400 station.

Findley belled the chippy hoistman to drop the cage to the 4500. Before they stepped off they saw a smokey haze on the timber station. They quickly realized there was no fire in the small area and the smoke was coming down the shaft, the source of fresh air for the lower levels. Findley belled the chippy hoistman to take them down to the 4800, but there was no answer.[4] Within minutes the smoke increased and burned their eyes. Findley belled the chippy hoistman again a few minutes later and received no response.

Gary Beckes, an electrician, had the tedious task of checking the motor car batteries and charging stations in the "motor barns" on each level. The electricians so disliked the assignment, they rotated the job every two weeks. He was glad to receive a call in mid-morning to repair an electric locomotive on the 5000 level. Because of the 2,500-foot trudge from where the locomotive had broken down

---

4 Why they belled for the hoist to take them to the 4800 level below when they were aware the smoke was coming down the shaft was never explained.

to the 5000 No. 10 station, he could not get back to the electric shop until 11:15. Fellow electricians Wayne Blalack, John Williams, and Norman Ulrich and lead electrician Arnold Anderson were half-way through their lunches. Blalack and Williams left after receiving instructions from Floyd Strand to check the wiring on one of the lower level stations, but missed the chippy cage carrying Peterson, Findley, and the others. There was little they could do except bell for a cage and wait at the station.

Beckes glanced at the clock on the wall at 11:45 and strapped on his tool belt, then stepped out in the drift and smelled smoke. He looked in the direction of the main haulageway to the Jewell shaft and saw a smokey haze. Before he could turn back, the smoke rolled toward him he described "like somebody pulled the plug."

Beckes stepped back in the electric shop and told Arnold Anderson: "There's smoke coming out of the drift."

Anderson ran out of the shop and yelled across to the blue room: "There's smoke in the drift."

Foremen Harvey Dionne and Gene Johnson strapped on their belts, donned their hard hats, and ran out of the blue room past the electric shop and followed the smoke in the 3700 drift toward the Jewell shaft.

"There's smoke in the drift, Jim," Bob Bush repeated in the rear of the blue room. Bob answered the phone and told Don Beehner in the pipe shop, who had called after seeing smoke, to go to the No. 10 station and wait for orders, then called Pete Bennett in 08 shop to ask if they had a fire. When Pete said no, Bob told him to check the area. The brothers grabbed their belts then ran to the cut next to the chippy hoist room and boarded a Mancha Midget (an open electric vehicle) to search for the source of the haze. When they saw the thick smoke in the drift, they knew it was a serious fire. A fire in a deep underground hard rock mine is feared and must be extinguished before it ignited something flammable near a shaft.

Harvey Dionne and Gene Johnson were the first to arrive at the 910 raise, approximately 900 feet from the blue room, followed seconds later by Arnold Anderson and Norman Ulrich. Smoke was roiling down the raise from the 3400 or 3550 levels directly overhead. The old raise, a six by six-foot shaft-like opening, was no longer used for ventilation or hoisting and had been partially filled with waste rock. Harvey, the most agile, climbed the ten feet to the top of the drift by grabbing and placing footholds on rockbolts and crevices in the rib until he could see over the 12 by 12-inch timbers anchored into the rib and laced with lagging (planks) over the raise bottom. He peered up through the narrow opening between the lagging and the edge of the mine roof, but was driven back by the acrid smoke streaming in his face. As he scampered down, Jim and Bob Bush arrived on a Mancha Midget.

The experienced foremen knew that the vast amount of smoke billowing down meant there was a major fire above the 3700 level, the normal way in and out of the mine, and it would soon be inundated with smoke and impassable. They feared the smoke would circulate with the ventilation airflow to the No. 10 shaft and down to the lower levels, contaminating the only source of fresh air and cutting off the only means of escape of the men below. There was no choice but to evacuate the mine through the 3100 level.

"I'm going back and get the men up," Gene Johnson said.

"I'll go and help Gene," Bob Bush said.

"Harvey, we'd also better close the fire door to the Jewell," Johnson said and started to run back to No. 10 station.

"I'll take Harvey to close the fire door then try and get over to the 08 Shop and see what's going on there." Jim Bush said.

Arnold Anderson and Bob Bush ran after Johnson. Harvey Dionne and Jim Bush hopped on the Mancha Midget, the fastest way to reach the air door eight-tenths of a mile west towards the Jewell shaft. Norman Ulrich jumped on the motor. The electrician said he knew how to close the door by cutting the circuits, which would allow anyone escaping out the 3700 level to open the door manually, an almost impossible feat if the hydraulic air door was triggered by the carbon monoxide alarm mechanism and automatically closed.

Several minutes after Roger Findley belled (signalled) and squawked the chippy hoistman on the intercom and the cage didn't move, Richard Breazeal stepped out of the cage and squawked the hoistman several times, but received no response over the archaic intercom system. Smoke pouring down the shaft was getting so thick he couldn't see more than a few feet. He hung on the signal bell cord and closed his eyes in an effort to stop them from stinging. The long steady pull on the bell signal cord kept the signal light on in the chippy hoist room that could not be ignored by the hoistman. After a minute or so, he could no longer tolerate the smoke and was gasping for air. Breazeal ran into the cage and unhooked the oxygen hose from the cutting torch and turned on the oxygen. Findley and Harris joined him taking turns breathing oxygen out of hose for five minutes. After they agreed that the signals must be out on the chippy hoist, Breazeal asked Findley, a cager familiar with the hoistmen and much younger, to fill up his lungs with oxygen then run out on the station and squawk the double-drum hoistman to pick them up.

As Gene Johnson ran past the blue room, he saw Jim Salyer on the phone attempting to determine the source of the fire. He went to the station to call Thomas Harrah, the maintenance foreman, in the surface machine shop.

"Tommy, turn in the stench warning, we have a fire underground." Without missing a breath, Gene told Harrah to instruct Robert Launhardt, the safety engineer, to bring the self-contained breathing apparatus to the 3100 level No. 10 station for the foremen to use during the evacuation.

Launhardt looked up at the clock as John Davis of the purchasing department entered his office above the warehouse to join him for lunch at the conference table. Davis was right on time. It was precisely noon. Not more than three minutes later, Launhardt opened his insulated "dinner bucket" miners carry their lunch in to keep it warm or cold and removed a sandwich. As he started to unwrap it, the phone rang.

"Bob, drop everything you're doing and meet me in the yard right now." Harrah said and hung up.

Harrah's brevity and the urgency in his voice told Launhardt something was seriously wrong. As he ran down the stairs to the mine yard, the dense smoke pouring out the Sunshine tunnel sent a chill up his spine.

Ira Sliger, hoistman in the double-drum hoist room on the 3100 level, was hoisting muck from the 5600 level pocket, a chute below the level connected to the shaft for loading ore and muck, when he received a call on the squawker from Roger Findley. Findley told him that three men were stranded on the 4500 timber station because the chippy signals were out. Sliger was about to remind the young cager that the double-drum hoist only picked up men during emergencies because it slowed the hoisting when Gene Johnson's voice came over the intercom:

"Ira, where is your cager?"

"In the 5600 pocket pulling muck," Sliger replied.

"Get him up to the 3700 as soon as possible."

Robert Scanlan, Sliger's partner on the double-drum hoist, broke in on the line: "Gene, what's the trouble?"

"We have a fire down here," Gene said.

According to the hoist trip recorders, Sliger was raising the south skip and lowering north in counterbalance when Gene Johnson called. *(See Appendix B.)* Sliger dumped the south skip in the chute on the 3100 level at 12:03 then brought it down empty to the 4400 level at 12:05.[5] He raised the loaded north skip to the 4400 level at 12:06, where it was clutched out and remained until 12:17. Therefore, Gene Johnson called Harrah to begin the evacuation before 12:03 p.m., which coincides with Launhardt's testimony that Harrah called *before 12:03, and possibly at 12:02.*

---

5 The south cage remained on the 4400 level until a few seconds after 12:06. It was never explained why Dusty Rhoads, Randy Peterson, and the others on the level did not board the cage. It is possible the cage was not sitting precisely on the level or was not noticed.

TIME IS OF THE ESSENCE

The Bureau of Mines "Final Report on the Sunshine Mine Disaster" issued February 14, 1973, listed nine major factors contributing to the number of deaths in the abstract:

2. Top mine officials were not at the mine on the day of the fire and no person had been designated as being in charge of the entire operation. Individual supervisors were reluctant to order immediate evacuation or to make a major decision, such as stopping the 3400 level fans.

3. Company personnel delayed ordering evacuation of the mine for about 20 minutes while they searched for the cause of the fire.

Time is of the essence in the event of an underground mine fire. The evacuation plan must provide as much time as feasible for the miners to escape. But while time is crucial, so is judgement. A safe evacuation route is necessary. As in the case of any disaster, individual accounts and the time vary due to the excitement and confusion. Later judgments differed due to the conflicting interests by mine management protecting Sunshine's liability, the United Steelworkers of America representing the miners, the press looking for a story angle, the Bureau of Mines responsible for the enforcement of mine safety, and politicians in search of headlines and votes. Of course, there were also lawyers pleading the victims' cases, suing everyone remotely connected with the disaster, and claiming one-third of the award.

The principal source of timing relied upon by the Bureau was the hoist trip recorders, devices that graphically record the time and number of hoist trips to the various levels on a paper tape. Their purpose is to record ore and muck production and idle time, hence the nickname "tattletale." Tattletales are not precisely accurate and are subject to interpretation, as witnessed by the pencil notations. *(See Appendix B.)* Robert L. Anderson, the Sunshine Mine's chief engineer, interpreted the recordings during his deposition on May 17, 1972, and testimony at the hearings on July 21, 1972, which contained minor conflicting interpretations. Ira Sliger, the hoist operator, admitted at the hearing that the tattletales could be off by as much as five minutes when they are installed each morning. Anderson determined they were out of synchronization by one and one-half minutes, which meant that one tattletale was one and one-half minutes faster than the other, as the north and south cages hoist were operated in counterbalance. The tattletale's squiggly line does not help interpretation either, Anderson conceded.

As for the distances traveled and the time the men testified they learned of the fire and when events occurred, many miners do not wear a watch in the harsh and wet mine environment. And, as one foreman told me off the record, "Who the hell checks their watch when they're running to save their ass and choking from [expletive deleted] smoke?"

After four days of hearings into the cause of the disaster and listening to testimony of disparate times and distances, I demanded to go down in the mine to check for myself on Saturday when the hearings were recessed. We could not enter the areas where the fire was still burning or the ground was unstable because of the burned timber support. Airtight bulkheads had been erected on the burning levels to choke off the oxygen and prevent the carbon monoxide from leaking. Entry behind the bulk-heads was barred except to trained crews using self-contained breathing apparatuses as they progressively constructed bulkheads closer to the fire to eliminate the oxygen feeding the fire. It was extremely hot near the bulkheads, in some locations in excess of 105°F, and there were still traces of deadly carbon monoxide leaking from around the bulkheads.

The Bureau assigned two Bureau mine inspectors and Sunshine management instructed Ewell "Hank" Day, a burly, quiet foreman with twenty-five years in the mines, to make sure nothing happened to the Washington lawyer and political appointee conducting the hearing. I insisted I was trained and qualified to wear a self-contained breathing apparatus in a contaminated atmosphere after taking the Bureau's twenty-hour mandatory training course in less than three hours earlier that morning. I also passed a ten-minute physical examination by a doctor who diagnosed me "crazy."

After four hours in the mine, my entourage of over a dozen sat in a drift to rest and further taint our lungs with cigarettes. My escorts included Laverne Melton, president of the United Steelworkers of America Local 5089, and Marvin C. Chase, vice president and general manager of the Sunshine Mining Company, both there to make sure I was not brainwashed by the other. The American Mining Congress sent Richard W. Bliss, a mining lawyer, to lobby me in the dark depths. Half of us were exhausted after climbing up ladders in a dark 200-foot raise, twice the height of my office building in Washington, D.C. The other half was smart. They rode up on a hoist.

One of the mine foremen laughed when he saw me reach for a pack of Camels in my shirt pocket only to discover they were soaked with perspiration.

After I took my first drag on a Marlboro he offered from an airtight aluminum can strapped to the outside of his hard hat, I asked: "How far did we walk from the raise we climbed to where we are sitting and how long did it take to walk here?" He estimated it was 600 feet and it had taken five or six minutes. A half-dozen voices chimed in disagreement to tell me it was anywhere from 300 to 800 feet and it took between three to ten minutes.

"So much for the time and distances you guys gave in your testimony this week and in your depositions," I said and laughed. "It was 525 feet, plus or minus 25 feet, and it took us exactly three minutes and forty-five seconds. I have been timing the distances we walked and counting my steps most of the time we were in the mine." Last, I asked everyone to check their watches and tell me what time it was. I received four answers spanning a difference of nine minutes.

Jim Bush grinned and asked me if I wanted to climb another 200-foot raise. I said: "Hell, no." He replied: "You were in your lawyer-world at the hearing this week asking questions and giving us a hard time. This is our world down here."

Jim was right. I never would have been able to recall the time and distances in dark drifts with only a light from a cap lamp in thick smoke that burned my eyes as I ran and staggered over railroad tracks and breathed deadly carbon monoxide that made me weaker every second. Nor could I have climbed a series of 200-foot raises several thousand feet under such conditions. At the hearings, I had learned that the self-rescuer on my hip was only guaranteed for one hour. Also, the chemical heat transfer eliminating the carbon monoxide would merely let one breathe carbon dioxide at temperatures in excess of 300°F and blister one's lips in high concentrations of the toxic gas. Jim Bush, a muscular foreman who climbed the raises regularly, testified that it would take him two or three hours to climb the raises between the 5200 and 3100 levels under ideal conditions. For the miners on the lower levels, there was no way out after the No. 10 shaft became contaminated with smoke or carbon monoxide.

Before I finished my cigarette, I made up my mind that the Bureau's regulations should be amended to require secondary escapeways equipped with hoists. One of the purposes of the public hearing was to determine the causes of the loss of life and prevent similar disasters occurring in the future. It was a no-brainer. But I was naive and didn't realize how long it would take to promulgate such regulations against mining company opposition, nor to cut through the federal bureaucratic red tape. [6]

After my hard day in the mine, I joined a few foremen and miners at the Broken Wheel Lounge for "after-shift beers to get the dust out of our lungs." There I learned things dared not mentioned at a public hearing attended by company officials and lawyers.

---

6 The Bureau of Mines "Final Report on the Sunshine Mine Disaster" issued February 14, 1973, recommended secondary escapeways be equipped with hoists.

CHAPTER 3

EVACUATION

The Hoistman

Ira Sliger had been the No. 10 double-drum hoistman the last ten of his forty-four years working in the mines. At sixty-one, he lamented, "I look big enough to eat oats and pull a plow, but if there is any exertion in it, I can't do it." Sliger suffered from what he called "dust on the lungs." Silicosis, the bane of hard rock miners, had resulted in the removal of one of Sliger's lungs.

Sliger squawked his cager, twenty-one-year-old Byron Schulz, in the 5600 pocket and told him to get his cage and come to the 3700 level. Schulz belled Sliger to stop at the 5600 station to pick up his partner, Elmer Kitchen. Kitchen, a fifty-four-year-old shaft miner, was working as a second cager because the new pocket required two cagers. Sliger dropped the south cage from the 4400 level at 12:06. For reasons never explained, the cage stopped above the bottom of the 5600 pocket for a few seconds at 12:08, then rose above the 5600 station and immediately dropped back down to pick up Schulz above the pocket and left at 12:10 without picking up Kitchen, wasting precious minutes.

The cage stopped on the 4500 timber station at 12:11 to pick up Roger Findley, Richard Breazeal, and Jack Harris and left a few seconds before 12:12. It arrived on the 3700 level a few seconds after 12:13. Until Schulz saw the smoke on the 4500 level and Findley told him there was a fire, he didn't know it was an emergency.

The 3700 Level

The precise times and sequence of events are difficult to determine with certainty. Typical of most disasters, the crisis occurred unexpectedly and the events unfolded rapidly, confusing memories of the turmoil. The toxic smoke not only clouded their vision, it could effect their thinking and physical ability to respond without their realizing it until it was too late. No one was aware of the debilitating effects of carbon monoxide, and they were facing a rapid release of deadly carbon monoxide in concentrations not believed possible in a hard rock mine.

The drill shop and connecting warehouse was a din of clanging metal reverberating against rock ceilings and walls supported by steel-mats and rockbolts. Even without the cacophony of machinery, the mechanics often had to raise their voices to be heard in the 25 by 40-foot drill shop and L-shaped warehouse measuring 30 by 40 feet and 15 by 20 feet.

Around 11:30, Les Mossburgh told Bill Bennett, whose normal work station was the 08 shop, "I'm going to ask Dusty if you can stay here and learn how to overhaul a raise climber." Mossburgh walked from the drill shop to the No. 10 station to obtain Dusty Rhoads's okay while the lead mechanic was waiting to board the chippy cage to go down to the 4400 level. When he returned, the pair filled a large metal basin with cleaning solvent and began washing parts of a raise climber and blasting the oil and grit off with "whiz-bangs," compressed air hoses with perforated metal heads.

A few minutes after 11:30, Clyde Napier ambled out of the drill shop for a drink of water at the No. 10 station. The fifty-nine-year-old mechanic preferred the colder water at the station fountain over that of the drill shop's fountain. Napier had worked in the mines since he was seventeen. With forty-two years in the mines, Napier and his fellow old-timers in the drill shop and warehouse, Les Mossburgh (thirty-seven years), Homer Benson (thirty-one years), and Hap Fowler (forty-four years), had seen and done all there was to do underground and had earned the right to work at their slow but sure and steady pace. Bill Bennett was the youngster in the group with thirteen years underground. Napier returned to his bench next to the entrance and put a jackleg drill in a vise, then started to disassemble the pneumatic couplings, something he could do and faster than the "young upstarts" at his methodical pace.

After stowing his lunch bucket under his bench, Hap Fowler gathered a stack of requisitions at his bench to take to the blue room for the foremen to sign. As he stepped out on the No. 10 station, he wrinkled his nose at an odor and noticed a slight haze on the station and the backs of several foremen running down the drift toward the haulageway in the direction of heavier smoke. The only man he recognized was Bob Bush, rushing out of the blue room.

"Did they find a fire?" Fowler called nonchalantly.

"No, not yet," Bob Bush said and continued running after his brother, Jim.

Fowler watched them disappear on the Mancha Midget then left the requisitions in the blue room and headed back to the warehouse.

Napier called to Mossburgh, washing parts of the raise climber, "I smell smoke."

"It's probably just somebody burning a rag on the station," Mossburgh said as Napier walked out the shop entrance to the drift.

Napier looked at the smoke in the drift and returned inside and told the others there was smoke in the drift "probably coming from the electric shop."

Homer Benson was leaning against a bench chatting with Jim Salyer, drift development foreman, in the corner of the drill shop set aside for sharpening saws and axes and putting new handles on axes and picks, when they overheard Napier say there was smoke in the drift. Benson told Salyer to stay sitting on a stool while he checked out the smoke, then walked through the warehouse to the No. 10 station. Salyer walked with a limp as a result of a mine accident.

Benson walked back in a few seconds later. "Jim, by gosh, there is quite a bit of smoke out there."

Salyer hobbled as fast as he could to the Blue Room with Benson trailing him as far as the shaft station. Benson stood and watched the smoke coming from the main drift for a minute before returning to the drill shop. It was foremen's job to find out where the fire was and let the men know.

Mossburgh had second thoughts about the odor. "That's not rags burning, it's wood," he said to Bill Bennett. He walked through the warehouse to the station and saw the smoke and Jim Salyer on the phone in the blue room attempting to call the shops to determine the source of the smoke. As he reached Jim Salyer's side he asked if the fire was serious.

Salyer shrugged and kept his ear to the phone. The phone system was a single-circuit between the shaft stations, hoistrooms, and shops, and there were others talking on the line. "I wish Dusty would get off the phone so I can talk," Salyer said.

Meanwhile, Hap Fowler had walked through the warehouse to the drill shop and saw that the smoke had started to seep into the shop. "We better get some air blown in here," he said to Homer Benson.

Bill Bennett turned on the oxygen from the welding cart for himself and Mossburgh while Benson and the others blew whiz-bangs in their faces. The five men stood inhaling compressed air and oxygen as the smoke increased without showing any anxiety, confident the foremen would return after finding the fire and tell them what to do. Years of experience taught them not to rush and attempt to escape out the 3700 towards the Jewell shaft and end up meeting a wall of flames or deadly smoke.

Gregory "Greg" Dionne, a twenty-three-year-old pipe fitter and the son of foreman Harvey Dionne, and Tony Sabala, a fifty-four-year-old pipe fitter's helper, spent the morning stringing compressed air and water lines on the 4000 level for a diamond drill. They did not get back to the pipe shop for lunch until around 11:40. Waiting to join them was Don Beehner, the 3700 No. 10 station nipper and union safety committeeman. Don's job was cleaning up the station area.

Tony never ate lunch and relied on his younger boss to pour him a cup of coffee from his thermos. He was taking his second sip when they were startled by a muffled explosion, he described "like a gale blew down a door." Seconds later a tornado of smoke roared up the drift and into the pipe shop. The pipe shop sat on the bottom of the former No. 8 shaft and sucked in 2,000 cubic feet of air a minute that leaked up to the 3550 and 3400 levels. When they looked out of the shop the smoke appeared to be pouring out of a bulkheaded crosscut 200 feet down the drift from the direction of the 08 shop.

Tony asked Don to call the blue room and ask a foreman to check for a fire. Aware the foremen could not reach the source through their drift, he added: "Tell them to go around the other way and check, we have a bad fire someplace."

After Don hung up, he said: "Bob said we should hurry to the ten station."

Greg led the others as fast as they could follow down the 600 feet towards the bulkhead door leading to the No. 10 station. Overweight Tony huffed and puffed on the two hundred yard dash to keep ahead of the wave of smoke. When they passed the oiler's station behind the air door to the No. 10 station, Greg told the oiler, James Lamphere, to come with them and pointed to the smoke behind him.

Lamphere had been sweeping the oil storage area oblivious to the smoke in the drift. He followed them through the door, where he was met by a slight haze on the station. Although thirty-two, Lamphere had only worked underground two years and the oiler did not have an experienced partner. Lamphere glanced in the drill shop and joined the mechanics breathing oxygen and compressed air.

After smelling smoke when he walked out of the electric shop, Gary Beckes followed Norman Ulrich and Arnold Anderson almost to the Strand electric substation, but turned back because of the thick smoke and the possibility that he could not make it to the Jewell. Beckes jumped to the side of the rib when Jim and Bob Bush raced past on the Mancha Midget. As he approached the fork in the drift leading to the electric and other shops on the left and the fan switches and ore chutes on the right, he ran into fellow electrician, John Williams. They discussed the best escape route and decided walking to the Jewell was too risky, so they returned to the electric shop to wait for instructions from a foreman or the lead electrician, Arnold Anderson, searching for the fire.

Beckes disconnected a 30 amp fuse to shut off the electricity powering 110 volts in the electric shop to stop a small ventilation fan blowing air into the dead end room and cut down on the smoke entering. Pulling the fuse also cut off the electricity to the clock on the wall, stopping it at 11:53. Two minutes later, Marcellus "Morry" Story, a mechanic, entered the shop. Story had walked from the 08 shop to the No. 10 station to take the cage to the 5600 level with fellow mechanic, John Gardner, but found it hazy and continued on to the electric shop.

Seconds later, Don Wood, the chippy hoistman, rushed in coughing and blurted that the chippy hoist signals were out and it was so smokey in the hoist room he couldn't see the dial indicator telling him where the cage was.[7] The 3700 chippy hoist room connected diagonally up to the 3550 level, where its headframe and sheave wheel dropped the hoist's cable vertically down the shaft to the lower levels. The opening exposed the hoistman to the smoke and carbon monoxide emanating from above before migrating to other parts of the 3700 level.

Beckes called the double-drum hoist room on the 3100, but received no response. Jim Salyer was on the party line phone system asking someone if the fans on the 3400 exhaust air level should be shut off to stop the exhaust air recirculating the smoke from the fire above back into the fresh air and down the No. 10 shaft. Beckes told him he could cut the fans off from the switch rack behind the electric shop, but it would also cut off the power to the double-drum hoist. As the chippy hoist rose only to the 3700 level and the smoke appeared too thick to escape out the 3700 to the Jewell shaft, the double-drum hoist was the only way to the 3100 level.

As Beckes hung up, Arnold Anderson stuck his head in the doorway and told Beckes, Williams, Story, and Wood that Gene Johnson was calling for the double-drum to raise everyone to the 3100 level and to head for the No. 10 station. The electricians gathered their lunch buckets and left for the station. Wood ran back to the chippy hoist room to retrieve his jacket and lunch bucket. Wood was never reported seen again. His body was found near the No. 10 station.

Pete Bennett answered the phone in the 08 shop. Two or three voices were coming over the line and he could not understand what they were talking about until Bob Bush's booming voice asked if there

---

7 Beckes testified at the hearing on July 20 that he found the signal bells operating after the fire area had been bulkheaded off and the chippy hoist room was accessible. However, it was common knowledge that the chippy hoist signals were occasionally out of order due to water leaking down the shaft. The hoist dial indicator was a old model with a six-foot diameter clock face located eight feet in front of the hoistman. The chippy hoist room was not equipped with a new vertical dial eighteen inches in front of the hoistman and an enclosed cab to protect the hoistman from smoke like the new 3100 level double-drum hoist.

was a fire in the 08 Shop. Bennett told him it was clear in the shop. Bush told him to check the area outside the shop. Bennett, the senior mechanic with nineteen years working at the Sunshine, asked Kenneth Tucker, his young partner with only two years underground, to help him search for a fire.

As they were leaving, Pat Hobson, a mechanic, entered the shop. Hobson had left a few minutes earlier to walk to the No. 10 station on the drift leading past the pipe shop, but when he opened the bulkhead door he had to turn back because of the smoke.

"It's smokier than heck that way out," Hobson said.

The mechanics ran to the bulkhead door, then closed it at the sight of huge cotton balls of smoke filling the drift. They walked along the 820 crosscut until they came to the mined out D vein, called the East Dog House, where fans, slushers, and heavy equipment were stored. Seeing no smoke, they headed back to the 08 shop to call the blue room, but were forced to retreat when they saw billowing smoke rolling towards them. It was impossible to return.

Gene Johnson stepped in the warehouse entrance to avoid the smoke curling over the edge of the shaft.

"Did you find the fire yet?" Hap Fowler asked.

"No," Gene replied, shaking his head.

"Well, I'm getting the hell out of here," Hap said and walked towards the blue room.

Gene returned to the shaft and was about to pick up the phone when Tony Sabala arrived.

"It's getting awful bad here," Tony said and coughed.

"Yeah, it is getting kind of bad, ain't it?" Gene said in a calm voice and called the double-drum hoist room. "What the hell is taking so long to get the cage to the 3700 level?"

Hap Fowler opened a cabinet in the blue room and dumped a box of self-rescuers on a table for Bob Bush, Gary Beckes, John Williams, and Arnold Anderson, then grabbed one for himself.

"Are you going out?" Hap asked Bob.

"I'll help Gene raise the men to the 3100," Bob said, "and then I'll be right behind you."

Hap opened a self-rescuer and adjusted it in mouth, then picked up his jacket and lunch bucket and started walking to the Jewell shaft by himself. The confident veteran miner had been trained in the use of self-rescuers and self-contained breathing apparatuses and had been a member of the rescue team in his younger days.

Bob ran to the station and handed Gene Johnson a self-rescuer as the cage arrived a few seconds after 12:13. Gene ordered Richard Breazeal, Jack Harris, and Roger Findley to stay on the cage to the 3100 level and walk to the Jewell station and instruct Byron Schulz, the cager, to take the cage to the 3100 and send it back to him. He would act as cager and take it up to save space on the cage.

Bob realized Gene and Jim Salyer had things under control and there might be too many men left on the level to fill a second nine-man cage. He told Gene he would walk to the Jewell shaft and make sure that there were no men left in the 08 shop area. Wayne Blalack told him that he shouldn't do it alone and fell into step with the foreman as he headed into the heavy smoke.

Gary Beckes could not get his self-rescuer to work. He had never been trained in its use and had to read the directions: "Lift lid and push button." When he put it in his mouth, he thought he could not breath through it. He left it on the table and went to the station drinking fountain and wet a rag to cover his nose and mouth. It seemed to strain out the smoke and stop his coughing. When he looked up the cage was at the station. Gene Johnson told him and John Williams to get in and make room for as many as possible.

Unable to obtain relief from a whiz-bang, Homer Benson staggered out of the drill shop and vomited in the drift. Heaving seemed to help as he ran to the station. A man he didn't recognize in the smoke handed him his self-rescuer, but he couldn't get it to work. Before he knew what happened, Gene Johnson pushed him on the cage. Benson later said, "I left the self-rescuer on the cage for someone smarter than I was who could figure out how the damn thing worked."

Jim Bush flashed the headlights on the Mancha Midget and pulled the signal light as he passed the Sunshine Consolidated crosscut, a signal to the ore train coming from the Jewell shaft to stop. Harvey Dionne told the motorman, Jasper Beare, and his partner-swamper, Robert Mathews, there was a fire and to back the train out to the air door and drop Norm Ulrich off so the electrician could close the door. Jim and Harvey drove back towards the No. 5 shaft along the old haulage road, the fastest way to get to the 08 shop without endangering anyone walking out the main haulageway in the blinding smoke.

Pete Bennett, Tucker, and Hobson walked to where the 820 crosscut and 808 drift intersected and ran into Bob Bush and Wayne Blalack in the smoky haze. Bennett told Bob there were no men in the 08 area.

Bob removed the self-rescuer from his mouth and said, "Go out the Jewell and stop anybody along the way and tell them to get out."

Bennett and Tucker headed towards the Jewell on the old haulage drift. Hobson joined Blalack and Bob Bush as they headed back to the crosscut to the 09 drift vein to help anyone attempting to escape on the main haulageway.

As Jim Bush and Harvey Dionne drove past the No. 5 shaft on the old haulageway they passed Bennett and Tucker walking towards them. Harvey yelled to them to keep heading towards the Jewell as they drove by. They rode the Mancha Midget into the smoke towards the 08 Shop for several hundred feet, but were forced to turn back. Jim stopped the motor where his brother had met Bennett and Tucker and few minutes earlier. They decided that Harvey should take the motor and ride back to make sure Ulrich had been able to close the air door. Jim said he was going to walk to the crosscut to the 09 main haulageway and check for stragglers and make sure his brother had made it out.

Jim met Hap Fowler a few minutes later on the main haulageway

"You better come on and get out," Hap said, yanking the self-rescuer out of his mouth and glancing around at the smoke circling them.

"Did you see Bob?" Jim asked.

"About five minutes ago, but he will be all right. He's right behind me."

Hap started down the drift. He didn't get more that 100 feet when he ran into a wall of heavy smoke and couldn't see three feet ahead of him.

Gene Johnson stuck his head in the entrance of the warehouse and shouted to the mechanics in the drill shop to get to the station. Les Mossburgh and Bill Bennett dropped the hoses from the oxygen tanks then wet rags at the water fountain to cover their noses and mouths before leaving. James Lamphere and Clyde Napier laid down their whiz-bangs and ran out the drift entrance to the smoke-blanketed station without any protection against the smoke and carbon monoxide.

Most men stood by the shaft as if they were waiting for the cage after their normal shift. Behind them in front of the safety room, Tony Sabala was on the ground choking and coughing. Lamphere, allergic even to cigarette smoke, fell to his knees gasping for breath. Don Beehner opened self-rescuers and activated them for both men and told them not to take the devices out of their mouths and keep the nose clamps on until they reached clear air. Greg Dionne, after getting his self-rescuer to work, led Tony to the cage when it arrived and guided him on.

Gene Johnson shoved Bill Bennett on the cage before hopping on behind him. The men in the second row held the their comrades standing on the outside edge of the doorless cage as it left the thick smoke. Gene faced those on board and yelled to everyone to walk to the Jewell shaft as soon as they hit the 3100 level. The cage rose at 12:16:30. Mossburgh and Bennett saw Jim Salyer's silhouette in the haze. Salyer was still talking on the phone.

3700 LEVEL EVACUATION

The smoke was so thick the men could not recognize everyone on the cage and many did not know which cage they boarded. In addition to Byron Schulz, Richard Breazeal, Roger Findley, and Jack Harris, who arrived from the 4500 station, it is known that Gary Beckes, Homer Benson, and John Williams boarded the first cage. It was corroborated that Arnold Anderson, Don Beehner, Bill Bennett, Greg Dionne, Gene Johnson, James Lamphere, Les Mossburgh, Clyde Napier, and Tony Sabala were on the second cage. William McKeen (4000 level motorman who had been working near the Jewell station and was on his way to a lower level) and John Gardner, Clarence Stanley, and Morry Story (mechanics from the 08 shop were near the No. 10 station when smoke was detected) were hoisted on one of the two cages. Thus, twenty men, including four from the lower levels, were evacuated from the 3700 level to the 3100 level on the two cages. Jim Salyer and Don Wood died on the 3700 level.

SELF-RESCUERS

Congress required all underground coal miners be provided self-rescuers and trained in their use when it passed the Federal Coal Mine Health and Safety Act of 1969. It was but one of many health and safety statutory standards included in the pervasive 1969 Coal Act. The weak Federal Metal and Nonmetallic Mine Safety Act of 1966 contained no congressionally-mandated standards under the theory that coal mines were notorious for fire disasters and underground "hard rock" mines were much safer because there was little to burn underground. Self-rescuers were not required in metal and nonmetallic mines by the Interior Department's Bureau of Mines until September 9, 1974 — two and one-half years after the Sunshine Mine disaster.

Of the fifteen mines in the Coeur d'Alene Mining District in 1972, only Sunshine and the Bunker Hill Mine provided self-rescuers. But unless miners are trained in their use and familiar with the toxic effects of carbon monoxide (CO), self-rescuers are of little use. As Hap Fowler commented: "If you're not used to them, you might just a well chew on a cork."

The self-rescuers converted CO by an oxidation catalyst (hopcalite) to breathable carbon dioxide in atmospheres containing up to 1% CO for 30 minutes. The manufacturer, Mine Safety Appliances Company (MSA), cautioned in the directions for use to keep calm and avoid exertion, thus their use was severely limited when climbing a series of 200-foot raises to escape.

Few Sunshine miners had been trained in the use of self-rescuers, but even they did not realize the deadly concentrations of CO they faced on the day of the fire. Nor did they know that the greater the concentration of CO, the self-rescuer's oxidation process created a higher temperature of the air breathed through the mouthpiece. In the pre-1969 self-rescuer models provided by Sunshine, the temperature increased 100°C for every 1% CO over the ambient air temperature in the mine, which ranged between 85°F in the vicinity of the 3700 No. 10 station to 92°F on the lower levels. Thus, 1% carbon dioxide flowing into the mouthpiece could reach temperatures of 297 to 304°F. If the CO reached 2%, the mouthpiece airflow could rise to an unbearable 509 to 516°F, which would blister the wearer's mouth and the paint on the self-rescuer. While the CO level during the evacuation of the mine is not known, three days later it was measured at 4.5%.

To the untrained miners, the extremely hot air caused the impression they were not getting any air, which should have been a warning that the concentration of CO was lethal. The intense heat also made them gag and cough, forcing them to remove the respirator from their mouth. The moment of the disaster was no time to read the MSA's instructions that the wearer must grip the mouthpiece in his mouth and seal his nostrils with the attached nose clips and warned:

> Mouth and nose have to be sealed carefully all the time. The appliance must not be taken out of the mouth in any case, nor is its wearer permitted to talk (danger of bypass breathing).

Most men did not know how to open the old model self-rescuers, thought to be an easy process by pressing a button to break the vacuum seal. Most hit them with the ten-inch wrenches every Sunshine miner was required to carry. Many miners complained that the seals on the canisters appeared "vulcanized," and several said they were rusty. Six of the 38 pre-1969 manufactured self-rescuers found in the mine after the fire and examined by the Bureau disclosed they had been stored in the heat and humidity of the mine for over twenty years and only three were less than five years old, notwithstanding the manufacturer's recommended a shelf life of five years. Sunshine also provided 36 new and improved MSA self-rescuers capable of reducing the air temperature inhaled from the mouthpiece to 117°F. in CO concentrations of 1?% and lasted for one hour.

CARBON MONOXIDE

CO is a product of the incomplete combustion of organic substances, such as wood, oil, and tobacco. It is a colorless, tasteless, and essentially odorless gas.

When normal breathing takes place, oxygen passes from the lungs into the blood and interacts with hemoglobin (Hb), a vital chemical in the red blood cells transported to all cells in the body. CO is lethal because its affinity for hemoglobin is three hundred times that of oxygen and creates carboxyhemoglobin (COHb). COHb deprives the body of oxygen and causes anoxia, which affects the nervous system, heart, brain, and other parts of the body.

The symptoms of COHb toxicity include headache, dizziness, dimness of vision, fatigue, muscle weakness, slowing of movements, nausea, and vomiting before collapse, convulsions, coma, and death. Levels of COHb saturation above 50-60% are likely to be fatal in healthy adults. Older people and those with reduced cardiopulmonary functions, such as bronchitis, atherosclerosis, and emphysema or blood disorders, like anemia, might die at COHb saturations as low as 25%. In healthy adults, a saturation of 30% may cause a headache, nausea, lack of concentration, and a feeling of "drunkenness." Between 30 and 40%, the results are vomiting, faintness, loss of visual acuity, weakness, and a slide towards stupor and coma. Over 40 to 50% causes progressive weakness, lack of coordination, and convulsions, which can progress to cardiorespiratory failure and death. Some fit young adults may reach 70% saturation before dying. Heavy smokers invite a disadvantage, their normal COHb level is in the range of 5-6%

Unfortunately, few, if any, of the miners knew the symptoms. Or that high CO exposures can be lethal in minutes.

CHAPTER 4

CONFUSION

Topside

Robert Launhardt, the safety engineer, ran down the steps and into the yard in response to Tom Harrah's urgent phone call. The sixty-year-old maintenance foreman was trotting between the surface machine shop and compressor room.

"Bob, I just got a call from Gene Johnson," Harrah said. "We have a fire in the mine. He wants you to dump the stench in the mine and get the breathing apparatus back at the 3100 No. 10 shaft."

Launhardt's background was unusual in Idaho's panhandle, where mining and logging were kings and every business depended upon the economic well-being of the twin rulers. He had returned as safety engineer on February 14, 1972, a mere ten weeks earlier, after holding the position between 1962 and 1967. He quit in 1967 to sell insurance. When that didn't pan out, he worked for an employment agency.

Upon graduating college in 1954, he was hired by Sunshine as a laborer. His second day on the job, he claimed to have been promoted to timber repairman's helper because of his three summers mining experience while attending college in one of the many small mines dotting Idaho's Salmon River Mountains. It wasn't an advancement. Both were entry level jobs. Launhardt shunned lucrative gypo mining and spent the next eight years as a pipe fitter, a days pay job generally filled by men too young to carry their weight as a contract miner, or older, burned out men who had their fill of the backbreaking labor in the sweltering stopes.

During his first year, Launhardt volunteered to take mine rescue and first-aid training and served as the union safety committeeman until he was promoted to safety engineer in 1962. "Engineer" was a euphemistic title. Launhardt had studied theology in college. His safety education was limited to two one-week courses in accident prevention and safety management offered by the National Safety Council and reading a few books available on industrial safety. The religious, quiet forty-year old was regarded by the miners as conscientious, but not aggressive on safety matters . . . "a company man."

Launhardt and Harrah jogged to the compressor room housing the stench warning system next to the compressed air after-cooler machinery. Launhardt removed the bolts to a metal plate protecting the glass cylinder holding the stench and opened the valves. The final step was to take the hammer dangling from a chain and hit the plunger, shattering the glass and allowing the stench to flow into the compressed air. The simple process injected the mercaptan stench, ethanethiol, which has an extremely unpleasant odor described to reek like rotten cabbage and garlic. When injected into the compressed air it flowed through the mine wherever compressed air is used, such as whiz-bangs, drills, and slushers. The stench acted as a fire alarm to warn men to evacuate deep mines unable to provide audible alarms throughout their miles of tunnels.

Launhardt ran back to his office above the warehouse and placed a call to James Farris, his supervisor and the personnel director attending the Sunshine Mining Company stockholders meeting at a resort hotel in Coeur d'Alene, Idaho, to advise him that there was a fire and the mine was being evacuated. This required going through the hotel switchboard and calling Farris out of the meeting. Then he called the Bunker Hill Mine, the system the Coeur d'Alene mines established to determine where the mine rescue station truck and driver were located. The switchboard operator reported the driver was at the Star Mine. He called the Star Mine, and was told the driver had gone home for lunch. He called the driver's home, and was advised that the driver would probably be at the 610 Cafe. When one of the men eating lunch at the table in his office suggested he call the sheriff's office and ask him to him locate the mine rescue truck and driver, Launhardt asked him to make the call. As an afterthought, Launhardt called the engineering department to bring the mine ventilation maps for the outside rescue teams that would be arriving.

Launhardt hurried down the steps from his office to the change room across the yard to don his hat, belt, and slicker and pick up his cap lamp and battery pack in the charge room, then ran back to his office to get a flame safety lamp and carbon monoxide testers. For the third time, he ran down the steps and across the yard towards the Jewell shaft topside station to deliver the breathing apparatuses to Gene Johnson leading the evacuation of the mine.

After Launhardt released the stench, Tom Harrah followed him to the safety office, hollering to several surface workers in the yard to come with them and carry the 45-pound McCaa self-contained breathing apparatuses to the Jewell shaft. In the rush and confusion Harrah handed a McCaa to a man who immediately put it down and left when someone told him to get more help. After the apparatus backpacks where on the way to the portal, Harrah raced to the surface machine shop and listened on the phone to determine if he could assist in the evacuation. Harrah heard Jim Salyer on the phone attempting to find the location of the fire and Bob Bush notifying the shifters on the lower levels to get their men to the No. 10 stations so they could be hoisted up. Harrah broke in and asked if there was anything he could do. Bob told him no.

Harrah ran out of the surface machine shop two hundred feet across the yard to the Jewell double-drum hoist room and asked the hoistman, Earl Stanfield: "Are you pulling the men out from below?"

"No," Stanfield replied, "I'm pulling muck from the 3700."

"You'd better change over and start getting the men out. There's a fire underground." Harrah said.

Stanfield squawked his cager, Clyde Dunlap, and told him to come out of the 3700 pocket and change the cages for evacuating the men.

No one told the Jewell chippy hoistman, Lino Castaneda, to prepare for the evacuation. An habitual eavesdropper on the party line phone system in the solitary chippy hoist room on the surface, Castaneda overheard one voice out of several he could not identify attempting to determine if there was a fire and a caller give a long ring, the emergency call for any foreman in the mine. A voice he recognized to be Bob Bush answered then called the 08 shop and talked to Pete Bennett. Then he heard Gene Johnson come on the line and ask Tom Harrah to activate the stench warning and send down the self-contained breathing apparatus to the 3100 level and order the No. 10 shaft double-drum hoistman, Ira Sliger, to hoist the men.

Castaneda knew it was the Jewell chippy hoistman's responsibility to hoist the men during emergency evacuations. The chippy hoist had four twelve-man cages and the double-drum hoist only had a single nine-man cage below its two skips. His duties were spelled out in the "Procedure to Follow in Case of Mine Fire" hanging in the chippy hoist room. It said it was the chippy hoistman's duty was to dump the stench, but the maintenance department had removed the stench from the chippy hoist room to the compressor room 200 feet away over one year ago, so it could no longer be his responsibility. Nor could he notify the list of company officials required in the procedures. The list was over one year out of date.

On his own initiative, Castaneda called his cagers, whose names he couldn't recall during his deposition taken four days later, and told them to put the doors on the three open decks of the four-deck cage that are taken off when not hoisting the shifts to make it more accessible to hoist equipment. Castaneda then ordered the cagers to stand by to evacuate the men on the *3700 level . . . not the 3100 level where the men where being evacuated.*

Underground

Ron Stansbury, a track repairman, had been working as motorman on the timber motor for three weeks with motorman Roberto Diaz. They returned on their daily man-trip to the 3700 Jewell shaft station from the No. 10 station scheduled to leave at 11:30, but were five minutes or so late, not that it mattered. Al Walkup, the mine superintendent, and the other "big shots" who usually rode the man-trip were at the company stockholders meeting. The only passengers were Floyd Strand, electrical foreman; Ken Ross, geologist; Larry Hawkins, sampler; and Johnny Reardon, mechanic. No one smelled or saw smoke during the trip.

Reardon belled the cage to take the four men to the surface. They chatted while they waited, ignoring the aggravating constant ringing of the phone at the shaft station for several minutes until Reardon became curious. Thinking it might be an emergency, he picked up the phone up and eavesdropped on the confusing chatter about a fire until someone mentioned Floyd Strand's name.

"There's a fire somewhere in the mine. Floyd, they might want you," Reardon said.

Strand did not say anything. The "Procedures to Follow in Case of Mine Fire" posted next to the phone instructed: "See that phones stay 'on the hook' so necessary calls are not interrupted." He attempted to listen to several conversations going on at the same time, but it was too confusing to determine the location of the fire. He knew it was serious when he heard a hoistman order a Jewell cager to come out of the 3700 ore pocket and go topside to change the muck skips to man cages in preparation to evacuate the mine.

In the meantime, the empty ore train driven by Jasper Beare and Robert Mathews had backed up to the Jewell station after having been ordered by Harvey Dionne to take to Norm Ulrich to the air door. Ron Stansbury and Roberto Diaz, who had left to follow the train and pick up a mucking machine at the No. 10 station, also had to return on the empty flatbed timber car. Ulrich arrived after cutting the air door electrical circuits and running the 400 feet to the station. Paul Johnson, shifter of a small crew working on the 4000 level west of the Jewell shaft, walked over to see what all the excitement was about.

The north double-drum skip arrived from the 3700 ore pocket with cager Clyde Dunlap in a hurry to put a cage under the skip at 12:14 p.m. According to the Jewell double-drum tattletale, Strand, Hawkins, Ross, Reardon, and Ulrich left at 12:14:30.

Robert Perkins, ventilation and refrigeration mechanic, was on his solitary daily rounds checking the fans and air coolers throughout the mine when he arrived at the 3100 Jewell shaft station. He belled the chippy hoist to take him to the 1900 level, his next stop was to check the 100-horsepower fan pushing exhaust air out the Big Hole and Sunshine tunnel to the surface. When the cage did not arrive and the station phone kept ringing for five minutes, he picked it up when it rang 3-3-3, the call for mechanics, thinking it could be for him. He thought he heard Bob Bush, but could not be sure because of the other voices on the line, however, he was positive someone said there was a fire and order a hoistman to get his cager.

Alfred Smith, the forty-two-year-old motorman on the 3100, and his swamper-partner, Gilbert Robles, a miner who had been filling in for two days, were parked next to the station. Perkins told Robles, dumping a load of muck, there was a fire in the mine. Robles yelled to Smith at the other end of the train that there was a mine fire.

Smith told Robles to hurry the dumping and climb aboard. When he became a motorman ten years ago, Smith was instructed by his foreman, if there was a mine fire to bring the muck train to the 3100 No. 10 station to help in the evacuation in case the 3700 level was impassable. It did not matter if the train was not fitted with seats and the men would have to ride in the muck cars, nor that the motorman's assignment in case of fire was not listed on the instructions.

They first encountered smoke coming out the crosscut leading to the No. 5 shaft, about half-way on the one-mile trip. It surprised both men. The area had been clear less than fifteen minutes earlier when they had driven the train to the Jewell station. The fire had to be big and below the 3100 level. The No. 5 shaft only went as high as the 3100 level.

When the first cage from the 3700 level arrived on the 3100 level a few seconds before 12:14, the men stepping off were relieved to find smoke was much lighter. Most sensed they were out of danger and mulled about waiting for their partners and co-workers to arrive from below. Gary Beckes and John Williams wandered into the double-drum hoist room across from the No. 10 shaft. Wisps of smoke wafted in the huge white-painted cavity, similar to a party where everyone was smoking. Beckes nodded to Ira Sliger operating the hoist in his enclosed cab. Sliger looked back at Beckes as if to say everything was under control.

Richard Breazeal and Jack Harris headed straight for the Jewell at a brisk pace, both having eaten enough smoke to last a lifetime. As they hiked towards the drift, they passed the muck train arriving in the drift behind the shaft leading to the loading chute pockets.

The second cage from the 3700 level arrived at 12:17. Gene Johnson jumped off and asked Greg Dionne, a level-headed-twenty-three-year-old and experienced cager, to start picking up men on the 4400 level, then asked twenty-one-year-old Byron Schulz to act as Greg's relief cager. Gene ordered Roger Findley, the nineteen-year-old cager, to head to the Jewell. Not wanting to be left out of the rescue effort, Roger volunteered to stay and count the men.

Alfred Smith ran from the train and asked Gene Johnson what he should do. He nodded his understanding when Gene told him to stand by and tell those coming up to walk to the Jewell or wait for him to haul them out if they didn't feel able to walk.

"When you get a load, take it back to the Jewell and pick up the breathing apparatuses and bring them back," Gene ordered. He put his self-rescuer back in his mouth and kneeled by the shaft to catch his breath as Sliger dropped the south cage to the 4400 level at 12:18:30.

The Jewell double-drum cage stopped at the 3100 level at 12:16 to pick up Robert Perkins on his way to check the fan on the 1900 level. The bosses on the surface would need to know the exhaust ventilation condition on the level during a fire.

Floyd Strand, aware the 3100 level was the evacuation route, asked Norm Ulrich, the able second lead electrician, to stay on the level in case an electrician was needed. The others continued up on the cage. Although they were never in danger, Strand, Reardon, Ross, and Hawkins were the first to escape when they arrived on the surface at 12:18.

Perkins walked through the air door next to the shaft on the 1900 level and 600 feet to a the second air door, not suspecting the extent of the fire. When he opened the door the smoke was so thick he could not see more than two or three feet into the drift. He closed the door and hurried back to the shaft and belled for a cage to take him to the surface. Ten of the longest and loneliest minutes in his life passed before the cage arrived and hoisted him to the surface.

Paul Johnson hopped on a Mancha Midget and drove 1,200 feet out the Syndicate drift west of the Jewell shaft on the 3700 level. The forty-seven-year-old shifter climbed down the 180 feet of manway ladders like a fireman, relieved he didn't find the two miners at the bottom of the 71 E stope on the 4000 level. Paul hollered to them that there was a fire and to climb to the 3700 level, so not to tie up the skips when the men were being evacuated, and go out the Jewell shaft.

The shifter waited on a sixteen-foot offset between ladders until forty-eight-year-old Jack Seagraves told him he could make it without any problems. Johnson didn't ask Seagraves's partner, Larry Hansen. At twenty, Hansen was expected to be able to climb 180 feet without any difficulty. After the miners gathered their coats and lunch buckets, Johnson started back up with Seagraves and Hansen under him. Two-thirds of the way up Seagraves became winded and rested for a minute. Hansen waited for his older partner while Johnson continued to climb up, hurrying to get back to the Jewell and help evacuate men. When the pair reached the 3700 level, they walked to the 1,200 feet to the Jewell shaft station.

Futility and Death on the 3700 Level

Harvey Dionne drove the Mancha Midget towards the Jewell to make sure Norman Ulrich had been able to close the door. He stopped to pick up track repairman Edward Davis west of the No. 4 shaft. Davis was walking towards the Jewell after being told by Ken Tucker and Pete Bennett there was a fire. He had been replacing track timbers on the old haulageway in fresh air unaware that toxic smoke was pouring from the No. 5 shaft. They passed Tucker and Bennett as they approached the air door and pushed it open with the motor. Waiting for Davis at the Jewell station was his partner, Richard Nickelby. Nickelby had been repairing the track 500 feet from the Jewell shaft station when told by Jasper Beare, the ore train motorman, to go to the Jewell.

Hap Fowler backed away from the wall of smoke and turned to look back at Jim Bush. For a few seconds, he saw Pat Hobson talking with Jim before both disappeared in the wave of smoke rolling down the drift. The sixty-one-year-old shaft repairman spun around and started running as fast as his aging legs could carry him over the railroad tracks and rubble in the dark. Holding the self-rescuer in his mouth slowed him down. He inhaled and filled his lungs and tossed the self-rescuer on the ground, then held his breath for as long as he could. A dozen desperate gulps of smoke-filled air seared his lungs before his cap lamp beam pierced through the smoke and he stumbled out of the blackness into fresh air. His legs were turning into rubber and his feet felt like they had lead weights tied on them when he fell by the side of the tracks five feet west of the No. 5 shaft. Unable to move, he lay on the ground until his energy sapped by the carbon monoxide returned and his breathing was almost back to normal.

Jim Bush asked Pat Hobson where Bob was as they stood in the swirling opaque smoke that dulled the beams from their cap lamps. Hobson told him that Bob was coming behind him. The fifty-seven-year-old mechanic held his breath, his only defense against the toxic smoke without a self-rescuer. Seconds later, Jim saw a cap lamp approaching through the smoke. He wasn't able to recognize Wayne Blalack until he was five feet from him. Blalack took his self-rescuer out of his mouth and told him that Bob was a few yards behind him and in trouble. Jim's eyes were watering and couldn't see Bob's cap lamp through the smoke. He walked back until he saw a bobbing cap lamp in the haze. Even in the murky gloom he knew the light was too low. Bob was sinking to his knees.

Jim pulled his brother up and laid Bob's left arm over his shoulder, then wrapped his right arm around Bob's back. He half-carried Bob about 500 feet, although he couldn't tell exactly to where, and caught up with Hobson laying on the ground. A few feet farther Blalack was stretched out. Still holding Bob up, he reached down and yanked Hobson to his feet, then told him to put his right arm around his shoulder while he wrapped his left arm under Hobson's arm and around his back. Jim urged Blalack to get up and walk in front of him. As Blalack stumbled along the tracks, Jim occasionally nudged him from behind with his knee.

In the smoke there was no way Jim could tell how far they had trudged or how close the No. 5 shaft and fresh air were. He felt himself getting weaker with each step, and Hobson and Bob were losing their strength and ability to walk and hold on to his shoulders. Every step become harder and Jim knew he couldn't hold Bob and Hobson up much longer. He couldn't stop his knees from buckling as he collapsed sending the three of them sprawling on the tracks. On his hands and knees he managed to roll Bob off one side of the tracks and push Hobson to off other side. Jim crawled to Blalack a few feet up the drift, but the robust foreman who normally could have carried two men was too weak from the carbon monoxide that was sapping his energy to even lift Blalack's leg off the track.

Jim rose to his feet and staggered, falling twice and crawling, before he made the 500 feet to the No. 5 shaft and fresh air. He woke up in the middle of the tracks unaware how long he had been unconscious, but knew he had to get help for the three men he left in the drift. He tottered 800 feet to the Sunshine Consolidated south crosscut in the drift bend. The forty-five degree turn had a signal light on the rib to warn the trains leaving the Jewell shaft station that a train was coming from the No. 10 station. He reached up and pulled the cord activating the red lights overhead and at the Jewell shaft station to instruct the motormen not to leave until the train arrived from the No. 10 station.

At the Jewell shaft station, Harvey Dionne saw the station's red signal light flashing as he talked to an exhausted Hap Fowler, sitting on a bench after staggering into the station. As the train was at the station, Dionne knew someone must be in trouble. Paul Johnson and Dionne ran for the train and yelled to the others on the station that someone needed help at the signal lights 1,500 feet down the drift and not visible from the Jewell station because of the air door. Ron Stansbury, Roberto Diaz, and Richard Nickelby jumped on the train and Pete Bennett and Hap Fowler followed on a Mancha Midget. As they approached the Sunshine Consolidated signals, Dionne and Johnson saw Jim Bush reeling down the drift towards them as if he was drunk, then plop down by the side of the tracks.

Fowler asked where Pat Hobson was, as his friend was with Jim when he last saw them in the drift.

"Pat, Bob, and Wayne are back in the drift and down." Jim said, barely able to speak. Although too disoriented to recall exactly, he added that he thought they were several hundred feet past the No. 5 shaft in the smoke and warned that Wayne Blalack's leg was on the tracks.

The men on the train climbed back on and headed down the drift as Hap leaned over and asked Jim how he felt.

"As soon as I get my legs under me, I'll go back in." Jim said, almost in a stupor and unable to stop his head bobbing.

"You can't go back in," Fowler said, "The smoke will get you. I'll follow you topside and see if we can get some equipment, then we'll go back in."

Jim nodded and got on the Mancha Midget with Fowler. Pete Bennett drove them back to the Jewell. Now more coherent, he told Bennett to go topside and get the McCaas while Fowler called to order them.

Fowler couldn't get any answers where the McCaas were, because two or three men were talking, until someone said: "I think some went to 3100."

"Can't you ring 3100 so I can get some pieces down here? We've got three guys in there that may be dead now."

"Can't you get them up on their feet?" a voice asked.

"Hell no, they may be dead. Get some down here," Fowler pleaded.

"I don't know what to tell you, I don't know anything about them," the voice said.

Fowler handed the phone to Jim Bush, but no one could help him.

In the meantime, Pete Bennett belled the chippy cage and started up. The cager, standing on the station and oblivious to Jim's orders, belled the hoistman to signal that someone had taken his cage. Lino Castaneda, the hoistman, stopped the cage and sent it back to the 3700 level before it got to the 3100 level, angry that someone should take the cage without the cager knowing it when he was waiting for men to be evacuated on the 3700.

"Why did you take me down?" Pete Bennett asked Castaneda over the phone.

"I took you down because my cager is down below and somebody else asked for the cage," Castaneda said.

"I wanted to come up because I have orders to get breathing apparatus," Bennett said.

Castaneda knew the McCaas were on the way down on the other cage from listening to the phone conversations. He laughed and said there was no use for Bennett to tell him, and held his the cage on the 3700 level. Castaneda's eavesdropping had not picked up that the evacuation was taking place on the 3100 level. He disregarded Jim

Bush's order. Nor did Castaneda know that his half-brother, Roberto Diaz, was going into the lethal smoke without a self-rescuer.

Paul Johnson stopped the man train in the fresh air. West of the No. 5 shaft the air was clear. Smoke pouring from the shaft formed a curtain hiding the drifts in front of the men and coursed into the juncture of the main and old haulageways.

Stansbury, the youngest at thirty-two, led the assault into the gray depths of the main haulageway followed by Dionne and Diaz, the oldest at fifty-five. Paul Johnson and Nickelby trotted into the old haulageway. None wore self-rescuers. After travelling 200 feet, Johnson and Nickelby realized they were in the old haulageway and returned to the fresh air. Johnson's brief encounter with the toxic smoke told him they would need the train if they were to bring out three men. He jumped on and drove it into the smoke with Nickelby following on foot.

It was impossible to recognize a man five feet away in dark tunnel, and the dense smoke stung their eyes and made them tear. With Stansbury in the lead, the trio kept going until they had traveled about 500 feet. Stansbury didn't recognize Blalack lying on the track until he and leaned down and his cap lamp lit Blalack's face. Several feet ahead the dim beam from his cap lamp outlined a form on the ground next to the track. When he kneeled down, he recognized Pat Hobson. The mechanic was gasping for air. Stansbury yelled back to Diaz to try and get them out while he tried to find Bob Bush. Several steps down the tracks he found Bob on his back. Stansbury tried to lift him, but discovered he didn't have the strength. He tried to drag Bob by the arms and found the exertion and noxious smoke made him choke and lightheaded. He had no choice but to run back for help from the others.

Meanwhile, Paul Johnson drove the man train slowly into the drift, unable to see where he was going over the two ore cars in front of the motor. He couldn't see the men in front of him when the front car struck Blalack's leg and sent the train sliding off the track. Dionne, Johnson, and Diaz lifted the car off Blalack's leg. Without being told what to do, they knew the only way to get the men on the ground out was to put them on the train. Twice they tried to lift the motor back on the track, the second effort with Nickelby's help, but they didn't have the strength.

Aware two men could normally lift a car back on the track, Dionne realized they were being weakened by the carbon monoxide faster than he believed possible. He yelled: "Let's get out of here." Having overseen the work to improve the ventilation on the main haulage drift, Dionne retreated several yards towards the No. 10 station to the crosscut to the old haulageway where he thought the smoke should be lighter.

Without warning, Paul Johnson fell like a toppled tree to the ground. Nickelby tried to lift him, but found he could barely lift Johnson's arms. He turned to ask Diaz for help, but was forced to helplessly watch Diaz fall to his knees unconscious. Nickelby could do nothing but run as fast as he could towards the No. 5 shaft or suffer the same fate.

Stansbury arrived seconds later and found Diaz on the ground. He tried to lift him, but couldn't. He took two steps and fell then crawled several feet before he could get up and stagger to the No. 5 shaft, stumbling against the rib and falling twice before reaching the life-saving fresh air.

After Dionne, Nickelby, and Stansbury staggered out of the smoke, they collapsed by the tracks to gather their strength and wits until the fresh air drove the carboxyhemoglobin from their system. Dionne, weak and unable to rise, asked Stansbury and Nickelby to go to the Jewell and phone topside for breathing apparatuses. The foreman leaned back against the rib, unable to believe what had happened. There was nothing he could do to save the dying men.

CHAPTER 5

TRAGIC ERRORS

The 4400 Level

The 4400, 4600, and 4800 levels were connected by raises, allowing the miners to climb from their stopes to the nearest level. The 3,500-foot long 4400 level was shaped like a dogleg. Two winding drifts in the west connected the bend near the No. 10 shaft. To the east a series of crosscuts to raises jutted off the lower leg like fetlocks.

Twenty-five-year-old William Mitchell and fifty-year-old Robert Waldvogel mined the only active stope, 10 E, 900 feet from the No. 10 shaft station. Drift miners Allen Sargent and Howard Harrison were extending the 625 west drift. Motorman John Peterson serviced both crews. Repairmen enlarging the 4400 shaft pocket limited the ability to hoist muck and ore, and the five men on the level did not justify a shifter. Jim Bush, production foreman, and Jim Salyer, drift foreman, dropped by once or twice a day to check their progress. Gene Johnson, shaft foreman, was scheduled inspect the 4400 shaft pocket that afternoon.

Shaft repairmen Benjamin Barber, Robert Barker, Irvan Puckett, and Jack Reichert were working in the shaft pocket and smelled and saw smoke coming down the shaft about the time Dusty Rhoads called from the 4400 shaft station around 11:45 to ask if they were burning anything. The repairmen climbed from the pocket and joined Rhoads and Randy Peterson, stranded on the station after they could not communicate with the chippy hoist. Puckett ran down the drift to warn the men on the level there was a fire and to go to the station. Rhoads and Randy Peterson stayed at the station attempting to signal for a hoist while the shaft repairmen waited around the corner where the smoke was lighter.

Waldvogel was up in the 10 E stope slushing ore by scraping it into the chute. Mitchell was on the level pulling the chute with fingerboards, a huge powered rake that dragged the rock out of the chute and into the ore cars. John Peterson was on the ore train motor waiting for Mitchell to fill the car before moving the second car in position when Puckett arrived. Puckett told Peterson there was a fire and to go to the station and to tell Mitchell and Waldvogel because he could not squeeze past the ore cars in the narrow drift. Peterson yelled the warning to Mitchell over the roar of rock tumbling out of the chute and into the ore car.

Mitchell yelled up the raise: "Bob, grab your water jug and come down out of the raise. There's a fire."

When Mitchell tried to leave the raise, he discovered Peterson had hurriedly left with Puckett, leaving the cars blocking the entrance to the raise. After a few angry expletives, Mitchell climbed over the ore cars to the motor in front and told his partner to get in the last ore car, then drove the motor to a stub drift to allow Waldvogel to squirm between the rib and ore cars.

They ambled in no hurry and met Edward Gonzales and Frankie Sisk, stope miners from the 4600 level working within 20 feet of the 4400 level. Both had climbed up after being notified by Puckett. A few steps later, they noticed a smokey haze coming up the No. 4 stope and the J-4 raise. The experienced miners knew the smoke was coming down the No. 10 shaft to the lower levels then circulating back up the raises under the fan ventilation system and contaminating the entire mine.

By the time they men reached the station the smoke was searing their lungs and making their eyes water. Hidden from their view, Robert Barker stood outside the shaft's north compartment squawking for the double-drum hoist. Dusty Rhoads was on the phone and Randy Peterson was squawking for the chippy hoist on the intercom. At first, in the smoke and without a shifter, no one could find the cabinet containing the self-rescuers. Mitchell and several others pulled off their T-shirts and soaked them with water. The wet T-shirts appeared to filter out the smoke and cooled their eyes. After one of the shaft repairmen found the locked self-rescuer cabinet, he busted the small lock with a swipe of his wrench and passed them out, but no one knew how they worked. Ed Gonzales, who could bend nails with his hands, couldn't press the button to get his open. Using a miner's solution to fix most anything, they hit the button with their ten-inch wrenches.

Still, everyone remained calm. Mitchell joked when he saw Jack Reichert: "I hope you didn't start it, Jackie."

As they bitched about the smoke and cussed the self-rescuers they couldn't get to work, they were joined by George Birchett, Gustav Thor, Floyd Byington, Roderick Davenport, Jack Ivers, and Leonard Rathbun from the 4600 level and Kevin Croker from the 4800 level, although the smoke made it impossible to recognize everyone.

Dusty Rhoads said he and Randy Peterson would stay on the station and bell for a hoist while the others went around the corner where there was less smoke. Out of sight of Dusty and the others, repairmen Benjamin Barber, Jack Reichert, and Robert Barker, who had been squawking for the hoist, and miners George Birchett, Gustav Thor, Jack Ivers, Leonard Rathbun, Floyd Byington, and Roderick Davenport got on the double-drum north cage that had been sitting there since 12:07 to make sure it wouldn't leave without them.

Ira Sliger raised the north cage with the nine men on board at 12:17. It arrived on the 3700 level a few seconds after 12:18:30. The men got off, expecting to he hauled out on the train to the Jewell as they were after every shift, minutes after the level had been evacuated by Gene Johnson. At 12:22 Sliger raised the north cage to below the 3100 level, where it arrived at 12:23. He left it idling until 12:27, then dropped it to the 4200 level, where it arrived at 12:28. The north cage remained on the 4200 level until 12:50.

Either Sliger did not know men were on board the cage or he made a tragic error. There was no reason to raise the cage to the 3700 level after it had been evacuated. Men had been signaling steadily from the 4400 level for over one-half hour. [8]

---

8 According to the testimony of Robert L. Anderson, chief engineer, the tattletales were not synchronized by approximately one and one-half minutes when set in the morning, as evidenced by the north and south skips not being raised and lowered in opposite directions during normal operations on the tattletales. If the north was faster, the men on the 3700 level would have seen the cage arrive from the 4400 level. Therefore the south cage tattletale was set faster than the north and the north cage missed the south cage leaving the 3700 level by around two minutes.

After discovering the north cage had left, William Mitchell and Edward Gonzales decided to stick with Dusty Rhoads and Randy Peterson at the station. Several minutes later, the older men couldn't take the caustic smoke. They yelled to Randy that they were going to the motor barn, a drift 100 feet from the station, and get a few whiffs of compressed air from a whiz-bang. Randy didn't hear their shouts and panicked when he couldn't see them and yelled, fearing he might have been left again. The three men ran to the station, thinking the cage had arrived, only to discover the frightened young cager. Randy insisted they return to the motor barn. He would stiff it out and keep squawking for the double-drum hoist.

While Sliger had the north gage on the 3700 level, he slowly lowered the south cage to the 3700 level. Without stopping, he dropped it fast to the 4200 and slowed it to a stop on the 4400 level at 12:21. Rhoads, Randy Peterson, Mitchell, and Gonzales boarded. Before the cage left, they told cager Gregg Dionne they were the only men left, thinking the others had been hoisted on the north skip. They were unaware that 125 feet around a bend in the drift shielding themselves from the smoke, Howard Harrison, John Peterson, Irvan Puckett, Allen Sargent, and Robert Waldvogel from then 4400 level; Frankie Sisk from the 4600 level; and Kevin Croker, the rugged Australian-born miner who had climbed up from the 4800 level, stood waiting for the cage.

The 4600 Level

Virgil Bebb, 4600 level shifter, and Charles Casteel, 4800 level shifter, were on the 4600 No. 10 station. Most 4800 stope miners were working close to the 4600 level and it was faster and easier for Casteel to climb down the raises to check their progress from the 4600 level. Bebb belled for the chippy cage several times and received no response. He decided to call and find out why he couldn't get a cage. Instead of getting the chippy hoistman on the line, he overheard several conversations about a fire.

"There's a fire somewhere," Bebb said to Casteel and Edward Fox, a miner working next to the station as grizzly man.

The shifters were listening on the line when they noticed smoke blowing in from the shaft. Bebb ordered Fox to go to the east and tell the men to come to the station. Casteel took off running west to tell his crews near the 4600 level to tell the men to go to the nearest No. 10 station. Seconds later, motorman Gordon Osterberg returned to the station after delivering powder to the stopes. Bebb told him to go west and round up the crew.

Dennis Clapp and James Sheppard were working in the H-6 stope, 1,500 feet from the station. Wayne Fister, a motorman, was slushing on the sill. Clapp was drilling when Sheppard said he smelled smoke. He turned off the drill and said he thought he smelled something, but it didn't smell like smoke, so he continued drilling until Fox yelled to Fister that there was a fire and to go to the station and to tell the men in the next stope.

They picked up their lunch buckets and jackets and walked to the No. 4 stope. Clapp climbed 60 feet down a raise until he could see the miners working in the stope. He shined his cap light at Ron Flory and Tom Wilkinson, stope miners from the 4800 level, and yelled that there was fire and they should head for the No. 10 station, then he relayed Casteel's message to send a motor to tell the drift miners, Richard Allison and Ronald Wilson, in the West Syndicate drift, almost one and one-quarter miles from the No. 10 shaft.

Roger Ostoj and Frank Norris were removing an Alimak raise climber with an acetylene torch in the J-4 raise 800 feet from the shaft station when they smelled smoke. Concerned they may have ignited wood in the raise, they sprayed the area with water then continued cutting the brackets off the raise climber.

When Norris climbed down the raise after lowering a load of Alimak parts to the sill, he yelled up at Ostoj: "The whole area is full of smoke."

By the time Ostoj climbed down, Fox was running towards them and yelling that they should go to the station.

Osterberg motored past Roger Koisti and Terry Jerome standing in the drift at the bottom of the service raise and told them to run to the station. Both had seen and smelled smoke that made Koisti ill, forcing them to leave the raise.

There was no way to count all the men working on the 4600 level. All Virgil Bebb could do was assure that his crew was notified. The only 4600 level men on the station were Edward Fox, Terry Jerome, Roger Koisti, Frank Norris, Bob Ostoj, Gordon Osterberg, Dennis Clapp, James Sheppard, Wayne Fister, and the Harold and Reuben Mendy, the motormen-brother team. No one appeared concerned about a fire. Norris and Ostoj sat on a bench and ate their lunch. Bebb could only pray that his crew in the stopes had been told to go to the nearest station and climbed up to the 4400 level or down to the 4800 level.

Charlie Casteel, 4800 shifter, could only tally 4800 level stope miners Robert Morris and Ernie Kienholz and grizzly man John Henry, scheduled to help out on the 4800 that afternoon. Remos McDaniel, a repairman working in the K drift on the 4800, had climbed to the 4600. McDaniel was sure that his partner, Kevin Croker, had continued climbing to the 4400 level.

There was nothing Bebb and Casteel could do but wait for the cage and count their men when they got off on the 3700 level, the usual evacuation route. When the smoke started to increase, the shifters handed out self-rescuers to the men, however, even Bebb and Casteel weren't sure how they worked. Five or six men retreated 300 feet to the motor barn. The air appeared clearer in the motor barn and it had a whiz-bang they could use to blow compressed air in their faces. Most insisted they didn't need self-rescuers.

A yell from Bebb at 12:22:30 that the cage had arrived brought everyone to the station. Greg Dionne got off and loaded the cage. As there did not seem any danger on the level, Casteel and Bebb decided they should go up on the first skip and count their men to make sure they all got up. Greg sent the cage up, but stayed to conserve room and assure they had a cager on the level. The cage left at 12:23:30.

When the cage returned at 12:27:30 with Byron Schulz, Greg had the men standing by to be crammed in the cage and belled on their way up by 12:28:30. Schulz and Greg stayed because there wasn't enough room, although Greg was becoming dizzy and the smoke was getting worse. Greg had broken the basic rule not to take his self-rescuer out of his mouth to show the others how to open and use theirs. As they waited for the cage to return, Ira Sliger called to tell them he was going to skip the 4800 level, contrary to Gene Johnson's orders to evacuate the levels in the order of depth, and take them to the 5000 level. Someone on the 5000 level had called that a man was down and seriously ill.

The 3100 Level

On the 3100 level, Dusty Rhoads and Arnold Anderson were on the phone asking for permission to shut off the 3400 fans. They believed the exhaust fans were recirculating the smoke and carbon monoxide down the raises between the 3100 and 3700 level and contaminating the fresh air intake. Electrical foreman Floyd Strand and maintenance foreman Tom Harrah were not ventilation experts and were hesitant to order the fans to be cut off. Both cited the danger of changing a ventilation system that men might be relying upon to seek fresh air. Dusty's reply that any damn air flow was better than the entire mine becoming contaminated fell on deaf ears. Dusty told them that he and Arnold were going to the 3400 level to wait for authorization when the mine management arrived.

Dusty told Gene that he and Arnold wanted to go to the 3400 level to shut off the fans. Gene told them to tell the hoistman to drop them off and be damn quick about it as the air was getting worse by the minute. Dusty ran to the hoist room to tell Ira Sliger to make a quick stop on the 3400 level and don't bother waiting for a signal to leave.

Gene Johnson cleared the second cage from the 4600 level and signalled it down in thirty seconds. Sliger dropped the cage from the 3100 at 12:30 and jerked it to a stop for a blink of an eye at the 3400 level to permit Dusty and Arnold to jump off, before stopping on the 4600 for less than 15 seconds to pick up Greg Dionne and Byron Schulz. The cage passed the 4800 level and arrived at the 5000 level at 12:33:30.

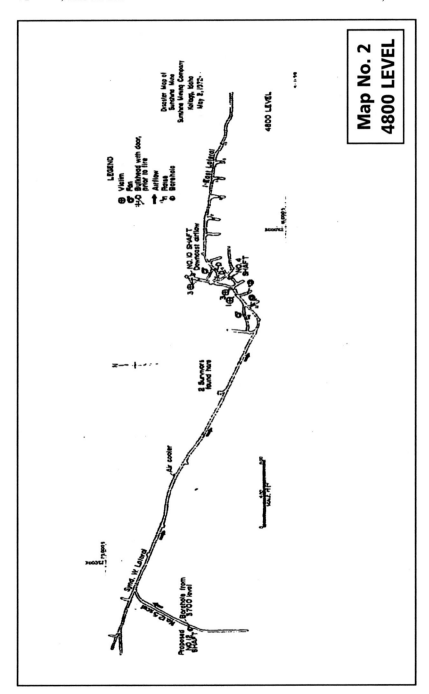

The 4800 Level

Twenty-eight-year-old gypo miner Ron Flory was endowed with a rangy athletic build. At six-two and 190 pounds, he stood a head taller than his 140-pound, twenty-nine-year-old partner, Tom Wilkinson. The partners worked well as a team, proving looks are deceiving. With his brooding eyes and close-cropped black beard, Ron looked the part of a rugged miner. On the street, Tom could have passed for an accountant with his horn-rimmed glasses and gentile smile, unless you noticed his sinewy arms, a product of eight years in the mines.

Instead of taking time out for lunch in the 4 E stope, where time is money and often only one can work at the face, Ron ran the slusher while Tom ate his lunch. Then Tom took over the slushing the ore down the chute while Ron gobbled his lunch so he would have time for a cigarette. Ron lit his cigarette and stretched out on a stack of lagging.

"Tom, I smell smoke," Ron yelled over the slusher's grating rumble.

Tom shut off the slusher and looked around to see if anything was burning and checked to determine if the slusher was overheating. Finding nothing wrong, he turned the slusher back on.

"I still smell something burning," Ron said and blinked at a cap lamp flashing in his eyes from above.

Tom turned the slusher off again and looked up the raise at the light. Dennis Clapp had climbed down from the 4600 level. Clapp yelled that there was a fire on the upper levels and Charlie Casteel wanted them to take a motor and ride out to the West Syndicate drift and tell the men to go to the station.

Tom and Ron ran 400 feet to the motor barn for a motor and drove out the mile and one-quarter on the West Syndicate Lateral drift to tell drift miners Richard Allison and Ronald Wilson to follow them on their motor. When the four arrived at the motor barn, they walked the 600 feet to the station and found it blanketed in smoke. Already at the station were David Mullen, Gordon Whatcott, Richard Bewley, Hubert Patrick, and Darrell Stephens. Stephens, a nineteen-year-old motorman, had started in the mine the day before, but maintained his composure among the older men. The boy's father had retired after a mining accident, and it wouldn't do to show fear.

Everyone picked up a self-rescuer from a stack on the shifter's work bench. Ron had no problem opening his self-rescuer after he gave the button a swipe with his wrench, but Tom couldn't get his to work. With only nine men on the station and eighteen devices sitting in boxes, Tom dumped his first on a bench and opened a second. After whacking it with his wrench and fiddling with the nose clips, he thought it might be working, but as he had never used one, he wasn't sure.

The increasing smoke on the station told them to get organized. They decided that seven should go back to the motor barn, a crosscut where the smoke was much lighter, and rotate two men watching the station, one to listen on the phone for instructions and the second to watch for the cage and continue belling for the hoist. The veteran miners knew the fan on the top of the No. 4 raise was sucking up the smoke to the 4600 level and keeping a good deal of the smoke from the motor barn. They figured, if they opened the two air doors in the drift between the East Lateral and the track line to the No. 10 shaft, it might stop the smoke circulating back to the motor barn. Ron gripped his self-rescuer in his teeth and ran to the first door. It opened easily; however, the suction caused by over 15,000 cubic feet a minute of air was so great he couldn't shove open the second door by himself. Another man came from behind him to help. With their combined brute strength, they pushed the door open, but the suction slammed the first door shut behind them. Behind them, Tom and Richard Allison, managed to push open the first door, but it didn't help clear the air. The fans in the nearby raises were drawing the smoke back.

Ron returned to the motor barn only to discover the smoke had increased. He walked back to close the air doors. As he turned into the crosscut, he heard the air door slam and saw that Tom had collapsed and Allison was unable to lift him. Ron tried to lift Tom, but couldn't for reasons he didn't comprehend. He ran back and told the others that Tom was down and to bring him back to the motor barn, then ran to the station. He belled 9-4-8, the nine-bell emergency signal and station number. The hoistman's reply signal was jumbled, so he belled 9-4-8 again. The hoistman signalled back with the emergency recognition that he would send the hoist as soon as possible. Ron waited for the cage until he began to get dizzy and felt his knees turning into rubber before running back to the motor barn.

Tom had not come to when Ron arrived. Someone suggested taking him to the West Syndicated drift where the air should be clearer because of the air cooler halfway up the drift. Three men lifted Tom on a motor. Ron drove Tom and Allison, who was gasping for breath and weak-kneed, 800 feet past the bend to the West Syndicate. Unable to think of anything else to do, Ron slapped Tom's face until he came out of his stupor. Feeling able and anxious to keep in contact with the others at the station, Ron left Tom and Allison in the crosscut and ran back to the motor barn.

By the time Ron arrived at the motor barn, someone had gone to the station to retrieve all the self-rescuers. They decided to give one motor to the two men at the station and keep the second at the motor barn with the others. Ron and Hubert Patrick ran back to where Tom and Allison were resting to get the second motor. After running almost the length of three football fields, Ron was dizzy again. He had not been using his self-rescuer and was tired from running back and forth. Allison said he was feeling better and he would return with Patrick and that Ron should stay with Tom.

The partners sat in the entrance to the crosscut gradually regaining their strength. After fifteen anxious minutes passed and no one had returned for them, Ron walked around the bend to make sure the smoke wasn't creeping up on them and check on their comrades. When he reached the H-6 crosscut, he saw the dim lights of two motors through the smokey haze by the entrance to the motor barn. Without a self-rescuer, he approached cautiously until he saw four bodies sprawled next to the motors. He ran back to get Tom to help him.

They pulled the first body back to the front of the motor and tried to revive him by slapping his face, but he was dead. The smoke and carbon dioxide was making them dizzy again and they knew they didn't have the strength to stay longer. Both had left their self-rescuers in the motor barn. They climbed on the motor and rode back to fresh air. Unable to talk, they sat exhausted from breathing the toxic smoke, hoping their other three comrades had found fresh air. There was also the ominous concern that the cage may had arrived and left without them.

CHAPTER 6

RUN TO THE JEWELL

Jewell Topside

Floyd Strand ran out of the cage on the Jewell top station at 12:18 and shouted: "Clear the station, they're bringing the men out."

Shaft repairmen Richard McKinney, Clifford Peterson, and James Zingler were building a new topside floor. Upon hearing that there was a fire and an evacuation ordered, they shut down their machines and stood outside the portal to see if they could help. The sight of surface employees lugging McCaa self-contained breathing apparatuses down the warehouse steps told them what needed to be done. Surface office workers were out of their element lugging the 45-pound aluminum back pack devices and were not dressed to go in the mine. Each grabbed two McCaas and carried them into the waiting cage.

Larry Hawkins, after arriving on the cage with Strand, ran to the warehouse and lugged two McCaas back to the cage, then waited outside the portal to see if he could assist in the rescue.

Zingler, trained in mine rescue, carefully arranged the McCaas on the floor of the cage. As the cage door had been removed, he stood in front so they wouldn't bounce out during the bumpy ride down. Richard McKinney and Clifford Peterson rode down on the cage above to help unload them on the 3100 level.

Launhardt arrived at the portal alone. Hawkins, also trained in mine rescue, was aware that Launhardt should not go into contaminated air alone and couldn't handle ten McCaas by himself. Hawkins volunteered to go with him. As they walked through the 200-foot long portal to the Jewell topside station, Launhardt told him they had to deliver the McCaas to Gene Johnson on the 3100 level as soon as possible and assist in the evacuation. No one had instructed a cage be held for Launhardt, forcing them to wait precious minutes for another cage.

The 3100 Level

Les Mossburgh stepped off the cage on the 3100 level and calmly laid his coat on a tugger, a small compressed air hoist used in raises sitting on the station, then took his cap lamp off his belt and put it on his hard hat. He looked back at Gene Johnson as he shoved his arms through his coat sleeves. Everything appeared under control. There was only a slight haze on the station when he turned and started walking to the Jewell. Gene was kneeling by the shaft attempting to catch his breath when Gregg Dionne left on the cage at 12:18:30. As Mossburgh walked from the station he saw the muck train sitting in the 3100 switch. He didn't think anyone would need a ride to the Jewell unless the smoke became worse.

Confused which direction to take, John Williams and Gary Beckes asked Clyde Napier if they should walk out the Silver Summit escape route. Napier advised him that it was over 6,000 feet to the Silver Summit shaft and it would be in exhaust air and too dangerous. Unsure of Napier's advice, Beckes asked Arnold Anderson, the lead electrician, if they should walk out the Silver Summit, the secondary escape route. Anderson repeated Gene Johnson's instructions to walk to the Jewell and said he going to stay in case Dusty Rhoads needed an electrician to cut off the exhaust fans on the 3400 level.

Beckes and Williams started walking to the Jewell shaft and soon passed Tony Sabala and Don Beehner. Tony was struggling to keep up with the string of men ahead of him barely visible in the opaque smoke. He was gasping and taking his self-rescuer out of his mouth as if he was smoking a pipe. It was one of the new models that didn't heat up to high temperatures, but excitable Tony didn't know if he was getting "good air" because it felt warm in his mouth. Greg Dionne had not told him he was staying to cage the men from the lower levels. Tony couldn't understand why Greg, his young partner he depended on and thought of like a son, had left him and was probably walking out ahead of him. But Tony was not left alone.

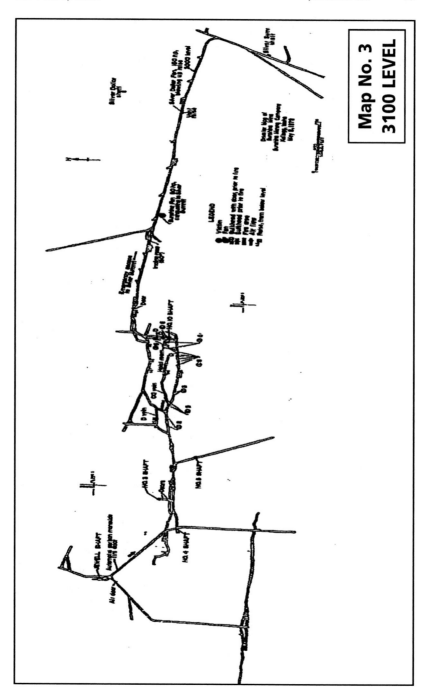

Map No. 3
3100 LEVEL

Don Beehner kept prodding him from behind and asking if he was okay. Don was trained in first aid and a member of the mine rescue crew. And Don would never let a fellow miner down.

Richard Breazeal and Jack Harris raced far ahead of the others. The smoke lessened slightly after they left the No. 10 station, but started getting heavier about 1,500 feet from the station near the first old bulkheaded crosscut leading to the D vein drift. Spotting smoke seeping from between the bulkhead and the country rock, they stopped and scooped up mud and dirt with their hands to pack in the crevices. The task appeared futile. They couldn't fill the deep crevices with their hands.

Harris pointed to a compressed air blow pipe and hose laying a few up the drift as Bill Bennett walked past and asked him to find if it was hooked up. Bennett only had to walk 20 paces to locate the connection and turn it on. He walked back to make sure the air was flowing and found Harris and Breazeal already using the compressed air to blow the mud in the cracks. Bennett watched them until Les Mossburgh walked by on his way out.

"I figure it don't take three men to run a blow pipe," Bennett said and joined Mossburgh.

Bennett mentioned he was concerned about fifty-nine-year-old Clyde Napier, who had been coughing down on the 3700 level. Mossburgh assured him he had seen Napier walk towards the Jewell ahead of them. As the pair proceeded, they noticed smoke seeping out of a second crosscut leading to the D drift. Another 500 feet further, they discovered smoke pouring out of the crosscut to the No. 5 shaft.

"I wonder if Dick and Jack are coming out," Bennett said.

"We better go back and get them two out of there," Mossburgh said and turned to walk back.

They hadn't walked a dozen steps when they saw two lights coming out of the dark drift. A few seconds later they recognized their fellow mechanics and turned and headed for the Jewell. The air west of the No. 5 shaft was clear, so they took their time walking. At the air door 400 feet from the Jewell station, they saw the reason for the clear air. The open air door was allowing 24,000 cubic feet a minute of fresh air in from the surface and coursing the smoke away from the Jewell shaft. They also realized it was blowing the smoke towards the No. 10 shaft . . . the escape route for the men below who would be following them.

Mossburgh counted heads at the Jewell shaft station as they waited to be hoisted to make sure Napier and the other mechanics from the drill shop who had walked out were there. When the cage arrived, Launhardt and Hawkins got off.

"Where is the motor?" Launhardt asked.

When someone replied it was at the No. 10 station, Launhardt said: "I have to get back there right away."

Launhardt picked up a McCaa and put it on his back, then lifted another to carry it one mile to Gene Johnson at the No. 10 station and announced he was going to walk. Hawkins donned a McCaa and slung the straps of a second over his arm and stood ready to follow Launhardt.

"I'm going with you," Zingler said, glancing at the six McCaa's laying at Launhardt's feet.

Don Beehner volunteered to walk back with them without mentioning he had been exposed to the smoke and carbon monoxide and had just walked from the 3100 level No. 10. station.

"Are you trained?" Launhardt asked, aware that Beehner was certified.

Zingler said, "yes." But he didn't mention he wasn't certified. He was overweight and had recently injured his leg in a mine accident that disqualified him.

Hawkins parroted, "yes." He didn't tell Launhardt that he wasn't certified in contaminated atmospheres because he was overweight. He had been 235 pounds at the time, but had since trimmed down to 215, although he still a had few pounds to go and take a medical exam before he was technically qualified.

"Fine, I will need all the help I can get," Launhardt said.

When the first cage arrived from the 4400 and 4600 levels on the 3100 level at 12:24:30, Gene Johnson told them to run to the Jewell and belled the cage to return to the 4600. The empty cage left within 45 seconds.

Charles Casteel and Virgil Bebb told Gene they would help him and count the men from their levels to make sure they got up. Few men were familiar with the 3100 level traveled only by the hoistmen, cagers, mechanics, and repairmen. Randy Peterson said it was similar to the 3700, the level they traveled every day, and to follow him. Dennis Clapp, James Sheppard, William Mitchell, and several others nodded and set off behind the cager. Harold Mendy insisted he couldn't leave until his brother, Reuben, came up.

The second cage from the 4600 level arrived at the 3100 level at 12:29:30 crammed with the last men from the 4600. Gene waited until the last man was out and signaled the cage down as Dusty Rhoads and Arnold Anderson jumped on as the cage left at 12:30.

Casteel and Bebb pushed the men in the direction of the main haulage drift and shouted: "Run for the Jewell. Any man who can't make it, climb in the muck train and they'll haul you out." The shifters couldn't leave. They still had seventeen men from their levels they couldn't account for and would not leave Gene Johnson with only young Roger Findley to direct the evacuation.

Several exhausted men climbed into the muck cars. The rest were soon strung out along the main drift, running, staggering, and pulling each other through the acrid smoke blowing in their faces. In the stretch near where Breazeal and Harris had attempted to stem the leaking smoke, it was pouring from another bulkhead and several raises. They couldn't see three feet in front of them and had to look down to shine their cap lights so they could follow the tracks and wouldn't run into the ribs. Those without self-rescuers covered their mouths and noses with their T-shirts or rags, coughing and spitting as they walked. Some with self-rescuers choked and gagged when they became hot and yanked them from their mouth. Several vomited by the side of the tracks. There was nothing anyone could do to stop the blinding smoke from making their eyes sting and tear.

After enduring nearly one-half mile of poisonous smoke, cries of "Fresh air" rang out as they ran passed the crosscut to the No. 5. shaft. To the man they sucked in the uncontaminated air blowing in their faces. Several sat down and enjoyed deep breaths until the strength came back into her wobbly legs. Osterberg, who had come up on the second cage and was near the rear of the pack, couldn't stop the tears running down his face until he was well into the fresh air.

The sight of a cage waiting at the Jewell station raised an undeniable urge to sit and rest while they waited for stragglers. Exhausted, they watched four men standing next to two rows of breathing apparatuses laying on the mine floor. Launhardt and Hawkins put one McCaa on their backs and picked up a second. As Zingler ran his arms through the straps of two McCaas and hefted one on each shoulder, Beehner slung a McCaa over each shoulder and joined them.

The four men disappeared down the drift, each lugging two 45-pound McCaas. By the time they walked the 400 feet to the air doors carrying a cumbersome 90 pounds, it became evident to Launhardt that they were not going to be able to walk the almost one mile to the No. 10 shaft in a short period of time.

Launhardt told them they would have to wait until the motor came back from the No. 10 station.

CHAPTER 7

THE LAST TRAIN OUT

The 5000 Level

The ride in the cages down the Jewell shaft to the 3700 level, train to the No. 10 shaft, cages down the shaft, and their walk or motor ride to the raises and stopes for the 25 men working on the 5000 level took up to 45 minutes each morning. The drift extended 3,800 feet east and 1,400 feet southwest from the shaft station. To the east the drift followed the relatively undeviating vein. On the west it meandered south from the shaft station then splayed like a claw, three talons pointing southwest and one to the east.

Robert Macartney and James Fenner were assigned by the shifter, Robert Anderson, to remove Alimak raise climber rails in the No. 7 raise, 2,000 feet east of the station. Fenner was the lead man. The twenty-seven-year-old miner had been at Sunshine two and one-half years and had worked at the Homestake Mine in South Dakota's Black Hills. Macartney, at twenty-five and with less than a year in the mines five years earlier, had started at the Sunshine last Thursday after serving a hitch in the Marines, including a tour in Vietnam.

The lack of the ability to communicate on the deep levels when far from the single phone at the shaft station is endemic in deep hard rock mines. Partners working in close proximity use hand signals to converse over the din of the drills and slushers and the protection of ear plugs. Another aggravating problem is maintaining tools and spare parts on the levels.

Fenner and Macartney's day didn't get off to a good start. A mechanic with an acetylene torch scheduled to cut the railing bolts supporting the raise climber to the rock didn't show up, and they had no way of finding Bob Anderson while the shifter journeyed on his rounds in the over one-mile of drifts on the level. There was little they could accomplish except square away the area in preparation for the real work to follow. While checking the tugger hoist required to lower the heavy machinery and Alimak rails, they discovered it wasn't secured sufficiently and needed bolts. As no mechanic carries heavy bolts unless he knows in advance they are needed, they decided to walk back to the station and take the hoist to the warehouse on the 3700 level for the bolts and ask the lead mechanic at the drill shop next door where the mechanic and acetylene torch were.

Walking to the No. 10 station, riding to the 3700 level, obtaining the bolts from Hap Fowler in the warehouse, and asking the whereabouts of the mechanic in the drill shop took about 40 minutes. Waiting for the chippy hoist wasted another 30 minutes. The chippy hoist had to stop on the 4600 level and unload ventilation pipe stacked in two cages, which took another 20 minutes. They finally arrived back at the raise around lunch time. They were in no hurry to finish eating. The mechanic had yet to show up to cut off the bolts. Around 11:45 they noticed a slight haze in the drift. At first they thought it might be from someone using a cutting torch in the raise to the east. As they eyed the smoke, it grew in intensity, so they decided to investigate. When they stepped into the drift, they met Leonard Bourgard and Charles McGillivary, miners from the 9 E stope 200 feet to the west, looking for the source of the smoke coming from the direction of the station. The four decided to walk to the station to see what was burning. When they opened the second air door, they were met by a cloud of thick smoke.

They could barely see the shaft through the smoke when they arrived at the station. Robert McCoy, the station nipper, told them to go to the other side of the grizzly where the smoke was lighter. Norman Fee, the grizzly man, had turned on the compressed air. Fenner and Macartney walked to the grizzly and joined the several men who had arrived earlier. Fenner glanced around for Bob Anderson, the shifter, and asked where he was. Fee said he had left after lunch to make his rounds on the west side. Concerned no one was in charge, Fenner asked if anyone had gone through the level to tell the others there might be a fire. Hearing no response, Fenner said he would take two men with him on the muck train to the west and asked Richard Lynch, a motorman, to go to the east.

As Macartney had never been in the area, Fenner dropped him off near the 4 W stope and told him to walk back to the station on the relatively straight drift without any forks. Fenner motored to the No. 10 raise and told Isaac Stevenson, a miner from 15 W stope who had volunteered to go with him, to go to the workings in the east drift and that he would pick him up on the way back. Fenner continued to the 12 raise to warn the men, then drove to the H-8 stope. He had to climb 150 feet up before getting the attention of Bob Anderson and the men in the stope. On his way back he picked up Stevenson and Macartney.

Thirty-two-year-old gypo miner Kenneth Riley had worked in hard rock mines in California, Montana, and Nevada for four years and at Sunshine for ten years. His thirty-eight-year-old partner in 4 W stope, Joe Armijo, had been in the mines since he was young. That was all most miners knew about the Mexican except that he wasn't afraid to work. Like many gypos, they didn't bother packing a lunch and wasting time eating when there was money to be made. Armijo was drilling at the face when Riley smelled something and told his partner to shut off the drill. Riley said the stope looked foggy. Armijo told him to check the drift. Riley climbed down to the drift and could barely see Macartney arriving to tell him to get to the station.

Robert Follette and Howard Markve were mining the face of the 10 W stope. Follette went back to the raise to change the drill steel and noticed smoke drifting up the raise. He turned to wave his light at Markve 128 feet back in the stope just as he heard someone climbing up the manway and shouting there was a fire and to go to the station.

Ernest Baillie and Wayne Johnson spent the morning barring down and rebolting the 12 W stope after a rock burst, a phenomenon in deep hard rock mines. Rock bursts occur when the rock is strained beyond its elastic limit by heavy pressure and it releases its energy instantaneously, rupturing and shattering with explosive violence into an open cavity.

After lunch, Johnson climbed down 110 feet in the manway to run the tugger hoist and raise the slusher and bucket necessary to clear the muck. Baillie signalled him to hoist from above, but received no response. When he looked down, Johnson was halfway back up the raise

"We'd better get the hell out," Johnson yelled.

Baillie climbed down the 110 feet to the sill after Johnson said there was a fire and they had been ordered to go to the station. By then, smoke was wafting in the drift towards them. They wet their T-shirts to cover their faces and walked to the station.

Thomas Watts and Jasper "Jack" Lovesee were relieving the ground in the 1 East drift, an unstable area that had caved and sloughed slabs off the ribs. The job required them to bar down loose rock and install new rockbolts and timber support. As was their custom, they broke for lunch at a convenient time instead of the scheduled 11:00 a.m. and ate late in a timber station 1,200 feet from the No. 10 station. Watts rose to go back to work. Lovesee hadn't finished his coffee. Watts shrugged and helped himself to a cup of Lovesee's coffee and rose again.

"Where are you going? Back to work?" Lovesee asked.

"Well, it's about time, isn't it?" Watts replied.

"Hell, it's only ten after twelve," Lovesee said as Watts walked back to the drift.

Watts was standing by his drill and reaching for his ear plugs and gloves, when Lovesee yelled from 25 feet behind that there was smoke in the drift. He told Lovesee it was probably someone blasting.

"I'm going to go find out what's going on," Lovesee said.

"Go ahead," Watts said and turned on the drill.

Thirty seconds later, Lovesee waved his cap lamp to get Watt's attention and yelled that there was heavy smoke in the drift. Watts shut down his drill. "Well, let's go find out what's going on."

Darol Anderson, timberman, and Delmar Kitchen, miner, were preparing the No. 5 raise. "Prepping" a raise included setting timbers, installing raise climbers, and mining out chutes for the stope miners. They ate lunch on the station with Bob Anderson, Darol's brother and the 5000 level shifter. Darol was twenty-nine and had been working at the Sunshine for six years and was a former Homestake miner. Thirty-year-old Kitchen had been at Sunshine for two years, but had worked there several times in the winters, preferring to "be in the woods in the summer" as a lumberjack, an indulgence many young workingmen enjoyed in the Idaho panhandle.

They were fifty feet up in the raise slushing and unaware of the smoke when Richard Lynch shined his cap lamp at them and yelled that there was a fire and to run to the station. Both climbed down, not believing the fire was serious until they walked out the drift into the heavy smoke. Kitchen panicked when he began to cough and gag. He ran through the air doors where the smoke was lighter and drank some water from a hose to relieve his coughing.

Forty-one-year-old Wilber "Buzz" Bruhn had been a hard rock miner for twenty-two years. His partner was thirty-one-year-old Dewellyn Kitchen, Delmar Kitchen's brother. They were the far end of the level up in the No. 27 raise and unaware of the smoke until the Richard Lynch shouted up the raise: "Buzz, you better come out, there's smoke at the station."

Bob McCoy told everyone arriving at the station to take a self-rescuer from the pile he had stacked on the bench and to stand by the grizzly, where the smoke was lighter. The grizzly and the powder and primer magazines were around a corner and 50 feet from the shaft. The men took turns standing by the shaft to signal the others when they arrived.

Eight or ten men were at the station when Darol Anderson and Delmar Kitchen arrived and picked up self-rescuers from the shifter's bench. Darol spotted that Howard Markve and Robert Follette didn't have one and handed them two still in boxes. Markve read the instructions aloud as they attempted to get them to work. It took them a few minutes to figure they had to bang the button with their fist or a wrench to activate them.

After Follette clamped down on the mouthpiece he stopped coughing. The fifty-two-year-old miner knew he had to pace himself and not take the device out of his mouth to talk. To get out of the way he and Markve leaned between two stacks of timber and waited for the cage. From his vantage point, Follette could see everything going on and hear if a skip arrived. He wondered why some men preferred to wet their T-shirts to cover their mouths and noses and watched with amusement a miner take out his false teeth and put them in his lunch bucket in order to be able to clamp down on his self-rescuer.

Thomas Watts and Jack Lovesee picked up self-rescuers from the shifter's bench. By the time they thought they had them working, Bob McCoy said he was going to the station to take a turn at watching for the cage. Watts and Lovesee followed him. Watts stood by the heavy wire door to the shaft, grasping the wire so he could get as near as possible and hear the skip coming. The smoke roaring down was so dense he couldn't see the other side of the shaft. He hadn't been there a few seconds when the skip came down and he had to back away. It was 12:33:30.

Greg Dionne and Byron Schulz, jumped off. McCoy yelled that the cage had arrived and covered his face with a rag because his self-rescuer was too hot and made him cough. Watts was the first to board, followed by Lovesee and McCoy. Someone yelled that Lando Rihtershik, a motorman, was choking and pushed him on the cage. Ernest Baillie, Isaac Stevenson, and Leonard Bourgard climbed behind Rihtershik and held him up. Darol Anderson pushed his way on and turned to see that Delmar Kitchen had stepped back. "You're going with me," Darol yelled to his partner and pulled him on board. Schulz slammed the shaft door shut and belled the hoist up seconds before 12:34:30.

The 3100 Level

Ira Sliger managed to hoist the cages from the 3700, 4400, and 4600 levels before he started coughing and having difficulty breathing, not surprising for a sixty-one-year-old man with silicosis and one lung working under pressure and in air contaminated with smoke and carbon monoxide. He asked his partner, thirty-eight-year-old Robert Scanlan, to take over while he ran the 200 feet to the station for self-rescuers. Scanlan took over as the south cage was descending to the 5000 level.

Sliger returned to the hoist room cab with a box of self-rescuers and took one for himself and laid the rest on the bench next to Scanlan. A moment later Gene Johnson ran into the hoist room.

"Ira, you better get out of here before we have to carry you out," Gene said. "Bob can run the hoist all right."

"Are you all right?" Sliger asked Scanlan.

"Yes, I'm pretty good," Scanlan said. "The only thing is the smoke is hurting my eyes."

Sliger walked out of the hoist room and the 300 feet to the muck train.

On the unbelievable fast 30-odd seconds ride up to the 3100 level, Delmar Kitchen held his breath as he stood on the edge of the door-less cage and Darol Anderson held on to him. The cage was emptied and left a few seconds before 12:36.

Gene Johnson, Charlie Casteel, and Virgil Bebb shouted in unison: "Run to the Jewell." Al Smith yelled that any men who felt they couldn't walk to the Jewell to climb in the muck cars and pointed through the haze to Gilbert Robles waving for them to hurry.

Watts, the first man on the cage and the last off, hadn't heard Gene's instructions. "Gene, did you say the Jewell?" Watts asked.

"Yes, damn it."

"Do you need any help?" Watts asked, seeing Gene's exhausted condition.

"No, get your tail out of here," Gene said.

The 5000 Level

Buzz Bruhn and Dewellyn Kitchen arrived at the 5000 station covering their faces with wet T-shirts. They grabbed self-rescuers from the shifter's bench and hit the buttons with a wrench to activate them after being told it was easiest way. Both stood in the smoke and tried to remain calm until the cage arrived. Bruhn looked around and saw that several men were ill.

Norman Fee, the grizzly man, was on the ground choking. One man was trying to get him up while Ken Riley was attempting to show him how to use a self rescuer. Robert Goff was sitting nearby coughing while his self-rescuer lay sitting next to him on his lunch bucket. Greg Dionne, who had helped Goff open his self-rescuer, lay stretched out on a pile of lagging breathing heavily.

After returning to the station, Fenner had given his self-rescuer to Isaac Stevenson, who had traveled with him without a respirator to alert the men on the level. Confident he now knew how to actuate it without any difficulty, he grabbed a box. When he opened it up, he discovered the canister and the device were rusty. He tossed it on the ground. Before he could open another, Schulz yelled that the cage was back.

Robert Macartney sat on a stack of timber trying to pace himself and get his breath back after his run in the drift, but didn't know if his self-rescuer was working. It made his throat dry. He didn't hear the call that the cage had arrived. Buzz Bruhn shook him. In the smokey haze, Bruhn thought he was shaking his partner, Dewellyn Kitchen. As Macartney approached the gage, Fenner pulled him the last few steps.

Robert Follette and Howard Markve walked to the cage after hearing Schulz's call and were the last two to board. As Schulz slammed the shaft gates shut, Follette looked out and wondered why others hadn't got on, as there was plenty of room.

The 3100 Level

Bob Scanlan dropped the cage seconds before 12:36. It arrived at the 5000 level at 12:38. It left less than one minute later and arrived back at the 3100 level at 12:39:30

Gene Johnson yelled: "Run to the Jewell and don't look back." Charlie Casteel and Virgil Bebb pulled the men off the cage if they hesitated two seconds. Gene hit the bell signal and Scanlan dropped the cage a few seconds after 12:40.

The 5000 Level

Byron Schulz had the men standing by the station when the cage arrived a few seconds after 12:42. Dewellyn Kitchen, Richard Lynch, Wayne Johnson, Norman Fee, Robert Goff, Joe Armijo, Ken Riley, and Howard Fleshman, who had recently arrived from the far off H-8 E stope, boarded. Schulz pushed Greg Dionne on the cage, belled the hoist and jumped in and held onto Dionne. Scanlan raised the cage seconds before 12:43 and pulled it up to the 3100 level seconds before at 12:44.

The 3100 Level

Schulz, Dionne, and Fee stumbled off the cage. Gene Johnson and Bebb pulled the others out and told them to run to the muck cars and not to look back. Gene told Al Smith to take the motor to the Jewell and hurry back with the McCaas, if they were not already on the way. Smith welcomed the order. He was feeling dizzy and light-headed. Fee collapsed on the station, and Riley bent down to pick him up. Gene and Casteel told Riley to run to the muck train and that they would take care of him.

Gene belled the cage and Scanlan dropped it empty seconds before 12:45 to the 5000 level to pick up Bob Anderson and Merle Hudson, a miner from the H-8 E stope. Bob Anderson was a shifter and capable of caging. The cage arrived at the 5000 level at 12:46:30.

Casteel dragged Schulz away from the shaft and blew compressed air until he seemed to snap out of it. He then turned it on Greg Dionne, Norman Fee, and Joe Armijo, who insisted he sit and rest for a minute. The smoke was thick and no one noticed several men were unable to walk fast enough to catch the train before it left or for Al Smith to see them in the smoke. Ken Riley was the only man on the third cage from the 5000 level to board the train.

Gene threw his self-rescuer on the floor and said, "This thing isn't worth a good goddamn," and kneeled to peer into the shaft. The cable hadn't moved in over a minute. Bob Anderson and one man should have been able to board and signal in a matter of seconds. He turned to Schulz and told him to run to the hoist room and tell Bob Scanlan to pick up Doug Wiedderick, an experienced shaft repairman on the 5800 level capable of caging, and hoist the men on the 5600 and 5400 levels.

Schulz stumbled to the hoist room and relayed Gene's orders.

"It's getting to me. My arms are beginning to shake," Scanlan said. Would you open me up a self rescuer and show me how to use it?"

Schulz opened a self rescuer and gave it to Scanlan, then watched the hoistman's body tremble with the effects of the carboxyhemoglobin in his blood that brought him closer to death by the second. Refusing to think about his own possible death, seconds before 12:50 Scanlan dropped the north cage like a rock to the 5800 level, where it arrived seconds after 12:51 and rose before 12:52. It hesitated at the 5600 for a few seconds before arriving at the 5400 at 12:54 and leaving seconds before 12:55. The cage paused at the 5000 level for a few seconds before 12:56, then slowly rose to 100 feet above the 3100, where it stopped a few seconds after 1:00 before dropping to the 3100 level around 1:01:30 p.m.

In the meantime, at 12:58:30 Scanlan lowered the south cage from the 5000 to the 5400 for about 15 seconds then brought it to the 3100 level around 1:01 p.m.

With the words "Run to the Jewell and don't look back" Darol Anderson and Delmar Kitchen put their heads down and stepped off at a quick pace on the mile trek to the Jewell. Few could keep up with the younger men. Behind them, Thomas Watts and Jack Lovesee wouldn't let the other get out of sight. The smoke blew in their faces and limited the visibility to less than three feet in the unfathomable opaque gray swirls illuminated only by their cap lamps. There was nothing to say and it was dangerous to take their self-rescuers out of their mouths to talk. Watts swore he had a mouthful of dry ice that burned his tongue.

Ernest Baillie and Robert McCoy's method was to plod at a consistent pace and conserve their energy. As McCoy's pace slowed, Baillie urged him to keep up and told him they would be out of the smoke any second.

One of the few on the second cage from the 5000 level to walk, James Fenner kept a steady pace without a self-rescuer, cussing that he had given his away. A few minutes into the hike, he asked someone he caught up with, but couldn't recognize in the swirling smoke, if he could take a couple of breaths from his self-rescuer. Renewed with a false sense of energy and security, he made it to the fresh air west of the No. 5 shaft and stepped aside to let the muck train pass.

Less than 100 feet west in fresh air, Thomas Watt and Jack Lovesee stopped to rest in the cool fresh air. When they saw the train, they stood to the side of the drift and waved it past. Watts remarked that he was feeling rejuvenated and it didn't look like there was any room in the muck cars anyway.

McCoy and Baillie had rested another 200 feet up the drift. McCoy was physically devoured by the carbon monoxide and shaking. There was nothing Baillie could do for the man 20 years his senior until he saw the lights of the muck train and was able to flag it down. The men in the last car pulled McCoy aboard and gave Baillie a hand as he climbed over the edge. Nothing needed to be said by the men in the cramped muck car, their arms and legs tangled with the man next to them. They crammed closer to each other to make room for McCoy and Baillie and still leave space for Lando Rihtarshik, curled up and semi-unconscious.

As the train neared the air doors, Al Smith slowed down at the sight of Robert Launhardt. Launhardt waved it passed and told James Zingler, Larry Hawkins, and Don Beehner to leave their McCaas in the drift and follow the train back to the station. They could pick up the ones they left in the drift on their way out.

The motor didn't stop for the last two men as it approached the Jewell shaft. Someone on the train mumbled that Darol Anderson and Delmar Kitchen should be in the friggin' Olympics.

The men climbed out of the muck cars and stood aside as McCoy and Rihtarshik were carried onto a waiting chippy cage. Their blood-red eyes, still stinging from the pungent smoke, circled the station for a glimpse of a missing partner or friend before looking back down the drift to see if any others from the 5000 level were walking out. Doubts lingered they would see a familiar face. Al Smith had stopped for everyone who needed a ride. By a rough count there were around a dozen still behind them in the smoke. When Watts and Lovesee walked in followed by Fenner, the number of missing came down to about nine or ten.

The chippy cager, Kenneth Wilber, filled up one deck on the chippy hoist, then told the others to board a second cage. He couldn't wait any longer. McCoy and Rihtarshik were having difficulty breathing and needed to be hoisted to the surface for oxygen and medical treatment.

Wilber didn't count how many were on the two cages. It was only 16 of the 25 men from the 5000. Nine men were missing, but who was counting?

WHY WEREN'T ALL MEN ON THE 5000 LEVEL HOISTED TO THE 3100 LEVEL?

In three trips, the nine-man cage hoisted 25 men from the 5000 level. Two men, foreman Bob Anderson and stope miner Merle Hudson, were probably dead when the cage returned the fourth time. The count based on the miners' depositions is as follows:

All nine men on the first cage lived: Darol Anderson, Delmar Kitchen, Ernest Baillie, Robert McCoy, Jack Lovesee, Leonard Bourgard, Thomas Watts, Lando Rihtarshik, and Isaac Stevenson.

Only six men were on the second cage and all lived: Wilber Bruhn, James Fenner, Robert Follette, Robert Macartney, Howard Markve, and Charles McGillivary.

Of the ten men on the third cage, only Byron Schulz walked out and Robert Riley road the muck train and survived. Eight died on the 3100 level: Joe Armijo, Greg Dionne, Norman Fee, Howard Fleshman, Robert Goff, Wayne Johnson, Dewellyn Kitchen, and Richard Lynch.

Robert Follette stated in his deposition that the second cage was not fully loaded. It is more than supposition that three nine-men cages had space for all 27 men on the 5000 level and Robert Anderson and Merle Hudson should not have been forced to wait for a fourth cage. The third cage hoisted ten men, eight of whom died. If the second cage hoisted more than six, it is likely that two or three more men would have survived, as all men hoisted on the first two cages survived.

CHAPTER 8

FUTILITY

The Last Man Out

Roger Findley counted 18 men stumbling off the cages from the 5400 and 5600 levels and 5800 shaft station. None had self-rescuers. The safety director had failed to supply the levels with self-rescuers and first aid supplies. The 5400 level was one-half mile long, had been under development for over one year, and had a regular crew of seven. Seven men regularly worked on the 400-foot long 5600 level, which had been open for over six months, and four men made up the crew in the 5800 level shaft. As a result, over 10 percent of the total men working underground had no protection from the deadly carbon monoxide.

The nineteen-year-old cager turned to Gene Johnson to tell him his count was 49, then stood panic-stricken as the foreman sank to the ground unconscious. Casteel yelling "Run to the Jewell!" woke him from his horrified trance. Never thinking he needed a self-rescuer until men began falling around him, he now realized he was dizzy and weak from whatever toxic gas was killing the others. He ran and grabbed a self-rescuer from a bench and stuck it in his mouth, not having the slightest idea how it worked, and started running for his life.

Casteel and Bebb, aware there was nothing more they could do, followed on Findley's heels.

Twenty-one-year-old Byron Schulz stared in horror at Bob Scanlan sitting in the hoistman's chair. Scanlan's entire body shook as he fought back death to raise the north and south cages filled with the men from the 5400, 5600, and 5800 levels simultaneously. Then the hoistman slumped over and died before Schulz's eyes.

Schulz opened the door to the hoistman's cab and stood aghast at the sight of Elmer Kitchen, his fifty-four-year-old partner, and several men unconscious on the floor. Unable to help the dying men, he ran to the station. He stepped around Duwain Crow laying across the track, his nose pouring blood from the effects of carbon monoxide, and ran past Casey Pena dunking his head in the water trough to ease his throbbing headache caused by the carboxyhemoglobin in his blood. At the shaft, Gene Johnson lay stretched out on the floor and unconscious. Schulz felt his pulse and found it barely beating. There was no way the slender youth could help the husky foreman. Fear of death, his greatest impetus, made him run back to the hoist room to get another self-rescuer.

"Bob's dead. There's no way to get guys up," Schulz yelled when he ran into Douglas Wiederrick in the drift.

"Hold it, I'm going to call topside," Wiederrick said. The thirty-seven-year-old shaft miner, weakened by the carbon monoxide, staggered to the hoist room and picked up the phone laying next to Scanlan's body. When he asked where the nearest fresh air was and was told the Jewell shaft, he dropped the phone and said, "Oh, God, we'll never make it."

Schulz tried to stick a self-rescuer in Wiederrick's mouth, but he spit it out and slapped it away then collapsed unconscious. The young cager grabbed a fresh self-rescuer from the table and ran out of the hoistman's cubicle. He shuddered at the sight of the men on the floor shaking with the last tremors before coma and death. He ran over the bodies lying on the station and pulled off his shirt and dipped it in the water trough, then wrapped it around his face and the third self-rescuer he would use during the most petrifying moments in his life and ran. In the main drift he tripped over several bodies. He didn't recognize them in the dark and blinding smoke, but he knew one was a shifter by his white hard hat. Schulz staggered to his feet and ran for his life.

After trudging back to the 3100 Jewell station, Launhardt told Beehner, Hawkins, and Zingler to couple the flatbed timber car sitting at the station to the rear of the train and load the two McCaas they had left on the flatbed. The safety engineer climbed in and kneeled in the front of the first of two muck cars. Hawkins drove the motor from behind the muck cars and Zingler and Beehner sat on the flatbed timber car in the rear. Launhardt signaled Hawkins to stop for the McCaas they had left at the air doors and load them on the timber car.

As they drove past the crosscut to the No. 4 shaft, Launhardt motioned Hawkins to stop while they were in clear air. "Let's stop and put on our McCaas and clear them," Launhardt said. He tested the air for carbon monoxide and warned the others he found traces of the deadly gas in the seemingly clear air. But he failed to notice that Beehner and Zingler had not put the McCaas on their backs.

Smoke was streaming from the crosscut to the No. 5 shaft as they passed. Hawkins slowed the train for fear of hitting someone running from the No. 10 shaft station in smoke so dense he could barely see Launhardt in the muck car in front of him. Hawkins leaned out of the motor so he could be guided by Launhardt's cap light beam as the motor inched through the smoke. Launhardt in the first muck car couldn't see the rails as the train crept along the drift.

They hadn't gone 200 feet into the smoke when Launhardt spotted a cap lamp in the haze. He raised his hand for Hawkins to stop. The ghostly figure was only a few feet away before Launhardt recognized Roger Findley staggering towards them, coughing and unable to catch his breath.

Beehner rushed to the front of the train and placed his McCaa mask over Findley's face and told him to breath.

"Someone take him to fresh air," Launhardt said.

"Beehner, you take him out," Zingler said.

"No, you take him out. I'll go in with Larry and Bob," Beehner said and gave Findley air from a McCaa sitting on the timber truck.

As Beehner held the mask to Findley's face, Launhardt, took another carbon monoxide test. He couldn't believe his eyes. The test tube turned black, indicating the carbon monoxide exceeded the maximum of 3,000 parts per million (0.3 of 1%) calibrated on the tube. He shouted his findings that the carbon monoxide was lethal and could kill in minutes and to board the train.

Zingler grabbed Findley's arm and led him back the 200 feet to fresh air.

"Get your apparatus on," Hawkins yelled to Beehner on the timber truck in the rear and mumbled that a man trained in mine rescue should know better.

The train crept down the track and as it approached where the D vein met the main drift. The drift was narrow and timbered. Fearing he could not see a man coming out the drift, Hawkins leaned out the side of the motor and found the smoke wasn't as thick along the rib. The aluminum backpack on his McCaa struck a timber post and knocked him back and sideways. Hawkins had all he could do to hang on and not be thrown off the motor.

Seconds later, Launhardt saw another light and could hear Byron Schulz gasping for breath before he recognized him holding his shirt over his face and self-rescuer.

At the sight of the motor's lights, Schulz screamed frantically: "I need oxygen, get me oxygen."

Hawkins stopped the train. Beehner climbed off and led Schulz to the flatbed timber car. Launhardt and Hawkins, both big men and wearing McCaas, had to squirm between the cars and the timbered rib to lift Schulz onto the flatbed timber car. As Hawkins turned, the cord from the battery on his belt that ran up his back to his cap lamp caught on a timber or a jagged rock, snapping his head back and pulling him off balance. For a moment, Hawkins was disoriented and could only see the back and timbers.

Launhardt pulled the self-rescuer from Schulz's mouth and told Beehner to put a mask from a McCaa on the timber truck over Schulz's face.

"They're all dead back there, they're all dead," Schulz repeated hysterically.

"Here's oxygen, breathe this," Beehner said, and covered Schulz's face with his mask.

Hawkins struggled to free his battery cord and turned towards the others as Beehner fell on his face. "Beehner's down!" Hawkins yelled and crawled over the timber car to the other side. He rolled Beehner face up and tried to gulp a breath of oxygen from his McCaa then placed his mask over Beehner's face. Hawkins held his breath as long as he could before taking his mask off Beehner's face. He tried to suck oxygen from his mask then jammed it back on Beehner's face as Beehner's body shook with convulsions and blood gushed from his mouth and nose.

"We have to get him up," Launhardt said, bending down to lift Beehner.

Hawkins wiped Beehner's blood from his mask and jammed it on Beehner's face, then tried to help Launhardt lift him. He couldn't breath and didn't have the strength to lift Beehner's legs. He yanked off his mask and wiped it with his sleeve, then held it to his face as he reached back to check his bypass valve.

"There's something wrong with my machine," Hawkins yelled.

"What's the matter?" Launhardt asked.

"I can't get any air."

"Did you check your bypass valve?"

"Yes, but it still won't work. I have to get out of here," Hawkins yelled.

"Do you think you can make it?"

"Yes, take care of the kid and Don, I can't stay any longer," Hawkins said and started running.

Launhardt tried to lift Beehner on the timber car, but couldn't lift his dead weight. He was now alone and had to leave Beehner to get Schulz, semi-conscious on the timber truck, to fresh air.

After leading Findley to the fresh air west of the crosscut to the No. 5 shaft, Zingler stood in the drift to see if he could help anyone else coming out of the smoke. He decided he couldn't help anyone standing in the fresh air and cussed the fact that he hadn't put on his McCaa in the fresh air or taken one from the timber truck. "Maybe I can go in a few feet and help someone," he said to himself, then ran into smoke. After less than 200 feet, he couldn't stand the smoke burning his eyes and lungs. Aware Launhardt said the carbon monoxide could be lethal in minutes, he was forced to retreat. When he arrived back in fresh air, Findley had left to walk to the Jewell.

Frustrated he couldn't help, Zingler walked 1,200 feet back to the No. 4 shaft. He squawked down to the 3700 level, where the shaft bottomed, and asked if anyone was there. He could operate the hoist, if anyone answered. After several unanswered squawks, he picked up the phone and listened to voices on the surface tell the men underground that they were doing everything they could to get them out. Aware he couldn't help and shouldn't add to the confusion, he could only listen to the men who had no chance of escape.

Hawkins stopped running and walked to conserve his ebbing strength. Walking allowed him to attempt to adjust his bypass valve and figure what was wrong with his McCaa. His training how to check his McCaa in case of a malfunction flashed before him, but nothing he did helped. Five feet ahead he saw a dark shadow next to a timber post. A step closer, he recognized Charlie Casteel leaning against the timber. It would have been easy to miss him on the other side of the rib on the north side of a thick timber when he drove in. He grabbed Casteel's arm, but Casteel didn't respond. Panicked at seeing the young shifter dead, a friend he admired, he started running again and tripped over the track and fell. He staggered to his feet disoriented, unable to determine which way to go where the tracks split and went in two directions. The smoke was too dense to see the signs at the crossroads posting the way to the Jewell and No. 10 station. His hazy mind spun with the thought that the 3100 level had been mined-out years ago and was used only to haul muck to the Jewell station. He kneeled and shined his cap lamp on the rails and followed the shiniest track that told him it was currently being used.

A few feet down the track he collapsed unable to take another step. At the sound of the train coming from behind, he managed to stand and lean against the rib until the train slowed.

"Bob, keep on going. I'll jump on the back of the muck car," Hawkins yelled.

Hawkins leaped on the back of the last car and hung over the edge, lacking the strength to climb into the muck car. After a few seconds he realized, if he stayed in that position, his McCaa backpack might hit a low timber and knock him off. He slid down and held onto the top edge with both hands. Afraid Launhardt would look back and think he fell off, he held onto the edge with one hand and held his cap lamp up over the rim for Launhardt to know he was still hanging on.

The train passed into fresh air seconds before he lost the strength to hold on. A few minutes later, it pulled to a stop at the Jewell station. Hawkins dropped to the ground until he was able to stand. As he walked to the shaft, he yanked off his mask and let it fall. Dangling, it kept bumping his leg with each step. He threw the mask over his shoulder and glanced at the inhalation hose. It had been torn in half when he had hit his backpack against a timber, allowing the carbon monoxide to enter his face mask and rendering the bypass valve useless.

Futility on the 3700

Ron Stansbury and Richard Nickelby raced to the Jewell station and told Jim Bush that Paul Johnson and Roberto Diaz had collapsed in the drift and they couldn't get Bob Bush, Pat Hobson, and Wayne Blalack up after they were overcome by the smoke.

Jim Bush called the 3100 Jewell station, where Pete Bennett had told him the McCaas had been sent, and asked Norman Ulrich to send down men with McCaas to rescue the five down men in the 3700 drift. Ulrich told him that Launhardt had taken all the McCaas to Gene Johnson at the 3100 No. 10 shaft station, but there were a dozen or so self-rescuers on the station floor that the men had discarded. Jim told them to bring them. They were better than nothing.

Ulrich, assigned to stay on the level by his foreman in case someone needed an electrician, figured there was little use hanging around. No men had walked out in the last ten or fifteen minutes.

"Come and give me a hand," Ulrich said to Kenneth Wilber, a twenty-six-year-old cager.

"Maybe I should stay here," Wilber said, unwilling to leave his post in case seriously ill or injured men arrived and had to be hoisted.

"No, he needs all the help he can get, come on," Ulrich said.

Wilber said, "Okay," and joined Ulrich picking up self-rescuers and tossing them in a box, unaware they should not be reused and were probably useless after being exposed to the air for over one-half hour. He asked Al Smith and Gil Robles, the 3100 level motor-men who had refused to leave in case they were needed to run the motor back to the No. 10 station, to stand by in case someone had to be raised to the surface.

Jim Bush, Ron Stansbury, and Richard Nickelby, still not recovered from their ordeal in the toxic smoke, were sitting on a stack of timber when Ulrich and Wilber arrived on the 3700 level. Jim told them where the five men were and staggered up to join them. He climbed on a small Mancha motor and motioned for Ulrich to drive and told the others to take the man train. Harvey

Dionne had not returned and might need help. Jack Beare, the motorman, and Wilber piled on the train and followed the motor. Jim did not realize how close to death he had been, nor that it would be hours before the effect of the carbon monoxide wore off. He almost fell off the motor twice because he hadn't regained his equilibrium, and Ulrich had to grab and steady him.

Harvey Dionne was sitting in the drift a few yards east of the No. 5 shaft, unable to stand since he had escaped from the toxic smoke. Ulrich stopped the motor and told Jim to stay with Harvey. Neither were capable of helping the rescue attempt. He told Jack Beare to get on the motor with Wilber.

Beare said it was suicide to go into the heavy smoke when they saw it pour from the No. 5 shaft crosscut and saturate the drift.

Ulrich shrugged and looked over the self-rescuers in the box and picked one that looked good, although he didn't know how it worked. He had heard one of the men who had walked out on the 3100 level mention that the button was hard to work. He pressed hard on the button and bit down on the mouthpiece with his teeth and started to walk into the smoke, but failed to put on the nose clips.

"Don't go in," Beare warned.

"If it's too bad, don't stay in," Wilber said.

Ulrich ran into the wall of smoke about 200 feet. His mouth began to feel hot and he began to cough from the heat. He assumed the device wasn't working and dashed back to the fresh air for a better self-rescuer.

Wilber was still attempting to figure out how it worked when Ulrich came out of the smoke. The only instructions on the device were *Do not use twice.*

"What's the matter?" Ulrich asked.

"I don't know how to open it, do you?" Wilber said.

"I don't know either."

Wilber tried several respirators and tossed them back in the box until he found one that didn't taste smoky. "I'll give it a try," he said and walked into the roiling smoke about 60 feet. His cap lamp light beam hit a gray wall of smoke three feet from his face and he couldn't see the track when he looked down. Before he walked another 30 feet his head started to spin and he felt he was losing his balance. He turned and started back. Panic gripped him, but he told himself not to run. Just as he was about to throw up his hands and scream, he saw the lights of the motor through the smoke and stumbled into the fresh air. He threw his self-rescuer on the ground and told Ulrich that it didn't work.

Ulrich thought he found a self-rescuer that worked and ran into the smoke. He lasted less than a minute before he began to cough and choke, forcing him to turn back.

"It's no use," Ulrich said as he ran out of the smoke.

Beare drove them back to the Jewell station. Harvey Dionne and Jim Bush were sitting on a bench still unable to fully function.

"Well, there was probably no use anyway. It was probably a foolish idea," Jim said. "Thanks for trying."

Harvey asked Wilber if he knew where the No. 12 borehole was drilled in preparation for sinking a new shaft and told him to go back and take the lagging off the hole so air could get down to the 4800 level. Harvey and Jim knew that with the 3100 and 3700 levels contaminated with smoke, it would be the only source of fresh air getting to the lower levels.

There was nothing the foremen could do and they had been out of touch with what was taking place on the 3100 level. Before they belled to be hoisted topside, Harvey picked up the phone.

Zingler was still at the No. 4. shaft station on the 3100 level listening on the phone,   pained that men were dying and no one could do anything to bring them up from the lower levels. He was hearing fewer voices from below and could only imagine the worst. Dusty Rhoads, who had been constantly on the phone asking for the okay to cut off the 3400 fans, hadn't called in several minutes and his last call said he and Arnold Anderson were in bad shape and repairmen Custer Keough and William Walty were on the ground.

Zingler heard someone call from the 4800 level: "Come and get us. If you don't hurry, we are not going to make it." Then he heard Harvey Dionne say: "We're coming to get you."

After the man on the 4800 disconnected, Zingler told Harvey: "We can't bring them up the 3100. The air's deadly up here and they couldn't make it out even if they did bring them up here."

"There goes our last lifeline out." Harvey said and hung up.

Zingler walked to the 3100 Jewell station. When he arrived, he saw the muck train and the McCaas sitting on the train. The train had passed the No. 4 shaft, set off 150 feet from the main drift, without him hearing it. It was worse than he thought, and Launhardt's haphazard attempt to bring the McCaa breathing apparatus to Gene Johnson at the No. 10 station had failed.

CHAPTER 9

CHAOS AND FRUSTRATION

The Surface

Robert Launhardt and cager, Clyde Dunlap, guided a stumbling Byron Schulz to the cage on the 3100 Jewell station. The safety engineer's curt statement that Don Beehner had been overcome by carbon monoxide and he and Hawkins couldn't bring him out shocked the cager. Launhardt's dazed expression told Dunlap not to ask what happened to James Zingler. The McCaas piled on the timber car said they never delivered the breathing apparatuses to Gene Johnson.

On the ride up Schulz sank to his knees and collapsed in the cager's arms. Launhardt pressed his McCaa mask on Schulz's ashen face until the cage reached the topside. Hawkins, still weak and his reaction time slowed by the effects of the carbon monoxide, could barely lift his arms and was unable to help. The half-dozen men waiting topside for a cage loaded with their friends stared and stood for a moment before two stepped in and carried a semi-conscious Schulz out the portal. Launhardt told Dunlap to get the McCaas left on the train and bring them to the surface then shook his head at the questioning eyes of Pete Bennett and walked head down behind the men carrying Schulz.

Bennett grabbed a glassy-eyed Hawkins's arm as he shuffled off the cage. Hawkins said he was okay and just needed some fresh air.

"Like hell you are," Bennett said, "You're as white as white can be," and led him over to a stack of timber and helped take off his McCaa.

Hawkins leaned back and stared at the confusion around him. Men were attempting to blow oxygen into the faces of the Robert McCoy, Lando Rihtarshik, and others having trouble breathing.

Few, if any, were trained in first aid. Two mechanics had wheeled oxygen tanks from the machine shop and were blowing it on gasping faces or catching it in their hard hats held in front of the victims' faces in an effort to create a pocket of oxygen. He didn't know how long he had been sitting in a trance when paramedics wheeled McCoy, Rihtershik, and Schulz to the ambulances.

A shadow crossing Hawkins's face made him look up. He recognized Martin "Mike" Castellan, a Bureau of Mines inspector.

"Larry, come with me, you need oxygen," Castellan said.

The inspector led him away and administered oxygen from a small tank with mask from where Hawkins didn't know or care. The oxygen entering his system cleansed his blood of carboxyhemoglobin. Slowly his pulse rate began to drop into the normal range and he felt less disoriented. He began to think how close he came to death and how futile and disorganized Launhardt's effort to reach the 3100 No. 10 station had been — over one hour after Gene Johnson had ordered the breathing apparatuses.

Castellan left Hawkins to his thoughts and viewed the chaos. He had been told of the fire at 1:15 p.m. while inspecting the American Smelting and Refining Company's nearby Galena mine and immediately phoned his Spokane, Washington, field office to advise his supervisor of the fire. Under the Federal Metal and Nonmetallic Mine Safety Act of 1966, mining companies were not required to notify the Bureau immediately. The Bureau's authority under the Act was limited to an advisory capacity during mine disasters. Castellan arrived at 1:35 p.m., but had verified the magnitude of the fire one-half mile away as he drove to the mine by the smoke pouring out of the Sunshine tunnel and Big Hole exhaust vents and blanketing Big Creek Canyon.

He was told by a harried Sunshine corporate official, wearing a shirt and tie, that all the men had been evacuated. The inspector's eyes told him the man had lied. Two men, obviously clerical workers by their clothes and shoes, were walking around the mine yard with clipboards asking the miners if they had signed out. His perception was confirmed when Hawkins told him that Don Beehner was killed during their aborted rescue attempt and Byron Schulz had screamed that everyone was dead on the 3100 level, including the shaft foreman, Gene Johnson and two shifters. Castellan's chats with survivors walking out the portal disclosed that three men had been overcome by smoke on the 3700 level and two men attempting to rescue them were also felled by carbon monoxide. That added up to five men dead on the 3700 level and no one knew how many on the 3100.

The inspector walked to the shifters shack Sunshine management had hastily set up to debrief the men coming out of the portal and determine what rescue routes to take. Castellan needed to brief his supervisor when he arrived from Spokane and couldn't rely on what he was told by mine management officials. Their information wasn't any better than what he had gleaned from miners who had escaped and most mine officials only told the Bureau what they wanted the government to know.

Parked outside the shifters shack was the Coeur d'Alene mine rescue truck containing 50 self-contained breathing apparatuses. A few minutes before Launhardt and Hawkins came out of the portal, volunteer rescue crews from the nearby Bunker Hill and Galena mines had started to arrive. It would be after 3:00, when day shift got off, before the mines could hoist the shift to the surface and transport them to the Sunshine mine. Although most rescue crews were trained in the use of self-contained breathing apparatuses, they had never faced the heat and toxic air generated by an actual mine fire. Not that it mattered to the volunteer crews. In the tight mining community they had friends and relatives in almost every mine and they knew their rescue crews would risk their lives for them. One of the Galena Mine miners was twenty-six-year-old Leonard Nickelby. His brother, Richard, and brother-in-law and father-in-law worked in the Sunshine.

Upon emerging from the portal a few minutes after 2:00, Launhardt had taken it on his own to order the air door on the 3100 level closed and the air door on the 3700 opened. The safety engineer believed he was protecting the Jewell shaft on the 3100 and the air coming down the Jewell to the 3700 would provide fresh air to anyone walking out on the regular escapeway level. In case survivors might attempt to walk out the secondary escapeway through the adjacent Silver Summit mine, Launhardt requested the Silver Summit mine manager to stop their fan that made the escapeway in the lethal exhaust air. The fan was turned off at 4:00 p.m.

It was obvious to Castellan that Launhardt hadn't asked Harvey Dionne and Jim Bush, experienced foremen, just emerging from the portal and looking like battle-weary retreating soldiers. He had been told that Jim Bush's brother, Bob, was one of the men assumed dead on the 3700 level. Castellan didn't know that the anguished gaze on Harvey Dionne's face was from knowing that his son, Greg, was likely killed on the 3100 level No. 10 station.

Ten minutes before Castellan drove into Sunshine's parking lot, Marvin Chase, Sunshine's vice president and general manager of mining and western operations, and Albert Walkup, the mine superintendent, had arrived from the stockholders meeting in Coeur d'Alene. In his late forties, Chase was a graduate mining engineer. Typical of mining engineers, he worked as a miner and shifter for several years prior to utilizing his engineering "book-learned" education and had jumped between four or five mining companies before taking over as general manager at Sunshine in 1969. Receding hair and a pale complexion blamed on wearing a hard hat and going underground three or four days a week was another characteristic of hands-on mine managers of hard rock mines. His speech was deliberate as was the man who always thought about what he had to say. In the three years the author dealt with the Sunshine mine, I never met a Sunshine employee who had anything bad to say about Chase. They thought of Chase as an honest and dedicated Westerner trying to do the "right thing," unlike the [expletives deleted] "New Yorkers who really ran the company and cared only about costs and the price of silver."

Sunshine's current management that took control of the corporation in a proxy battle six years earlier were more interested in corporate takeovers and mergers than mining and ran the company into debt with their risky investments while the mining operation continued to show a profit even during times of low silver prices. The former company president made all the major decisions until he was ousted. The position remained vacant for over one year until ten months ago when the chairman of the board, a New York corporation lawyer, was named president. Chase was given the authority to manage the mine, but he was still a vice president. Unlike other corporate division heads awarded the title of president of their subsidiaries, Chase reported to the president in New York.

Chase was alone in making decisions how to rescue possible survivors except for the relatively new mine manager, Al Walkup, and the veteran chief engineer, Robert L. Anderson. Electrical foreman Floyd Strand and maintenance foreman Tom Harrah were well-qualified in their fields, but were not familiar with the mine's ventilation system. None of Sunshine's other officers, including the president, Irwin Underweiser, had mining experience, and the day shift underground supervisors were decimated. Three of his five day shift underground foremen were probably dead, leaving only exhausted Harvey Dionne and Jim Bush, both of whom had lost family members in the mine. All five day shift production shifters were in the mine and likely dead. Ten members of Sunshine's twenty-four-man rescue team were missing. Chase would have to rely on his night shift foremen and shifters who were beginning to arrive.

The First Rescue Attempt

Chase and Launhardt briefed the rescue crews from the nearby mines and Sunshine employees trained to use breathing apparatus making the first rescue attempt. The crews entered the mine at 2:45 p.m. Launhardt led them to the No. 5 shaft on the 3700 level and stayed with the backup crew in fresh air. The safety engineer hadn't taken a refresher course in the use of the breathing apparatus in over five years and was not technically qualified to enter contaminated atmospheres.

The rescue crew walked a few feet into the smoke and tested the air for carbon monoxide, a basic precaution. The standard carbon monoxide test instruments used by the Bureau and mining industry were only calibrated up to 0.3 of 1% carbon monoxide. The test confirmed Launhardt's earlier reading that the device turned black in seconds, a warning that the atmosphere was deadly. At the news, the reflex action of every crew member was to run his hand over his mask to make sure it fit snugly. Before they walked 200 feet, the heat carried by the exhaust ventilation recirculating over the fire 300 feet above saturated their clothes in sweat. As they slowly progressed beneath the fire, the heat began to reach oven temperatures that would soon become unbearable. Visibility in the smoke was less than three feet, making their cap lamps almost useless. The only way they could keep track of the man in front was to keep their arms extended and touch the backpack of the aluminum breathing apparatus. Soon that became impossible when the aluminum backpack burned their finger tips without gloves.

They were about to be forced to surrender to the intense heat when they came upon the bodies of Pat Hobson, Bob Bush, Wayne Blalack, Roberto Diaz, and Paul Johnson approximately 500 feet into the smoke. Without body bags, they were helpless to do anything other than go to the surface and return. And it had to be accomplished quickly. Heat does horrible things to bodies left in high temperatures.

Dejected, the crews returned to the surface to deliver the bad news around 4:30 p.m. They were not equipped to reach the No. 10 station in the heat and high carbon monoxide levels without building bulkheads to establish fresh air bases.

The Surface

Roland V. Wilson, Supervisory Mining Engineer at the Spokane Field Office of the Seattle Subdistrict, Western District of the Metal and Non-metal Mine Safety and Health Division, was far down in the Bureau of Mines hierarchy. Averaging 70 miles per hour on the 85-mile drive from his office, he pulled into Sunshine's yard at 3:00 p.m. The stocky mining engineer had done his mandatory apprenticeship as a laborer and engineer in several mines before joining the Bureau. Wilson was never concerned that a situation was too big or small for him to handle. At times, one might not know he was in the room while everyone else was talking until he spoke. His slow, deliberate style cut through a rock-hard problem and said what had to be done without raising his voice or using a surplus of emotion or syllables.

Wilson insisted on a complete briefing from Marvin Chase and Al Walkup, then issued a closure order banning all persons from the mine because of the imminent danger caused by the fire except for those necessary for the rescue of survivors, recovery of bodies or extinguishing the fire. At first glance, a Bureau closure order looks like a federal bureaucrat's version of a parking ticket even in size. Although it warranted no monetary penalty, it gave the inspector power. [9] While an inspector could not order mine management how

---

9 Civil penalties for violations under the Federal Mine Safety and Health Amendments Act of 1977 are mandatory and cannot be waived. Under the Federal Civil Penalties Inflation Adjustment Act of 1990, penalties currently range from a minimum of $70 to a maximum of $60,000 for each violation of the health and safety standards. As this is written, MSHA is revising the maximum penalties to $220,000 for flagrant violations under the Mine Improvement and New Emergency Response Act passed in June 2006. The 1977 Act's statutory formula requires consideration of the mine's history of previous violations, size of the mine and company, negligence, potential gravity of the injury and number of persons that could be injured or killed, and the demonstrated good faith of the mine operator in correcting the violation.

to proceed during a fire or when men were trapped, he had the authority to judge whether they were acting in a safe manner and endangering possible survivors, rescue crews or any person on the mine property, and order the action stopped. The Bureau's so-called advisory capacity became an invitation to management's strategy meetings and their advice was not taken lightly. Chase was also aware of the Bureau's vast rescue capabilities, including the best trained rescue crews in the nation, and he needed expert help.

Wilson's first suggestion was to provide a comfortable location for the relatives of the miners beginning to gather near the mine portal to prevent accidents and provide a safe access to the mine. Many of the miners who had escaped had called their families to tell them of the fire and assure them they were okay, and the news was already on the local radio. His next step was to debrief the rescue crews coming out of the mine and Jim Bush and Harvey Dionne, experienced witnesses to the conditions in the mine and the most capable of analyzing where the fire was and the likely location of survivors.

After Jim Bush and Harvey Dionne were interviewed, Chase told them to be checked out by a physician in the mine yard and to go home and rest. But the foremen couldn't leave. They had to face their toughest task of the day. Jim stayed at the mine with his mother and his brother's wife. Even after being told that her husband was dead, Bob's wife refused to leave. Bette Bush volunteered to pass out sandwiches to the waiting relatives and urge them to have faith. Harvey had to tell his wife and young daughter-in-law, the mother of his five-month-old granddaughter, that things looked black for twenty-three-year-old Greg and to ask God for a miracle.

For most relatives and friends of the missing men, there was nothing to do but wait and pray in that special corner in purgatory reserved for miners' families when their men are trapped underground. Tears flowed from the women unable to hold in their emotions, but most stood alone and stared into oblivion, too shocked to share their fears.

When the late afternoon sun dips behind the mountains, the chill hits the canyons first and shadows blanket the ground like an ice shroud. At an altitude of 2,600 feet in Northern Idaho's panhandle, the temperature can drop to near freezing in early May. Standing on a concrete slab surrounded by ugly, gray metal buildings, stacks of steel pipe and rough timbers, and parked heavy machinery added to the cold and the realization of the crude life faced daily by their missing husbands, fathers, brothers, and sons to earn a living, but the men knew. The men of the Silver Valley had been miners for generations.

Chase insisted the families be allowed to remain where they could see the mine portal from behind a rope stretched between a warehouse and the machine shop. During the first hours the families raised their expectations each time the Jewell hoist's cable and sheave wheel above them started moving. They could tell from the direction the wire cable traveled whether the a cage was coming up or going down. When the cable told them the cage was rising, they would watch for their loved ones to walk out or gaze at the faces of the men walking out the portal to tell them if there was good news. The sight of men entering the portal with their aluminum backpacks was comforting. It meant that someone who knew more than they did still had hope and was doing something.

The first news from Sunshine corporate officials came from someone they didn't know. Wallace C. Wilson, a Sunshine Mining Company vice president, briefed local reporters. The local press and reporters from Spokane, Washington, wrote stories that would be picked up on the wires by the Associated Press and United Press International for the nation's newspapers, which would be placed on the inside pages or at best a spot low on the first page until the editors determined it was national news. Wilson announced that five men had been found dead and 108 had been evacuated, leaving 77 unaccounted for in the mine. The obvious death of Don Beehner was not admitted because his body had not been discovered, a practice Sunshine would follow to maintain hope and shield the relatives from the bad news. Wallace Wilson's pathetic message of hope was: "There is fresh air as well as smoke-filled areas." Nothing was mentioned about the specific levels the women knew their husband toiled.

Obviously wanting to cut the interview short and return to the search for survivors, Chase announced that fresh air was being forced down the area where the trapped miners were believed to be. A man wearing a tie and quoted as a company official by the reporters answered a question about the cause of the fire as "probably an electrical failure." His response raised a wince from Chase, aware it was a wild guess and improbable. Jim Bush and Harvey Dionne were sure the fire started on the 3400 or 3550 level and there was no electrical wiring on the levels except for the exhaust fans that Chase knew were working.

If the miners' relatives and friends did not recognize Wallace Wilson, it was little wonder. Wilson was a Sunshine Mining Company vice president and president of its Piezo Crystal Division subsidiary from Carlisle, Pennsylvania, a manufacturer of radio quartz crystals, who happened to be in the area to attend the stockholders meeting.

The Second Rescue Attempts

The crowd watched several rescue crews pile into vans and drive toward the Silver Summit Mine in an effort to enter the Sunshine through a mile-long tunnel connecting the mines. The first crew was led by a Sunshine mine rescue team member familiar with the tunnel between the mines on the 3100 level. They faced no obstacles the first 2,000 feet to the Silver Dollar fan in clear air. When they entered the smoke they were forced to retreat. One of the Galena Mine rescue crew's McCaa leaked and he had to be replaced. After walking another 1,500 feet, they were driven back by the extreme heat and impenetrable dense smoke before reaching the Sunshine fan, far short of the No. 10 station. *(See Map No. 3.)*

The third rescue crew team entered the mine on the 3100 level through the Jewell shaft around 10:00 p.m. They faced the same insufferable heat, thick smoke, and deadly carbon monoxide as the first two rescue teams and returned to the surface around 1:00 a.m. in the morning of May 3.

It was apparent to Chase, Wilson, and the other tired and coffee-saturated men around the table at 2:00 a.m. that the two approaches to the No. 10 shaft station on the 3100 level and only access to the station on the 3700 level were too far to travel under the harsh conditions. The only method of reaching survivors was to build bulkheads to seal off the smoke and carbon monoxide and establish fresh air bases to shorten the distances. This required not only constructing bulkheads spaced at sufficient distances in which the heat could be tolerated, it meant rebuilding the old wooden bulkheads on the 3100 and 3700 levels, where smoke was leaking from the mined-out drifts and old raises.

The hardest decisions were whether to stop or alter the direction of the fans in the complex ventilation system. They had to estimate the possible damage and changes to the system caused by the fire and the effect it would have on areas that potentially provided fresh air to survivors. Reversing the Sunshine fan on the Silver Summit escapeway was risky, but it would force fresh air towards the 3100 level No. 10 station and down the shaft to the lower levels. It was worth the gamble. Opening the doors on the 3100 and 3700 levels would also force air towards the No. 10 station, which reversed Launhardt's decision to close the air door on the 3100 level. Harvey Dionne and Jim Bush's decision to open the No. 12 bore hole to the 4800 level was deemed quick thinking. The bore hole was providing the only fresh air to the 4800 level and there was a chance the air might migrate up to the 4600 level. They were hesitant to alter the main fans on the 3400 and 5200 levels for fear of disturbing the ventilation system that men trapped below might be depending on in fresh air pockets.

Building the bulkheads would take days, maybe weeks, too long to hope that the men could stay alive. It would also take more men trained in the use of self-contained breathing apparatuses than they had on hand working around-the-clock. Roland Wilson mentioned that he recalled reading about a Bureau research program for using inflatable rubber bags instead of building wood bulkheads in emergencies, but no one at the late-night meeting had heard of them. Wilson called a friend in the Bureau's Washington headquarters and asked him, only to learn the following morning that the research project had been cancelled.

By midnight, the bitter chill without warm coats and the need to pick up children at a neighbor's and tell them their father wasn't coming home had thinned out the crowd. Local reporters looking for anecdotal stories circulated through the fifty relatives and a handful of miners who refused to leave until they had word of their partners still underground. Miners, many still in their hard hats and diggers, comforted the women with descriptions of possible places for fresh air and that their husband was "damned good miner and knew how to take care of himself." They spoke quietly among themselves outside the glare of the floodlights in front of the portal and turned their backs when approached by reporters.

Eugene Stephens, a retired miner whose nineteen-year-old-son, Darrell, had started to work in the mine the day before, couldn't help telling a reporter as he walked to his car holding his wife's hand: "I know he's down there. He's just a kid. . . We're hoping, that's all."

The 4800 Level

Darrell Stephens would never learn the reporter misspelled his name as "Stevens." He died that afternoon.

Twelve hundred feet from Darrell's body, Ron Flory and Tom Wilkinson sat talking over their options. It would be foolhardy to attempt to climb the raises. The raises were near the No. 10 station and filled with smoke and toxic gas. Even if one cleared, they had no idea where the fire was or what the smoke and gas conditions were above. They had left their self-rescuers in the motor barn and feared all their friends were dead near the station. It seemed logical to wait. How bad could the fire be? There was nothing to burn in a hard rock mine except old timbers and garbage tossed in the old workings on the upper levels before the mine began sand-filling the mined-out stopes with the granulated waste rock left after the ore was removed.

Ron's calendar watch only made the minutes seem like hours. The urge to do something as day ticked slowly into late evening was overpowering. They knew there was a bore hole drilled in preparation for the new No. 12 shaft somewhere in the Syndicate drift and it couldn't be hard to find. It would be wise to check it out in case smoke was coming down and crept up on them when they were sleeping. It might also be a place where they could climb up if there was no smoke. The search would also satisfy their ache to do something. They conserved their cap lamp batteries by only using one when they walked the dark 4000 feet to the where the drift split in two, but couldn't find the bore hole in either of the 300-foot stub drift ends. The only other place was a crosscut they had passed 800 feet back. They walked back and followed the crosscut for 900 feet until they saw a telephone and a wire coming down a four-foot diameter hole from above.

Ron rang the military-type field phone a half-dozen times, but there was no answer. They were about to give up when Ron noticed that the batteries were popping out of a back receptacle. He shoved them back in and rang again several times. Unlike their phones at home, it didn't have a dial tone and they were unable to determine if it was working. They surmised it wasn't connected. No one had been working on the borehole for weeks and a phone wouldn't be needed until the shaft was being constructed. It didn't cross their minds that the phone had been dropped earlier in an attempt to contact anyone who might be alive on the level. And the electrician crew that lowered the phone 1,100 feet down the four-foot hole hours earlier was unaware that a sharp rock had cut the wire.

It was a simple decision. The four-foot hole was too wide to climb 1,100 feet without a place to rest and they didn't know the condition of the hole all the way to the 3700 level. The only consolation was that fresh air appeared to be coming down the hole.

They walked back to the drill station, a niche carved out of the rock to store equipment during the mining of the West Syndicate drift, where they had been keeping vigil. An air cooler in the drift to the west seemed to make the air fresher. The spot was close to the No. 10 station if help arrived and they could watch if the smoke started to migrate towards them. Both were tired and hungry and sleep would help ration Ron's few remaining cigarettes. They took turns sleeping on lagging stacked in the drill station while the other stood watch. The timber was cleaner and felt softer than rock. Neither could sleep for more than a couple of hours. To Tom it was the silence and the scene of death of his fellow miners that wouldn't let him sleep.

CHAPTER 10

WEDNESDAY, MAY 3, 1972

Organization and Politics

As usual, the wives and mothers of missing miners woke to an alarm before six o'clock, not to fix their men's breakfast and pack their lunch, but to drive to the mine. By the light of the moon they left their clapboard houses, apartments, and trailer homes in Mullan, Wallace, Moon Gulch, and Smeltersville. They joined the cars and pickups driven by miners on their way to work at the Lucky Friday, Bunker Hill, Crescent, and a dozen other mines in the Silver Valley. The main route, Interstate 90, paralleled the Coeur d'Alene River and towering banks of gray mine waste streaked yellow by acid drainage. They turned off in Kellogg, the town with the most missing men to cry over.

The last two miles ran up Big Creek Canyon along its cascading creek roaring down with the mountain's spring runoff. After passing a valley filled by millions of tons of gray waste mine rock higher than your neck can crane to see the top, they crossed a wooden bridge and entered the mine parking lot. The first pale streaks of dawn were breaking over the mountain when they walked to the mine yard and saw the faces of the shivering men and women who had kept vigil through the chilly night. There was no news except for a ray of hope in the form of another rescue team that had entered the portal.

Chase insisted it was his responsibility to give the bad news at the 10:00 a.m. press briefing. The mine manager showed emotion for the first time when he reported a rescue crew had discovered 19 bodies on the 3100 level. No names were given. The crew had to retreat under the oppressive heat and smoke and didn't have time to identify them. Chase announced he still had hope men would be found alive. The relatives didn't have to be mathematicians to calculate that 19 bodies out of 77 missing men meant that one-quarter were dead.

Roland Wilson was still at the mine at 7:00 a.m. He had to brief Bruce Grant, a Bureau Technical Support mining engineer, and Robert Campbell, Westinghouse Electric Corporation's Mine Rescue Project program manager. Westinghouse was under contract with the Bureau to supply emergency services and supplies during mine disasters and maintain the Bureau's mine rescue equipment and facilities in Charleston, West Virginia. The corporation's enormous technical, logistics, and purchasing capability was retained to locate and deliver every conceivable type of equipment that might be needed any place in the country around-the-clock. En route on their U.S. Air Force flight from Baltimore, Grant and Campbell determined the basic radio communications, seismic equipment, and personnel needed to be airlifted from Pittsburgh and Charleston.

Wilson asked Grant and Campbell, a pair proud of their inherited nothing-is-impossible Scottish engineering heritage, if they thought large inflatable rubber bags would work to speed up the process of building bulkheads in the mine honeycombed with 112 miles of old drifts and crosscuts. They listened to the concept Wilson had heard of filling and sealing rubber bags around the edges with a rigid polyurethane foam supported only by timbers. Neither saw any reason why it shouldn't work. Campbell told a Westinghouse employee to get on the phone and find suitable bags and foam.

Aware he would no longer be in charge of the Bureau's efforts after the arrival of the Director of the Bureau of Mines, Dr. Elburt F. Osborn, and Assistant Director for Metal and Nonmetal Mine Health and Safety, Stanley M. Jarrett, Wilson inquired about a "torpedo," a rescue device he had read about developed at the Atomic Energy Commission Nevada test site and a New Mexico uranium mine for escape through a borehole. He believed the only survivors would be found on the 4800 level and it might be possible to reach them through the No. 12 borehole. Wilson admitted he had discussed it with Al Walkup, the mine manager, who was of the opinion that the hole was too irregular and jagged. The trio agreed it was extremely dangerous to send men 1,100 feet down a four-foot diameter hole and came up with the idea to first drop a low-light TV camera down the borehole to survey its condition and determine if there was smoke on the 4800 level. Campbell called his Westinghouse logistics team in Baltimore and told them to ship the TV camera and sufficient TV cable and locate the capsule at the Atomic Energy Commission, then standby to have it flown to Spokane.

Wilson left them at 9:00 a.m. to meet Jarrett; Allen D. Look, the Bureau's Metal and Nonmetal Mine Health and Safety Western District Director; and Kenneth Russell, Wilson's immediate boss and the Spokane Subdistrict Manager. After they arrived, Wilson would be at the bottom of the Bureau's management totem pole. On his own, Wilson had called in five Bureau inspectors to assist in the rescue effort and two instructors from the Bureau's Education and Training Division to train and certify as many men as needed in the use of self-contained breathing apparatus.

Sixty-nine-year-old Stanley Jarrett came out of retirement as a safety engineer for Kennecott Copper Corporation in 1969 to take the position as Bureau of Mines Assistant Director for Metal and Nonmetal Mine Health and Safety. He enjoyed the prestige the title gave him in mining industry circles and the Bureau's bureaucracy. Jarrett's lack of knowledge of safety standards and evasiveness when asked technical questions astounded the author during his testimony at the public hearing on the disaster months later, as it confounded Bureau employees under him daily. The Bureau's mine inspectors and mining engineers, all of whom had been miners, had little respect for the political appointee and his pro-industry leanings. Jarrett and his Washington staff appeared in the same blue coveralls worn by his inspectors. Jarrett's coveralls were new and pressed, while the inspectors' were worn and dirty from going into mines. Nor did the inspectors display a starched white shirt and tie between the lapels or wear shiny shoes.

After Jarrett was briefed by Chase and Walkup on the conditions in the mine, he advised them they must get organized for the complex rescue and suggested they form an advisory committee of Bureau members and local mine managers and engineers who had volunteered to help. To Wilson's surprise, he was named a member. Not a surprise to Bureau personnel, Jarrett insisted Sunshine management delegate responsibilities and draw up an organization chart. Jarrett's next move was to organize the Bureau and order his assistant to create an organization chart that had to be updated regularly as 115 Bureau personnel arrived during the coming days. Serving on the advisory committee and sending three or four reports every day to Washington kept Jarrett and his assistant busy and permitted the Bureau engineers and inspectors to devote their time working on the rescue effort.

W. Carl Griner, Idaho State Inspector of Mines, arrived at the mine around 8:00 a.m. and was assigned to the advisory committee. Griner had learned of the fire over a Boise radio station at 4:30 p.m. the previous afternoon. He was surprised when he called the Governor Cecil Andrus at 6:00 p.m. to advise him of the disaster. The Governor told him he had dispatched two of his political staff members to Kellogg hours earlier. Griner, a dedicated, self-conscious man in his early forties, had worked 22 years as a miner. His political appointment as the State Inspector of Mines and membership on the first Metal and Nonmetal Mine Advisory Committee on health and safety standards were a result of his labor union and Democrat political connections during the Johnson administration and a Democrat Governor of Idaho.

To Griner's credit and the admiration of many miners and the author, he testified at a congressional hearing that Idaho's mine safety regulations were "loosely written." He also complained that the federal standards had been "watered down" under a system that required unanimous agreement on mandatory safety standards by a nine-member advisory committee made up of industry, labor, and state political appointees. Standards approved by only a majority were deemed "advisory." A single member's objection, which generally came from an industry representative, excluded a standard from being mandatory. Advisory standards were merely considered a good safety practice the mines were not required to follow to the consternation of Griner and the Bureau.

The Idaho State Inspector and his office were deemed unqualified by the Bureau staff charged with overseeing state plans and inspections, however, the author believed Griner was quite capable. Two and one-half years earlier, Idaho had applied to implement a State Plan permitted under the Federal Metal and Nonmetallic Mine Safety Act of 1966 (1966 MNM Act) federalism concept that allowed states to enforce the law subject to the Bureau's approval. Griner struggled with two inspectors to inspect Idaho's 160 mines funded under the Federal Emergency Employment Act of 1970. His 1972 budget request for $104,000 was slashed to a meager $72,000 by the Idaho legislature for five inspectors, his salary, travel, and administrative overhead. Without sufficient funding, the Bureau was reluctant to approve the State Plan, although Idaho's safety standards were deemed equal or superior to the Bureau's, as required under the 1966 MNM Act. Two other drawbacks were that the Idaho mining law required advance notice to the mine before inspections and Griner and his inspectors were political appointees lacking any engineering education or experience.

The Bureau opposed the Idaho congressional delegation's effort to require the federal government to fund 50% of the salaries of state mine inspectors. It would erode the Bureau's turf if the appropriation passed. Congress had entrusted the enforcement responsibilities to the states under the Coal Mine Health and Safety Act of 1952 and determined the law was not enforced uniformly because of the coal industry's political power and the lack of adequate funding in most states. The Federal Coal Mine Health and Safety Act of 1969 (1969 Coal Act) removed the enforcement authority from the states and granted it to the Bureau.

In the battle of bureaucracies, Idaho was to play as little a role as the Bureau decided in assisting in the disaster, not that the State had the assets and ability to provide meaningful assistance. The resources available to the federal agency were evident that afternoon when two U.S. Air Force C-130 cargo planes landed at the nearby Fairchild Air Force Base with seismic equipment to help locate trapped miners, underground radios, and equipment. From there, Air Force helicopters ferried the equipment and Bureau and Westinghouse employees to the mine.

Democrat Idaho Governor Cecil D. Andrus arrived in the morning, followed a few minutes later by the Republican Secretary of the Interior, Rogers C.B. Morton. They attended a joint briefing by Chase and Jarrett that portrayed a confusing and dark picture for the 58 men believed trapped. The Andrus and Morton meeting was ironic. Morton was aware of congressional and public criticism of the Bureau's mine safety enforcement record and a movement on Capitol Hill and by the labor unions to transfer its mine health and safety jurisdiction to the Department of Labor. Andrus would be the Secretary of the Interior in 1977 under President Jimmy Carter after two coal mine disasters occurred, which provided the impetus for the mine health and safety functions transfer to the Department of Labor under the Federal Mine Health and Safety Amendments Act of 1977 (1977 Mine Act).

Andrus spent most of the day surrounded by reporters talking to the families of the missing miners and promising money, food, and an investigation into the cause of the disaster. The lanky congenial Westerner was in his element. Miners and their families voted straight Democrat. Andrus moved easily among them grasping hands instead of a politician's handshake and offering his sincere prayers for the rescue of the trapped miners. But it was Morton who captured the local and national reporters' attention in the two hours he spent at the mine. A national figure was big news in the Idaho panhandle; and a Western governor was not news in national newspapers. Morton was an impressive figure. Handsome and six-foot-seven, the snow-white-haired former Congressman towered over the crowd. He told them he personally spoke to President Richard Nixon that morning and together they promised the best government technicians and equipment were on the way and that he would order a full-scale investigation into the disaster.

Morton lost the audience for a moment when three station wagons drove out the portal carrying the bodies of Don Beehner, Charles Casteel, William Hanna, Floyd Raise, Nick Sharette, and William Wilson. Tales of Beehner's heroism and ultimate sacrifice by giving his life-saving oxygen mask to save the life of a fellow miner rippled through the crowd. Rescue crews were not allowed to disclose the names of the men whose bodies were discovered, nor mention they were bloated by the baking heat. The bodies of Beehner and Casteel were found less than 500 feet from the No. 5 shaft on the 3100 level. The four shaft miners had been hoisted from the 5800 level in one of the last cages raised by Robert Scanlan to the 3100 level before he died. The shaft crew had staggered 1,100 feet from the No. 10 station without self-rescuers before dying 600 feet from fresh air between 100 to 200 feet from where Launhardt's aborted rescue attempt turned back.

Morton concluded his remarks by pointing out that the present federal law governing hard rock mines did not provide penalties, like the law regulating coal mines, and that the Bureau has assessed $12 million in penalties against the coal companies for violations of the 1969 Coal Act. Never one to face tough issues or confront opposition, Morton said it was too early to determine whether the 1966 MNM Act should be amended to provide financial penalties. He failed to mention, of the $12 million assessed against the coal companies, less that $500,000 had been collected. Tens of thousands of scurrilous administrative appeals filed by the coal companies had succeeded in creating a log jam in the Bureau's pathetic penalty collection system. Its unbudgeted six-man penalty assessment office staffed with former coal mine inspectors was overwhelmed. It was also denied access to the Bureau's computer system used to generate mineral production statistics. Thousands of inspection reports and assessments documents couldn't be found in two huge rooms stacked in cardboard boxes. Not even file cabinets were provided.

The American Mining Congress (AMC), the mining industry's lobbying arm in Washington, exacerbated the Interior Department's lack of preparedness by supplying the coal companies with a printed "fill-in-the-blanks" appeal forms demanding formal hearings. Although the 1969 Coal Act went into effect January 1, 1970, the Interior Department's Office of Hearings and Appeals (OHA) responsible for the hearings was not established until April 1970. As the first OHA director, I was overwhelmed when appointed in May. I faced the tasks of hiring the administrative law judges (ALJ) to conduct the hearings and support staff, drafting and publishing the appeals procedural rules, and organizing the office, including finding office space. Through the dedicated work of the new OHA staff, the appeals process was in operation by the end of June, but faced a backlog of cases that would take almost two years to adjudicate.

The Director of the Bureau of Mines, Dr. Elburt F. Osborn, arrived at the mine at 5:00 p.m. He avoided formal press briefings when possible after Assistant Secretary Dole determined he lacked experience in coping with mine disasters and appointed Lewis Helm, a tough former news reporters, to handle the press.

The Bureau mine safety engineers believed Dr. Osborn was like his politically appointed predecessors from university circles, whose primary interest was research to improve mining methods. Only after major mine disasters were grants made for mine health and safety research, which resulted in Britain and Germany being far ahead of the United States in many areas. If Dr. Osborn had asked the rescue crews entering the mine filled with toxic gases what they thought of the Bureau's antiquated self-contained McCaa apparatus, he would have be told it was obsolete, to say the least. After I was trained on a McCaa in order to enter the mine when it was on fire, the Bureau's chief of training, Wayne Grames, told me, "The McCaa was a piece of crap," and insisted I wear a cooler-operating and lighter German-made Draeger self-contained apparatus. Most volunteers used the superior Draeger. A cutting insult to the Bureau's McCaa came when the press learned that the Bureau's rescue team asked the Atomic Energy Commission to send twenty British-made units they believed safer and cooler operating.

Another example of the lack of adequate safety research was the use of rubber bags filled with polyurethane foam that could be used as temporary barricades against toxic gases while fighting a mine fire, which could be installed in hours, instead of building barricades out of wood and other materials that took days. A request by the Bureau's safety division to test their use had been denied years earlier. The Bureau rescue teams experimented with the rubber bags by trial and error for the first time at the Sunshine Mine under hazardous conditions and made them work, eliminating hundreds of man hours of labor.

Congress recognized and alleviated the lack of funding for coal mine safety research and development (R&D) in the 1969 Coal Act by authorizing annual appropriations of up to $30 million. Coal mine safety R&D leaped to $23.5 million in 1971, over three times the 1970 budget, and reached $30.1 million in 1972. In contrast, metal and non-metal mine safety research was but $505,000 in 1971, but jumped to $2.9 million in 1972 and 1973 as a result of the Sunshine disaster. Nevertheless, little heed was paid to the research requests of the practical engineers responsible for health and safety. Jack Crawford, an experienced mining engineer and Assistant Director for Coal Mine Health and Safety, publicly categorized most coal mine R&D as "An academic attempt to reinvent the wheel."

After mine health and safety jurisdiction was removed from the Bureau in 1973 and transferred to the Mining Enforcement and Safety Administration (MESA), the division between the Bureau and MESA exploded before the 1975 public meeting of the Bureau's

Research Advisory Panel (RAP), primarily made up of university professors and companies holding Bureau research grants. MESA's Technical Support Division, which had made R&D recommendations when part of the Bureau, was virtually ignored. The RAP witnessed MESA's infamous "Smucker's Rebellion," named after the jam company's boxes MESA presented each RAP member containing documents claiming the Bureau's safety research was inadequate. As a result, MESA was granted a token $2 million for "technical applications to existing devices." The Smucker's boxes held Bureau research contracts disclosing that the salary charged by a university for the then Bureau director when he was dean of the mining school totaled 138% of his annual salary. It was blackmail, but it helped. In 1976, the Secretary of the Interior, not desiring infighting within his department, forced the Bureau and MESA to agree to a method of coordinating mine health and safety R&D. Nevertheless, coal continued to receive the lion's share. The 1976 R&D safety budget for coal was $29.2 million and metal and nonmetal $5.1 million out of a total Bureau R&D budget of over $120 million. The hardrock mine safety and health R&D inheritance was still that of an illegitimate son.

Osborn had to be ordered to go to Kellogg by Assistant Secretary for Mineral Resources Hollis M. Dole. Dole was aware that the Bureau's director had no interest in mine safety, as evidenced by his agreement to accept the political appointment on the condition that he would not have to become involved in health and safety. Osborn's lack of knowledge of mine safety resulted in him contributing little during his eight-day stay at the mine. His single appearance before the congressional committee investigating the disaster was to accompany Dole, and the transcript reveals that his testimony was approximately one hundred words in response to questions from the panel. The academic discovered he wasn't cut out for the job and resigned shortly afterwards. Jarrett turned in his resignation when he heard that mine health and safety responsibilities were about to be transferred from the Bureau to MESA and rumors that he would be the first one fired.

In Washington, press releases flew out of Idaho congressional offices to tell their constituents what they were doing and demanding on their behalf. Republican Senator Len Jordan asked the Office of Emergency Preparedness to provide disaster assistance to the families of the victims and called for an investigation. Democrat Senator Frank Church alerted all federal agencies that might aid his constituents and promised there would be a thorough investigation. Republican Representative Orval Hansen said the House Education and Labor Committee, of which he was a member, would appoint a special committee to investigate. Astute and likeable Republican Representative James McClure boarded a plane and flew to his district to personally tell the voters he would join in the House committee's investigation.

With the pressure of Congress and the United Steelworkers of America demanding an investigation, Osborn appointed Jarrett to head the Bureau's investigation. Irate at not having been consulted and not trusting Jarrett, Assistant Secretary Dole, a crusty, tough geologist, told Secretary Morton that the Department of the Interior must conduct an independent public hearing.[10]

Rescue Attempts

On the 3100 level the rescue work was slow, but not sure. The rail tracks had been removed from the mined-out areas, forcing the crews approaching from the Silver Summit Mine to carry the heavy timbers, burlap, and sealants over a mile to the "hook" area, a mined-out drift north of the air door leading to the No. 10 shaft station. When they opened the air door, the smoke and heat was impenetrable. Behind them the mined-out area swiftly began to leak toxic smoke and had to be bulkheaded at several locations before they could create a fresh air base for crews to reach the shaft station, the only way down to possible survivors.

Unknown to the crews, Westinghouse had found large rubber dunnage bag manufacturers in Rockmart, Georgia; Mishawaka, Indiana; and Portland, Oregon, and had made arrangements for them to be flown to Spokane, Washington, where waiting National Guard trucks would deliver them the following morning. An Air Force C-130 would land that afternoon with a rubber-tired mine vehicle to transport the men and materials over the mile stretch where the rail tracks had been removed.

---

10 Thirty years later, while the author was researching Dole's and John B. Rigg's (Dole's deputy) personal files, he discovered that Dole wanted the author to lead the independent investigation.

People and the News

The mining communities listened to the promises of help and investigations from the politicians. They sounded good, but the relatives only concern at the moment was getting their men out of the mine. For that they relied on Marvin Chase and the men risking their lives going in and out of the mine. Rescue teams were streaming in to assist the Sunshine, Bunker Hill, Galena, and Bureau crews from the nearby Lucky Friday and Star Mines and the faraway Anaconda Mine in Butte, Montana; Kennecott Copper's Burgin Mine in Eureka, Utah; Kaiser Resources's mine in Fernia, British Columbia; and Cominco's Sullivan Mine in Kimberly, British Columbia.

The missing miners' relatives and friends came dressed to weather the night cold. They soon found they were not alone in their time of need. The Red Cross set up a nurse's station and tables laden with coffee, milk, soft drinks, and sandwiches that would soon be overwhelmed by the support of the mining communities. Churches and the local miners' womens' auxiliary set up nurseries and organized centers to make sandwiches and soup in such abundance the Red Cross had to bring three refrigerators to the mine. To ease their nighttime vigil, a call to the Forest Service in the Coeur d'Alene National Forest brought a truckload of beds and mattresses from its ranger fire stations to be set up in a warehouse. With blankets furnished by the Red Cross, those staying through the night could catch catnaps and have a warm place for their children to sleep. The Red Cross also quickly realized the volunteer rescue crews had to be fed lunches and took over the task of feeding 200 men.

Clergy members of every denomination volunteered to ensure there were three pastors in the mine yard at all times to console and comfort the families. Unable to recognize the wife or mother of every missing man and tell each individually that the body of their father, husband, brother or son had been identified, Chase refused to allow the callous announcement of a man's death publicly. He welcomed the clergymen's cooperation to issue name tags to the nearest relatives of the missing men and allow the pastors time to circulate through the crowd and personally tell the families the tragic news privately.

Every store and bar in the Silver Valley echoed with a radio or television, and customers, bartenders, waitresses, and clerks stood stone silent when news came over the air. Miners could only talk of the fire and the times they were in fires or almost killed in mine accidents as they sipped their drinks in a local bar. Everyone had a friend or relative at the Sunshine Mine and the tales of death were too common. Earning but four inches of print and buried in an inside page of a local newspaper that day was the death of Gerald McDaniel, a thirty-three-year-old miner, killed in a rock fall at the Galena Mine four miles from the Sunshine.

School teachers allowed students to keep their ears to radios and turn up the volume for the classes to hear when there was news about the mine. They also had the heart not to give tests or homework. Flags flew at half-mast over the government buildings and schools. Time stood still in the small mining communities along the Silver Valley except for the rescue attempt at the Sunshine. All baseball games, parties, after-school events, church socials, and community meetings were cancelled.

At Chase's afternoon press conference, the haggard mine manager attempted to be optimistic. Compressed air forced to the lower levels was being tapped, a possible sign men were opening the valves to get air. His response to the question how the fire started was he believed it was spontaneous combustion of timbers and waste in the abandoned workings that had been smoldering for a considerable time before it built up pressure and burst a bulkhead on the 3400 level. He reported that a miner (Tony Sabala, although his name wasn't mentioned), had heard a bulkhead blow on the 3700 level in an area connecting with the upper levels. Standing behind Chase and nodding in agreement was Carl Burke, an influential Boise attorney listed on Sunshine's table of organization under the press staff of Lem Jones, Sunshine's Madison Avenue public relation's consultant. Jones, a former 20th Century Fox vice president, admitted to the press that he had never faced a tougher assignment.

Dr. Osborn noted in his personal log on May 4: "Burke was generally helpful to Chase on advising on public relations. Burke informed me of the State Workman's Compensation provisions, payments up to approx. $34,000 maximum." Apparently, Osborn thought it was important information to know when miners might be dead.

Reporters from the major newspapers arrived and mingled with the families when they were not standing off by themselves complaining of the lack of news and poor hotel accommodations. Many rented campers and vans and parked in the mine's visitors parking lot to be at the mine 24 hours a day. After Morton and Andrus left, the press searched for their next story, but few family members wanted to talk.

Morton and Dole appointed Lewis M. Helm, a former newspaper reporter and public relations executive and now a political appointee, to manage press relations and protect a naive Osborn from the press. Helm did not suffer fools lightly and took full control over Osborn's relations with the press. Experienced at media management during a crisis, Helm had the mellow voice of a TV anchorman when handling the press and the gruffness of a general when barking orders, which he later became in the U.S. Army Reserve.

Helm enlisted James Winston, a Bureau mining engineer, to aid him in the technical aspects when he briefed the media. Helm's first challenge was to hand out and have Osborn explain the Bureau's inspection reports on the Sunshine Mine. The press thought they hit a gold mine. The inspection reports listed thirty-five violations of safety standards that had been issued to the Sunshine Mine in November 1971 by inspector William. S. McCullough. Bureau inspectors were ordered by Helm not to talk to reporters. McCullough and Mike Castellan, mentioned in the reports as the inspector conducting a follow-up inspection, found it easy to avoid the press. They were underground with the rescue crews.

Few papers reported the violations had been corrected or had little or nothing to do with fire hazards. A *New York Times* article headline read: "Idaho Mine Got Safety Warnings — Failed to Correct Hazards Found by U.S. Inspectors," even though the material handed out by the Bureau stated that Castellan had reported all violations had been corrected. Two of the distant fire-related violations reported were quoted by *New York Times* reporter Felix Belair, Jr.: "A no smoking sign was not posted at the paint storage in the No. 8 paint shop;" and "Magazines on 5400 level were not posted with 'danger, explosives' signs."

The press handout included the Sunshine Mine's fatality statistics. At the press briefing, Sunshine and the Bureau claimed that Sunshine's record was "average or above average." Upon examination, it was clear that Sunshine had a fatality rate based on per million man hours that was three time the national average and had suffered on fatality each year during 1969 through 1971 and two fatalities in 1968.

Next the reporters shifted their attention to Byron Schulz, the young cager who was the last man to escape. He gave the press an angry voice needed for anecdotal reports about the mine's lack of safety precautions. Erroneously reported as the hoist operator, the twenty-one-year-old was quoted: "There was no organization. Nobody knew what to do or how to do it. If there had been more organization, there wouldn't be 72 men down there. The resuscitators gave out after only 10 to 20 minutes."

Schulz was a perfect example of the reason why safety and evacuation training should be required. The "resuscitators" he referred to were self-rescuers and designed to last one-half hour, but in the presence of carbon monoxide they can become extremely hot, causing Schulz and many other miners to believe they were not working. Training would have taught them that the hotter the air coming through the mouthpiece, the more lethal the concentration of the carbon monoxide.

The friends and families of the missing miners stood silent during the press briefings, wary of the sophisticated "Eastern reporters." One local school teacher and daughter of a miner told me the "Eastern reporters had an attitude that civilization ended at the Hudson and Potomac Rivers," after reading Leroy F. Adams's article in the *Washington Post* describing the scene at the mine as having "The bizarre look of a set from 'McCabe and Mrs. Miller.'" She and many others had seen the comedy at the Rena Theater in Kellogg depicting the dirty and dishevelled characters in the turn-of-the-century Western mining town.

At sunset, an announcement over the mine yard public-address system ordered the press to leave the area reserved for the missing miners' relatives and friends and that the press would be provided an area near the entrance. There were a half-dozen cheers from the friends and relatives. Most rural Idahoans were polite and merely breathed a sigh of relief.

The 4800 Level

Without food, Ron Flory and Tom Wilkinson knew they had to conserve their energy until they were rescued. Topside had to know that the men on the level were missing. Charlie Casteel, their shifter, was reliable and would tell them he was missing nine men. Not taking any chances, they periodically banged on the pipes to let anyone above know they were there. But their hopes of hearing a faint rapping back went unanswered. Unknown to the trapped men, the seismic equipment on the surface was unable to pick up their rapping on the pipes from 4,800 feet below.

The drill station selected for their underground home was relatively clean, having recently been built. Over 2,000 feet from the smoke and carbon monoxide, it gave them a sense of security. Still tense and fidgety, Ron said he wanted to check if the smoke had crept closer around the bend in the drift. He told Tom not to worry, he would ride the motor and be able to get out in a hurry if the smoke was to bad. When he rounded the bend, he saw that the smoke was worse than yesterday. He took a big breath of air and raced into the toxic smoke on the motor to get what he really came for — cigarettes off the hats of the men on the ground. He grabbed the several packs and hopped on the motor and drove back dizzy and weak-kneed. A few minutes passed before he felt well enough to smoke one of the cigarettes he had risked his life for.

CHAPTER 11

THURSDAY, MAY 4, 1972

Another Day in the Mine

Mine rescue work is dangerous. Men risk their lives to save others. But there are no mad dashes into deadly smoke and crawling down burning shafts to save men trapped in a blazing inferno. Rescue work at the Sunshine Mine was strenuous construction labor building bulkheads to cut off oxygen to the fire while wearing an uncomfortable rubber mask and a 45-pound backpack in roasting temperatures, smoke, and lethal carbon monoxide. The tools were hammers, saws, jackleg drills, and steel bars to knock down sloughing rock. The bulkheads were supported by 10- and 12-inch square timbers and spanned up to 40 feet wide and 10 feet high in the larger entrances to permit heavy equipment to traverse. Boards and plywood were nailed to the timbers then covered with burlap with a plastic backing. The last step was to spray a rigid polyurethane foam over the burlap to seal the pores and crevices next to the rock to make the bulkhead air-tight.

Air under pressure from 150 horsepower fans the size of a Boeing 747 jet engine is powerful and illusive. The drifts resembled crude wind tunnels. Thousands of cubic feet per minute of air blasted its way through the path of least resistance and streamed through bulkheads constructed years before modern plastic technology. Bulkheads shift and warp under the heat and pressure of millions of tons of rock over the decades. The only solution was to repair it or build another, sometimes two or three, adding tedium to the hazardous work. They hoped the next bulkhead would be in a narrow drift or crosscut and the air pressure wasn't too great to allow the use of the new inflatable bags.

The crew approaching the 3100 level from the Silver Summit turned on the 150 horsepower Silver Dollar fan, forcing fresh air to the No. 10 shaft and down to the 5200 level, where they hoped to find two dozen survivors. They needed the hoist to go down the shaft to bring anyone up that was still alive. Within minutes the fan drove the air into the mined-out "hook" area containing smoke and carbon monoxide and out the back of old wooden bulkheads, contaminating the fresh air.

In the brief interval before the leaking smoke and carbon monoxide became oppressive, the crew entered the station area to check the hoist room and No. 10 shaft for damage. The shaft had been soaked down by the fire emergency water deluge. Their only discovery was eight bodies. It was time for strong men to control their emotions. The real name for their task is "rescue and recovery," that is recovering bodies. Without body bags, the crew members could not carry out the bloated and cherry-red bodies discolored by the carboxyhemoglobin. They gently turned the bodies over and wrote down the number on each victim's cap lamp battery to identify the bodies. It was up to someone else to tell the relatives their men were dead. It would be days later before they could return to recover the bodies.

At the No. 12 borehole, Sunshine workers installed a 30 horsepower fan to increase the air flowing down the four-foot diameter hole to the 4800 level. They couldn't keep their eyes off Westinghouse and Bureau employees slowly lowering a camera down in an effort to determine if it was safe to send a crew 1,100 feet down the jagged hole. Behind them were Gene Rapp, a Bureau photographer, snapping pictures, and a twenty-two-year-old law student with a droopy mustache, Mark Savit, making a video tape of each step in the borehole operation.[11]

---

11 Eugene "Gene" Rapp and Mark N. Savit were with the Bureau's Education and Training Division. Both trained in mine rescue, their assignment was to record the events to aid in the disaster investigation and training. Several of Gene Rapp's underground photos were furnished to the press and released with a UPI or AP credit. His photos were also released by MSHA for this book. Mark Savit is currently one of the nation's preeminent mine safety and health and environmental lawyers.

Hidden from the press in a corner of the mine yard, three Bureau Education and Training Division instructors were in their second day teaching a 20-hour course to certify Sunshine miners to wear self-contained breathing apparatuses. At the end of the day there would be another 20 "helmet crew" volunteers ready for any task in the toxic air. After a quick supper, the instructors started training two dozen more volunteers for the hazardous work. During the ordeal, they would train 174 miners.

Inside the surface machine shop, Bureau inspectors worked around the clock with Sunshine mechanics checking self-contained breathing apparatuses after they had been used and preparing them for the next shift of rescue crews. Part of their job was teaching the Sunshine mechanics to clean, repair, and test the devices. They never ran out of work, nor could they permit a shortage of the apparatuses.

The Press

The laborious work of the Bureau, Sunshine miners, and volunteer rescue crews earned few headlines. Announcements of the installation of fans and building bulkheads didn't excite the national press. But it was hope the local papers could write about. Readers in the mining communities knew the trapped miners would die without fresh air and the rescue crews couldn't reach the survivors unless they built fresh air bases.

The press corp had ballooned to over fifty and was weary standing by the entrance waiting for news. The major news media included *Newsweek, Time, National Observer, Life, AP, UPI, Reuters, NBC, CBS, ABC, BBC, Chicago Tribune, Washington Post, and New York Times,* and scores of regional publications and radio and television stations. By far, the best reporting came from the Spokane press, the *Spokesman-Review* and *Spokane Daily Chronicle.* Reporters combed the papers to read what others were writing. Several headlined Ralph Nader's off-the-cuff remarks criticizing the 1966 MNM Act and calling it "totally fraudulent." Nader had made a speech in Spokane complaining about the lack of enforcement of the Clean Air Act of 1969. The story ran 18 column inches on clean air and only three inches on mine safety, but the headline blazed "Nader Criticizes Mining Safety Act."

News stories grew like weeds. Helm lashed back at Nader's naivety and told the press that Idaho was well-represented on the 1966 MNM Act's nine-man advisory committee by a vice president of the Hecla Mining Company, Gordon Miner of Wallace, Idaho, now working with Chase to rescue the miners, and W. Carl Griner, Idaho State Inspector of Mines. Griner took the opportunity to complain that the Idaho legislature didn't budget enough for his office to be effective, but boasted that four of his inspectors were assisting in the rescue work. Helm, tired of pointless technical questions from the press, asked Jim Winston to prepare a glossary of mining terms and arrange for a press tour of the nearby Bunker Hill Mine to indoctrinate the media in underground mining and the obstacles the rescue efforts faced. Few reporters attended.

Delmar Kitchen, a miner who had escaped from the 5000 level, told reporters hovering in the parking lot that he was joining his family in the mine yard. His father, Elmer, and brother, Dewellyn, were trapped in the mine. He lambasted Sunshine's safety program and lack of training in the use of self-rescuers and fire drills. In an attempt to counter the allegations, Carl Burke, a private lawyer for the Sunshine Mine, was quoted as a Sunshine Mine Co. official from Boise, "The company tries its best to maintain safety precautions for all of its employees . . . We also issue pamphlets on safety rules and regulations they are supposed to read."

Ed Gonzales, a miner who had climbed from the 4600 level to 4400 level and was hoisted to the 3100 level during his escape, said what most miners believed. "I think most men read the safety pamphlets and memorize the escape routes. But safety knowledge is only as good as how well persons exercise it. We're hired to go to work, not go to school for fire drills. I look out for myself on safety matters and I think most others do also."

At the noon press conference, Chase reported continuing fluctuations in the compressed air pressure meant that trapped miners might be getting fresh air. Irwin Underweiser, Sunshine's chairman of the board and president, commented, "Fresh air might also be coming in the lower levels from other inlets." Before Chase could whisk Underweiser away, he made another disingenuous remark. He told the reporters that Sunshine had insurance to cover a short-term loss caused by the fire and "might even show a profit this quarter."

The Bureau announced it would start its investigation into the cause of the disaster the next day by taking miners' depositions. It had assembled a team of six Interior Department attorneys from its Boise, Idaho, and Portland, Oregon, field offices and six Bureau inspectors and engineers to assist them. It sounded like the Bureau's investigation was serious unless one knew that few of the desk-bound government lawyers had ever taken a deposition and none knew anything about mining and mine safety. The Interior Department's Solicitor sent an attorney from Washington, D.C., Richard V. Backley, to head the deposition team. Backley, experienced in prosecuting coal mine health and safety cases and a former Assistant U.S. Attorney, discovered he could not teach six bureaucrat lawyers how to practice law in a few days.

An article in the Spokane *Spokesman-Review* drew the ire of Sunshine management and miners. Robert Launhardt, Sunshine's safety engineer, in response to the question why the miners hadn't been trained in the use of self-rescuers, was reported to have answered: "We haven't tried to teach our hourly employees how to use them, but if we did, we would have to train them again a month later." [12]

In the late afternoon, Chase announced that eight more bodies had been found at the 3100 No. 10 station and in the hoist room, but only six had been identified: Douglas Wiederrick, shaft repairman from the 5800 level; Grady Truelock, miner from the 5400 level; Duwain Crow, drift miner from the 5600 level; Fred "Gene" Johnson shaft foreman from the 3700 level; Elmer Kitchen, shaft miner in the 5600 pocket; and Dewellyn Kitchen, miner from the 5000 level. Delmar Kitchen, after hearing he had lost his father and brother, drove his anguished family home.

After the news that the number dead had reached 32, the evening shadows drove several relatives home to check on the children or to take a hot shower. One miner said he needed a drink after hearing of the loss of Gene Johnson, "The best damn foreman in the valley." They left alone and in groups, some holding hands, as they walked towards the parking lot and a horde of reporters, frustrated at being denied access to the mine and families. A half-dozen newsmen

---

12 Launhardt denied "having made a statement to that effect," at the hearing on July 21, 1972. Off the record, several miners swear they heard him say it.

rushed in their path and tried to talk to them or overhear their conversations, but were pushed aside by a woman, saying she didn't want to be bothered. When they persisted, they found they were surrounded by angry miners and told to leave "or else." Their good fortune was a Sunshine foreman capable of cooling miner's tempers. He reminded the newsmen that they were on mine property and mining folk protected their women from outsiders. One of the veteran reporters told his colleagues that a story about reporters getting the hell beat out of them by miners for pestering a widow wouldn't make a good headline.

The 4800 Level

It was Thursday according to Ron's calendar watch, the third day of being trapped without a sign that anyone was attempting to get them. Ron swore he heard voices when he woke from a nap. Tom strained to hear the voices, but couldn't.

Feeling rested, they decided to see if they could make it to the station and call topside or signal for a cage to let someone know they were still alive. Their banging on the pipes obviously wasn't working as far as they could determine. When they reached the H-8 crosscut the smoke was so dense they turned back.

Their survival looked hopeless, but when either became despondent or showed signs of panic, the other calmed his partner down. Maybe tomorrow things will get better. And prayers couldn't hurt.

CHAPTER 12

FRIDAY, MAY 5, 1972

The Space Capsule

Roland Wilson's idea of borrowing the Atomic Energy Commission's (AEC) capsule to send a two-man rescue crew down to the 4800 level was rejected by Sunshine as experimental and dangerous. Wilson complained to Helm, who had faith in Wilson and the Bureau engineers, and added that there would be no shortage of volunteers for the dangerous task. Helm telephoned Dole in Washington, who called Osborn and ordered him to be aggressive and demand that the Bureau use the capsule under the threat that the Bureau would take over the rescue effort. Helm instructed Osborn to hold a press conference to announce the encouraging news that the Bureau was going to drop a "torpedo" holding two rescue crew members from the 3700 level to the 4800 foot level in the four-foot diameter No. 12 borehole. Osborn's mention that two capsules were being sent by the AEC raised the imagination of the press, and several reported the arrival of "space capsules" and "terra space capsules."

To the Bureau's engineers, the capsule was a crude 38-inch diameter steel cylinder cage on the bottom half with an open top supported by two steel bars running its seven-foot length that could be hooked to a steel cable — an elongated metal basket. Bureau engineers and Sunshine mechanics had built a similar cage from rough sketches. As they had no way of testing their primitive device, Osborn insisted the AEC's tested capsule be used, even though it had not been employed in an actual rescue under adverse conditions.

Osborn called the AEC capsule "a risky thing," and added, "If we were inspecting a mine, we wouldn't let them use it." The capsule's

38-inch diameter only allowed a five-inch clearance in the crude 48-inch diameter hole and a man would have to be a contortionist to climb out the top, where they planned to install telephone communication to the surface in case the capsule jammed in the hole. One imaginative reporter wrote it required "one man sitting on the shoulders of the other." His conception wasn't totally outlandish, if you picture squeezing two men in a 38-inch diameter hole, especially two brawny miners wearing self-contained breathing apparatuses.

The capsule wasn't the only problem that concerned the Bureau and Westinghouse engineers. They had to build a hoist in the confinement of the 3700 level capable of lowering and raising a heavy steel capsule holding two men and their equipment and furnish it with sufficient power. They didn't yet know the weight of the capsule. The one item the engineers could calculate was the weight of 1,200 feet of one-half-inch steel cable necessary to hoist 1,100 feet. It would weigh slightly over one-half ton, far more than two men, their rescue equipment, and the capsule combined. To be on the safe side, they determined the hoist must be able to lift two tons.

There were also conditions not mentioned by Osborn. The risky scheme could not detract from the three separate efforts to reach possible survivors down the No. 10 shaft through the Silver Summit and the Jewell shaft on both the 3100 and 3700 levels. Osborn, Jarrett, and Sunshine management decided that no personnel could be reassigned from their current assignments. Jarrett sent out a call for Bureau Metal and Nonmetal Mine Division-trained mine rescue volunteers to go down the No. 12 borehole through Roland Wilson and Kenneth Russell, who were each running 12-hour shifts in the rescue effort. The volunteers were told the risks and to bring sleeping bags and their breathing apparatus. Every room for fifty miles was taken by the press, Bureau employees, and volunteer rescue workers. Many Bureau employees were already hot-sheeting, sharing a bed with a man on another shift. The borehole rescue volunteers would be housed dormitory-style on the sofas and floor in a local country club.

Twenty-two Bureau volunteers from Arizona, California, Colorado, Indiana, Minnesota, Missouri, Nevada, Tennessee, and Utah were on planes to Spokane the next day. Many were in the mine hours after they arrived, irritated they hadn't been called earlier to join the rescue effort. Five Sunshine miners trained in the use of breathing apparatuses insisted they be allowed to volunteer. *(See Appendix D, Borehole Rescue Volunteers.)*

The Vigil

The rescue crews gave comfort to the relatives. A Wallace mother, after spending the last thirty hours at the mine waiting for word of her missing son, told a reporter she only had praise for the rescue crews. "You know there is an air of calmness, quickness, and sureness to the way the rescue miners walk in there. They seem so confident and competent."

Families had an unwritten rule to maintain their hope. The missing men were referred to "he is," never "he was." But by the fourth day the strain showed on their faces and friends' inquiries were often answered: "We haven't heard his name yet, and that's good news." But the news was not encouraging. Three more bodies were reported found, bringing the total known dead to 35. One body found earlier on the 3100 level was identified as 5600 level drift miner Wayne Allen, age 39 from Big Creek, a mere mile down the canyon from the mine. There would be one less wife and two less children praying at the mine tomorrow.

Progress was exasperatingly slow. The No. 10 hoist couldn't be used by the rescue crews until the Strand electric substation was given at least 24 hours to cool down and could be inspected by the electricians. Completion of the construction of the eleven bulkheads on the 3700 level, thanks to the first-time use of heavy rubber dunnage bags, offered heartening news, but raised eyebrows when Osborn called them "balloons."

Those with relatives on the 5200 level, the largest single group of miners believed to have a chance of surviving on the lowers levels, learned that a phone dropped down the No. 10 shaft from the 3100 to the 5200 level had not been answered. But that could be explained claimed those desperately grasping for hope. It was possible survivors were in a remote stub drift or raise where there was breathable air and didn't see or hear it. The 5200 level extended over one-half mile east and 2,000 feet to the west.

The families with men on the 4800 level were not giving up hope merely because no one answered the phone. The phone lowered down the No. 12 borehole was over a mile from the No. 10 station and almost one and one-half miles from the east end of the 4800 level.

The 4800 Level

The only glimmer of hope for Ron Flory and Tom Wilkinson was the air was still fresh around the drill station. The roar of the fans reverberating in the distance told them the mine power was on and men were working to rescue them. Time and hunger were their worst enemies. To pass the time, they talked about their children and wives and hunting elk and moose in the mountains. Their cap lamp batteries now depleted, they had to rely on the lights on the motor. Much of their time was spent sitting in a darkness blacker than the devil's soul braiding blasting cord to take their mind off being "between a rock and a hard place."

They cured their hunger by wetting their T-shirts and covering their faces for a daring ride on the motor into the smoke. In less than two minutes they grabbed several lunch buckets and cigarette packs from their dead comrades bodies and rode out, slightly dizzy, with their feast of dry, four-day-old sandwiches. Tom thought the stale sandwiches were more dangerous than the slimy water from the condensation they wiped off the compressed air pipe cooler to drink. The rest of the food was stockpiled for the future, how long, they didn't want to think about. A can of sardines, a can of fruit cocktail, a cup of pudding, and one slice of apple pie wouldn't amount to a meal for one hungry miner.

PRESIDENT RICHARD NIXON'S
TELEGRAMS TO LOCAL MAYORS

"The disaster at the Sunshine Mine was tragic news that captured the hearts of all Americans. On their behalf, I want to send my deepest sympathy to the families affected. Our prayers now are with those making the heroic rescue efforts. I have directed the Secretary of the Interior and the Office of Emergency Preparedness to keep me personally informed of the developments to assure all federal assistance be expedited."

President Richard Nixon

Northern Idaho Press, May 5, 1972.

CHAPTER 13

SATURDAY, MAY 6, 1972

A Slow News Day

Newsmen with a nose for news slept late. It was a rainy Saturday and they hadn't been tipped off that new bodies had been found or new major developments. Sunshine management decided to withhold the news that a second rescue crew could not find the three bodies reported discovered west of the 3700 No. 10 station late yesterday. It would only confuse an embarrassing revelation. Sunshine's personnel office suspected that more than 47 men were missing as was being announced by management. The personnel office was instructed to recheck their records and not mention it to the Bureau. The failure to maintain an accurate record of the men in the mine was a violation of mandatory safety standard section 57.11-58 and management would have to explain the error to the press. The Bureau would also have to defend why their inspectors had determined Sunshine's check-in and check-out system was adequate under the standard.

Announcements about more leaking bulkheads were not newsworthy. Sunshine's estimate that it would be another 24 hours before the No. 10 hoist could be used by the rescue crews to reach the lower levels was a repeat of yesterday's news. It meant no progress had been made during the past 24 hours or Sunshine had painted a cheerier picture than was warranted yesterday. Bulkheads on the old workings holding back smoke and carbon monoxide near the No. 10 shaft on the Silver Summit side of the 3100 level had sprung leaks again because of the tremendous air pressure from the fans attempting to clear the air around the No. 10 station. That wasn't regarded as newsworthy by Sunshine either. Nor did Sunshine think it was news that the battery-powered vehicle used by the crews to carry equipment along the one-mile Silver Summit tunnel had two flat tires and had been used for such an extensive time that its battery went dead during the graveyard shift and had to be taken out to be recharged.

Sunshine announced a 250 horsepower fan the size of a house was being installed on the surface over the exhaust Big Hole to clear out the carbon monoxide on the 3100 and 3700 levels. Although the fan construction was visible from the mine yard, the story was only picked up by *Spokesman Review* reporters Tom Burnett and Stefanie Pettit. The reporters were not told that the carbon monoxide level coming out of the exhaust air at 0.27 % meant it was lethal in most of the mine, but was not dangerous at the elevated location on the hill when exhausted into the breezy atmosphere. Measurements of the carbon monoxide in the exhaust air on previous days were also not reported: May 3: 0.82%, May 4: 0.76% and May 5: 0.79%, all of which were deadly.

The good news was the rubber bags helped speed up the construction of the bulkheads to the extent they ran out and 90 more were delivered that day by two small jets. The news didn't come from the press at the mine. It was an AP story based on a public relations press release by the manufacturer, Goodyear Tire & Rubber Co. in Akron Ohio.

As Helm was holding a press conference in the rain, a flatbed truck arrived loaded with two AEC capsules. One reporter exclaimed: "Come on, Helm, knock off this 'Mission Impossible' crap." Another said: "Yeah, and how do you like his timing in the use of props?"

Osborn and Jarrett gave the press their first photo opportunity near the mine portal in mid-afternoon. Portly Jarrett displayed how a man would look standing in the capsule and gave credence to the previous day's story that one man might have to sit on another man's shoulder when the 38-inch diameter capsule was lowered. The borehole crew rushed the capsules into the mine, aware at first glance they would have to remove the top to allow the men to escape should the capsule become lodged in the bore hole. The engineers were pleased with the TV pictures of the hole after the camera was lowered the entire 1,100 feet. No obstructions or dangers were spotted, but it was determined prudent to let independent eyes study the video tapes over a larger screen and better light on the surface.

The rescue advisory committee had another concern. The bulkhead construction crews on the 3700 reported scalding water and steam coming down the 910 raise less than 100 feet from the Strand Electric substation that could endanger the electric power for the hoist going to the lower levels.

If analyzed, the most intriguing story of the day was written by Rick Zahler of the *Spokesman-Review*. His "Miner Tells of Escaping, Raps Safety," based on an interview of twenty-five-year-old stope miner William Mitchell, should have raised questions. Mitchell told of waiting for the skip (cage) on the 4400 level and not being able to squeeze on several skips "carrying some 30 men." Twenty minutes later, another skip arrived and raised him to the 3100 level, where he was able to walk out to the Jewell. After reaching the surface, Mitchell realized the others he thought had left him and Ed Gonzales hadn't made it to the surface. He correctly believed "some men" (actually nine) got off at the 3700 level and died. Mitchell and the others did not realize in the smoke and confusion that seven men were around the corner from the shaft waiting for the cage and were left stranded. Not being able to get on the cage that stopped on the 3700 level was the luckiest thing that would ever happen to Mitchell.

Marvin Chase, the exhausted mine manager, took part of the day off to attend the funerals for the first men found and brought to the surface. He returned to the mine even more drained. He had known every miner who died.

The 4800 Level

Ron and Tom decided inaction was necessary to conserve what little energy they received from the stale peanut butter and jelly, tuna fish, and cold cuts sandwiches yesterday. It was their fifth day trapped and there was no sign of a rescue crew. They continued to braid the blasting cord and chat in the dark. When one would become irritated or felt that there was no hope, the other calmed him down or assuaged his fears. They weren't religious men, but they got on their knees and prayed in silence and out loud.

If no one came tomorrow, they decided to risk going into the smoke and carbon monoxide at the station to telephone topside and signal the hoist room.

CHAPTER 14

SUNDAY, MAY 7, 1972

No News Is Good News?

The installation of the giant 250 horsepower fan continued through the night until it was completed and tested at 5:00 a.m. A rescue crew arriving at the 3100 level No. 10 station at 6:30 a.m. found the fan had cleared the smoke and carbon monoxide. With the smoke gone, the crew discovered 15 bodies in the drifts bordering the station. It wasn't their task to announce the grisly discovery, nor was it within the Bureau's jurisdiction. Sunshine management claimed they were not sure if the 15 included the eight bodies reported found on May 4. They decided not to make the grim announcement on a Sunday morning. In the surface machine shop next to humming lathes and drill presses repairing equipment for the rescue crews, relatives and friends were attending a Sunday non-denominational prayer service. The delay would give Sunshine time to confirm the number of missing miners was not 47 as they had originally calculated. The personnel office and payroll accountants had determined the correct number of missing men was 58.

A review of the ventilation system by the advisory rescue committee concluded the two 3400 level exhaust fans were feeding air to the fire and recirculating the smoke and toxic carbon monoxide to the other levels, as Dusty Rhoads had determined shortly after the fire was discovered. They decided to send a crew to turn them off at the switch station on the 3700 level. When the crew passed the cable shop, they discovered four bodies.

By 4:00 p.m., the ventilation on the 3100 level No. 10 station had improved considerably. Several hours later, the rescue crews entering from the Silver Summit and the Jewell met for the first time on the 3100 level. At 5:13 p.m. the compressed air pressure dropped from 90 to below 25 pounds per square inch, a sign of a rupture in the 12-inch compressed air pipe system that would cripple the use of compressed air throughout the mine. Minutes later, the electrical crew reported the 13,800 volt line to the Strand electric substation had failed, cutting off the power to the hoist. Without the hoist there was no way to get down to the possible survivors on the lower levels. Around 6:00 p.m., the exhaust fan on the 1900 level sputtered to a stop, eliminating the ability to draw the smoke and carbon monoxide from the 3700 level.

The discovery of the 19 bodies would not be reported for several days, nor would they and 24 other bodies previously found be taken to the surface. It was more important to continue with the efforts to save any possible survivors and not risk the lives of the rescue crews, a decision Sunshine could say was the consensus of the rescue advisory committee that included the Bureau and experienced engineers from other mines. As the bodies had not been identified, the Sunshine officials wouldn't be holding back the news of a miner's death from his family. No one thought of the stress on the Sunshine miners on the rescue crews. To Don Capparelli, a twenty-two-year-old Sunshine miner and rescue crew member, it was torture. He saw the bodies of men he knew, but was forbidden to disclose what he had seen. Afterwards, Capparelli talked to the several family members and couldn't tell them he had seen the distended bodies of their loved ones. The young miner locked himself in the bathroom when he arrived home and cried.

The News

The press was told there were still only 35 confirmed dead and 17 identified. They didn't question the bad news that the number of missing men had increased from 47 to 58. They accepted a tired Chase's explanation that the exact names of the men underground on the lower levels were maintained by the shifters on their books each morning and the records were still underground with the missing shifters. Sunshine continued to report 108 had escaped from the mine. That number turned out inflated. During the Bureau's investigation, they would comb payroll records that revealed only 80 men had escaped.

The media listened to Frank McKee, the United Steelworkers of America district director, complain about the Interior Department attorneys lack of probing questions into the cause of the disaster during the depositions.   His gripe had merit, although the union's lawyers didn't do any better when given the opportunity. McKee admitted safety conditions at the Sunshine were about the same as other mines in the region and on a par with the rest of the nation. He promised that the union, which represented a majority of the hard rock miners in the country, would step up its efforts to bring about stronger national safety measures. McKee was forced to make the pledge after union members complained that the Steelworkers had not backed them up on their safety complaints.

The most ardent anti-mining company advocate was J. Davit McAteer, a twenty-eight-year-old lawyer from West Virginia and consultant to "Nader's Raiders." McAteer, an attorney for the Miners for Democracy in their battle to take control of the United Mine Workers of America (UMWA), arrived with a press release demanding a congressional investigation. He later became an assistant to the president of the UMWA and an attorney for the Center for Law and Social Policy. In 1993 he was appointed by President Clinton as Assistant Secretary of Labor for Mine Health and Safety.

To attract attention, McAteer handed out copies of *Coal Patrol,* a poorly printed diatribe that lumped Interior officials: "The motley crew of ex-businessmen, former lobbyists, public relations flacks, and Republican political hacks who run the Interior Department." Several reporters showed copies to Helm, who laughed at the invidiousness.   No reporter quoted its baseless accusations, denying McAteer's credibility. McAteer attempted to participate in the taking of the miners' depositions as a representative of downtrodden miners, but Richard Backley, the Interior Department's lead attorney at Sunshine and a hard-core Democrat, advised him the miners were represented by their union, the United Steelworkers of America. The Steelworkers did not want the militant outsider's interference either.

McAteer was quoted by *New York Times* reporter Steven V. Roberts that "even those measures that were required by law were not always carried out and Federal inspectors passed over violations." It was a statement MSHA inspectors would hold against him during his tenure as Assistant Secretary. McAteer held the position almost the entire eight years of the Clinton administration, during which he diverted his time as the acting Solicitor of the Department of Labor for several years. His distrust of MSHA employees was reciprocated, and McAteer's term resulted in MSHA's morale reaching its nadir. Under his tenure the number of mining engineers and technical support staff declined and decimated the agency's expertise.

The Price of Silver

Cotton farmers talk about cotton prices and oilmen watch oil prices. In Idaho, they kept their eye on silver prices. In 1971, Idaho's 3,700 miners accounted for 5% of the total wages paid in the state, and the Silver Valley's 15 silver mines employed over 2,600, 70% of the state's miners. The Sunshine Mine produced 20% of the nation's silver and had 429 underground employees and 93 on the surface in administration and ore processing. It was inevitable that the press would report the local businessmen's concern about the potential loss of the Sunshine Mine's payroll.

Irwin Underweiser, Sunshine's forty-four-year-old president and chairman of the board, assured the press that the mine would only be out of operation for two months, but its employees would not be out of work while the mine was closed, as it would take all the employees to get the mine operating again. (He lied. The mine would not start operating for seven months and over one-half of its employees would be out of work.) He reported insurance would pay the company $6,200 a day during the closure and Sunshine might even show a profit. As the producer of 20% of the nation's silver, he expected an increase in the price of silver that "could enable the mine to wind up with a profit despite it closure." He added, "The price has gone up about "$1.56 to $1.599 per ounce since the disaster occurred last week," and "could rise another 10 cents in the next two months."

Underweiser was not only talking to the local press and assuring the miners they would not be out of work, he was trying to get a message to Sunshine's shareholders. Not all the shareholders believed the glib New York attorney. Sunshine's stock fell 18% the week after the disaster from $9.75 to $8.00 a share.

The No. 12 Borehole

The borehole team of Bureau, Sunshine, and Westinghouse employees was joined by Frank Solaegui, an engineer with Reynolds Electrical and Engineering Corporation (the Atomic Energy Commission's prime contractor), to build the capsule. Solaegui was welcomed by the crew rigging the hoist. "He's the only one who has seen one these #@%&* capsules before," a Bureau engineer said.

After the compressed air line ruptured, the pressure was not sufficient to operate the hoist. A portable air compressor was lowered down the Jewell shaft and transported to the borehole. The first test involved sending the capsule down the borehole loaded with 600 pounds of sand, well over the maximum two men and their equipment would weigh. The strain on the compressor caused them to lower it to the 4800 level a second time. Again the compressor labored heavily when the cage snagged on a jagged rock on the side of the hole. They decided to replace the original compressor with two larger compressors, all of which took valuable time.

On the surface, Osborn and Jarrett returned from dinner at 8:00 p.m. and met with Chase. According to Osborn's log of May 7: "[We] told him we had 22 experienced rescue men (USBM) arriving tonight that we wanted to get on the job helping to take out the bodies." After going to the borehole "to see situation," and being told by Wilson it will take four hours to set up the hoist, Osborn added another unfathomable notation in his log showing his ignorance: "There apparently will be a delay in getting our capsule down, although I don't see why we shouldn't go ahead. Our men have oxygen equipment good for two hours."

Osborn's log also noted the arrival of experts from the Bureau's Denver Technical Support Center. Mining engineers Ralph J. Foster and J. Warren Andrews were mine ventilation specialists and, at the request of Sunshine's then safety engineer, James R. Atha, had made a ventilation survey of the Sunshine Mine six month earlier. As the mine's ventilation system was crucial to the rescue efforts, the question must be asked: Why weren't they called to assist earlier?[13]

---

13 In April 1974, Sunshine sued the United States for damages resulting from the fire, alleging one of the causes for its claims was the Bureau's ventilation system report advising the mine's ventilation system was adequate.

Wilson, the Bureau's night shift supervisor, had pulled "four hours" out of his hat to get rid of Osborn. The men on the first crew knew they would be working until relieved at 3:00 a.m. replacing the hoist cable with a heavier cable and installing shoes (brakes), sheave rollers, and communications equipment. The crew chief, Robert E. Riley, was a no-nonsense engineer with 15 years experience in underground mining. Riley was going to be one of the first men to go down in the capsule and was backed up by a capable and experienced crew of engineers and inspectors, E. Levi Brake, James D. Pitts, Michael Munoz and Paul Talley. [14]

The 4800 Level

Ron and Tom were scared and hungry. They talked about climbing out, but decided it was madness without cap lamps and not knowing the way up through a series of raises that did not offset exactly one above the other. In many cases, the escapeways up through the raises between the levels were over 100 feet apart and would be impossible to find in the dark.

When the sound of the fans grinded to a stop, an eerie disquieting silence enveloped them. It meant the power was off. Panic set in. Had the fire forced closing the mine? Did the fire cut off the power? If the electric power was destroyed by the fire, the hoists could not get them to the surface. They had to know.

They dampened their grimy T-shirts reeking with sweat to hold over their faces before making a dash to the station on the motor. The motor's lights outlined the bloated bodies of their fellow miners through smoke. With only the dim lights from the battery-operated motor, they jumped off at the station. Tom desperately rang the

---

14 Osborn's list of the first crew in his personal log failed to mention Horst S. Gottschalk and Thomas J. Caster. The author knew the entire crew and can attest to their dedication and professionalism. However, the author cannot venture a guess what Riley, a perfectionist, would say if he knew Osborn spelled his name "Ruby" in his log. Helm, always thinking of public relations, instigated to have Riley, Brake, and Pitts on the first crew because they were tall, rugged, and handsome, aware the media and photographers favored such stereotype heroes. He also believed they were articulate and could handle the press.

emergency hoist signal while Ron attempted to call on the phone. Both lines were dead. Unknown to them, a cave-in of the 910 raise had cut off the power and the water deluge released to protect the shaft from burning had short-circuited the electricity and signals in the shaft.

They returned to the drill station weakened by the carbon monoxide. There was nothing either could say to lift the other's spirits. Things couldn't get any worse.

CHAPTER 15

MONDAY, MAY 8, 1972

Another Setback

The smoke and carbon monoxide on the 3700 level were far worse than the rescue crew had faced since the fire began. Under a tight-fitting rubber mask the 125- degree heat was suffocating. Their trek into the sweltering hell told them the fire raging above had increased in intensity. The aluminum backpacks on the man in front were too hot to touch without gloves.

It was almost 4:00 p.m. when the crew approached the 910 raise. Fallen rock and charred timber blocked passage to the No. 10 station. Even if they could squirm around the rubble, the possibility of more debris falling from the raise and the rock overhead after being exposed to tremendous heat made it unstable and too danger-ous. The 910 raise had caved in, breaking the 12-inch compressed air pipe and severing the 13,800 volt power line to the Strand electric substation. The heat coming down the raise like a gigantic hair dryer dried their perspiration-soaked shirts in seconds. Along the upper corners of the drift the fiberglass compressed air pipe had melted and globs of white goo hung from the bolted metal brackets like stalactites. Crews could not repair the compressed air pipe and electric cable until the 910 raise was sealed off, the unstable rock removed, and new rockbolts installed, tasks that could take days.[15]

---

15 The mined-out areas north of the main drift could not be used to reach the No. 10 station after suffering worse damage, as shown in the sketch of the 919 raise, 400 feet from the 910 raise in the 09 vein. The 919 raise caved-in from the 3550 level to the 3850 level and the heat blast-ing down like a blowtorch reached such high temperatures it melted the railroad rails on the 3700 level. *(See Appendix C.)*

Chase and the advisory committee discounted the break in the compressed air pipe. The installation of fans and erecting bulkheads on the Silver Summit side of the 3100 level had resulted in fresh air flowing down the No. 10 shaft to the lower levels. Their primary concern was furnishing power to the hoist on the 3100 level. Before the power could be turned on, the moisture had to be removed from the hoist and electrical connections in the shaft to prevent a short circuit that would endanger the rescue crews going down the shaft and possibly destroy the electrical equipment. Without electricity and compressed air, the electricians' only tools to remove the moisture were rags, and their frantic efforts were painstakingly slow.

Floyd Strand, the chief electrician, asked for every available electrician and repairman to help string a power cable from the main line entering the mine down the Jewell shaft to the 3100 level No. 10 station. Without the substation, he had to devise a method to step down and control the voltage throughout the mine. A power surge could cause an overload, trapping rescue crews in the shaft and destroying the power system and electrical equipment. Strand contacted the Washington Water & Power Co. in attempt to control the voltage during hoisting. In the end, the cooperation of the Bonneville Power Administration, then part of the Interior Department that generated hydroelectric power in the Northwest, was required to reduce and maintain a stable voltage on their transmission lines.

The Press

During Chase's press briefing attended by the 200 weary relatives and friends of the missing miners, he attempted to sound optimistic as he reported the setbacks. He told them there was still hope for the men on the 4800 and 5200 levels. With few exceptions, the press felt there weren't any headline stories and regurgitated recaps about the fire and rescue efforts that were like warmed-over hash.

The May 8 *Northern Idaho Press* reported "The Price of Silver Continues to Rise." But that wasn't what caught the eye of the missing miners' relatives and friends and caused them to see if they could spot Jerry McGinn, a UPI reporter. McGinn's story picked up by the *Northern Idaho Press* told of his arrival on Tuesday and how he and another reporter volunteered to help the Red Cross hand out coffee after the press was told they were no longer allowed in the area with the relatives. As a Red Cross volunteer, he had wormed an opportunity to chat with the relatives and eavesdrop as if he was one of them. At best, the story was a filler to be printed when there was no real news. McGinn's description of the people drew the "folk's" attention:

> They looked like ordinary, small town folks. The regular stereotype: thin ties, baggy cuffed pants, white sox, boots. Some of the kids wore mod dress, indicating the effect of television and an impending generation of new thinking in the area.

The women in J.C. Penny's dresses waiting for news of their missing husbands, a waitress still in the uniform she left work in to find out if her brother had made it out, men in Levi's or Sears' jackets standing in silent dread for word that their son was dead, and children in school clothes wondering if they still had a father were not dressed in the latest fashions. What McGinn failed see in their eyes and mention as they stared at the mine portal waiting for news of their loved ones was that these small-town Americans were paying the true price of silver.

The No. 12 Borehole

The second borehole crew leader, Wayne D. Kanack, was a stickler for detail. His experience as a miner and mining engineer had been in underground coal and hard rock mines from Alaska to Oklahoma. His veteran crew of former miners included Bureau men Donald K. Morris and Frank DeLimba and Sunshine miner Wilfred "Sonny" Becker. They were backed by capable Bureau engineers and inspectors James A. Fraser, Larry O. Weberg, and Warren M. Yenter running the hoist and communications. The lengthy time required to prepare and check the hoist before the capsule could be lowered earned them the right to be the first to venture down the hole at 9:00 p.m., half-way through their 12-hour shift.

Anyone who knew Kanack, expected him to go by the book and triple-check everything before he and Morris were lowered into the hole. By the time they descended a few feet, they discovered the 48-inch hole was irregular and rough. Worse, it was plagued with loose slabs of rock that could fall at any moment and injure or kill men in the capsule. Kanack notified the men on the 3700 level over the phone that the rock was "incompetent," a miner's term for unstable. Every foot of rock would have to be checked for telltale crevices and fractures and scaled with steel pry bars as they were lowered two or three feet at a time. It was sweaty, time-consuming work in a cramped space. One man had to push the heavy cage from the wall in order for the other to provide space to pry the rocks off the side so they would fall between the cage and the rock wall. In several locations the 48-inch drill had ripped through the incompetent rock and caved holes on the sides 10 to 12 feet deep, leaving the cage dangling too far for them to reach with their short pry bars to check for loose rock.

After one hour they had only scaled 150 feet. "Only 950 feet to go," Don Morris joked. With both men exhausted, Kanack signaled for the cage to be hoisted up. It was obvious when they looked up at the dim light from above that the hole wasn't exactly vertical and the capsule would become harder to push off the wall to prevent it from scraping against the rock and catching on jutting rock as it descended.

Kanack insisted the two-man crews work one-hour shifts, as exhaustion while doing physical labor leads to mistakes. By the time Riley's crew came on shift, Kanack's crew had scaled down 450 feet in six hours. They yelled to Riley's crew as they left to hurry and finish the last 650 feet.

The 4800 Level

Tom and Ron beat on the compressed air pipe with their wrenches. The effort was tiring on empty stomachs and seemed more useless with each attempt. Braiding blasting wire no longer took their minds off the futility of their entrapment. Maybe the other men on the level were lucky, at least they died fast and wouldn't starve to death. To survive, they knew they had to conserve their energy. Fortunately, weak and hungry men fall asleep easily.

Ron woke and swore he heard voices for the second time. Tom couldn't hear anything but the faint drone of a fan. That meant the power was back on and men were working. It was the first good news.

CHAPTER 16

TUESDAY, MAY 9, 1972

The No. 12 Borehole

Kanack reported his crew had scaled 450 feet, but below 350 feet it needed to be checked and scaled again. The last crew had been exhausted at the end of their 12-hour shift. Riley divided the two-man scaling crews into one Sunshine miner and a Bureau engineer. As they methodically barred their way down, the ground became more competent. When they reached 580 feet, the hole became more stable. Nevertheless, the work remained tedious and took all the strength of one crew member to keep the capsule from scraping and jamming against the side of the slanted hole with his hands. The hole deviated 30 feet from the vertical in a slight arc down its 1,100 feet and caused the cable to grate against the sides of the hole.

The team of J.D. Pitts, a Bureau engineer, and Donald Tiedmann, a Sunshine miner, made it to the bottom at 7:00 a.m. They called out but received no response. As instructed, without gas detection gear, they didn't leave the capsule and phoned to be hoisted to the 3700 level. The slow trip took 25 minutes to allow them to push the capsule away from the wall to prevent it from hanging up on protruding rock.

Riley assembled the other three men making up the crew, Levi Brake, Mike Munoz, and Horst Gottschalk, and checked that each man had the equipment they were assigned to take down. It would take two hours to send four men to the bottom. The capsule had to be manned when it was raised to make sure it didn't get caught on a rock. Gottschalk drew the unenviable job making two return trips by himself. Gottschalk and Brake were the first to be lowered down around 10:00 a.m. Half-way a rock broke loose and fell from above and crashed down on the cage and smashed Brake's hand.

Brake had to be hoisted topside to have a half-dozen stitches in his fractured hand. The rangy, handsome Arizona mining engineer had to be content jawing with the doctor and nurses in his Southwestern drawl and miss doing what he was trained for because of a "damn one pound rock." He joked that J.D. Pitts had dropped the rock 500 feet down the hole so he could replace him and get the glory.

When finally on the bottom, the four-man crew tested the experimental radio Westinghouse supplied and backup telephone phone system with spools of line running to the top. The voices over the radio came over load and clear, but that didn't mean they did not have to lug a spool containing over 500 feet of wire for the "wireless radio" aerial. After taking readings for carbon monoxide and oxygen, they walked to the West Syndicate drift and turned to the west. They had been advised that drift miners had been working in the far west end and it was logical miners seeking shelter from the smoke and carbon monoxide might take refuge at the farthest location from the No. 10 station. Finding no compressed air in the pipes and the water line broken was disheartening. But as the air was fresh, there was still a chance of finding survivors. They searched two stub drifts in the west, but found no survivors. They knew miners had been working there at the time of the fire when they saw two jack-leg drills and drilled holes containing explosives. No good miner would leave explosives in a hole and leave unless it was an emergency.

The crew turned back towards the No. 10 station and walked approximately 1,500 feet, periodically shouting and hitting the compressed air pipes with a steel bar in an attempt to get the attention of any survivors. By then, their cap lamps were growing dim and carrying the heavy gear in over 100-degree heat was beginning to tire them. If they turned back now, by the time the first two crew members were hoisted, Kanack's crew would be waiting to take over.

Wayne Kanack's crew of Don Morris, Frank Delimba, and Sonny Becker descended into the hole and began retracing the previous crew's steps. No one was optimistic, the heat became worse as they walked towards the No. 10 station, and the humidity was so dense a mist formed in the drift. Every 100 feet they banged on the pipes with wrenches to tell any survivors taking refuge in a raise or stope that help was coming. But they heard nothing.

An hour earlier, Ron and Tom had decided it was hopeless and drifted off into an exhausted sleep in the diamond drill station. When Ron woke and looked down the drift, he thought he saw lights. He shook Tom awake and told him, Ron had heard voices for several days and Tom didn't believe him until he saw several flashes of light. Both men started banging on a pipe with one hand and trying to get their boots on with the other as they listened to the sweet sound of someone knocking on the pipes 200 feet down the drift. Ron ran to the motor and put the lights on. Its battery no longer had enough power to run the motor, but its dim beams outlined four men walking down the drift.

It wasn't the type of exciting rescue one sees in the movies or television. The rescue crews were too professional to make it exciting. Kanack recorded the time his crew found the pair as precisely 5:43 p.m. Even hoisting rescue crew member Don Morris up the borehole after he collapsed from heat prostration was routine.

Joy, Reality and Despair

Kanack's phone call to the 3700 level advised that Ron Flory and Tom Wilkinson had been recovered alive and in good condition. The bad news was the survivors told Kanack that the seven others on the level were dead and in contaminated atmosphere near the station. The message was relayed to Osborn, Jarrett, and Chase, who sent back word for the crew to bring the survivors up. The bodies of the seven dead men would be recovered after the No. 10 hoist was in operation.

Ron was the first to be hoisted to the 3700 level. Waiting was Dr. Ernest E. Gnaedinger and a paramedic. He was handed a cold can of Gatorade as he climbed out the capsule, but the doctor only allowed him to take a few sips. When led towards the Jewell shaft, Ron balked. "I'll wait for my partner," he said. "We came in together and we'll walk out together."

Cheers of joy and hope welcomed the two miners as they walked from the portal. Frances Wilkinson, age 27, and Myrna

Flory, 18, hugged their bearded husbands, grimy and reeking with sour sweat from the heat. Ron had dropped from 195 pounds to 180 and Tom from 140 to 126 in eight days of heat with little food. Wrapped in blankets to shield them from the drizzling rain, they walked to the waiting ambulances and were driven to the hospital for physical exams and their first meal in a week of soup and sandwiches. The ambulances were followed by a caravan of cars packed with friends and relatives. The West Shoshone General Hospital called the cafeteria workers back to work to feed the expected onslaught of relatives and friends, something they can do in small towns that care about their people.

Marvin Chase's afternoon announcement in the drizzling rain that four additional bodies had been found on 3100 level and one more had been located on the 3700 level brought despair. His early evening news that Ron Flory and Tom Wilkinson had been rescued had raised everyone's spirit and hope. After the two men were driven to the hospitals, he advised the crowd that the seven other men on the 4800 level were dead. The somber reality set in that the fire had killed 47 men and 44 men were still missing. But there was a silver lining gleaming with the belief that if two could survive, so could others.

CHAPTER 17

WEDNESDAY & THURSDAY, MAY 10 & 11, 1972

The Dirty Work

The impersonal hard facts recorded by the Bureau's Ken Russell, the Spokane Subdistrict Manager in charge of the day shift, and Roland Wilson, running the night shift, revealed the details of the work and the number of men building bulkheads, investigating the 3700 level cave-in, rescue crews, and body removal. Exact times were recorded as Wednesday merged into Thursday without notice by the men working underground where there is no day or night.

> Wednesday, 2:15 p.m.: Voltage from Bonneville Power Administration reduced to accommodate hoist circuits.
>
> 3:15 p.m.: Hoist operating. Due to failures in shaft signalling system, it is necessary to repair the signals on each level before proceeding to the next level below.
>
> 9:22 p.m.: Crew descended to 3400 level and found four bodies.
>
> Thursday, 12:40 a.m.: Crew reported the atmosphere contaminated at No. 10 shaft on 3700 level and seven bodies found in tail drift behind the shaft.

> 7:13 a.m.: Seven bodies were found on 4400 level.
> Victims had attempted to remain alive by inhaling
> oxygen from a cylinder on a welding unit.
>
> 8:15 p.m.: Initially no bodies were found on 4200
> level, but three were later located at the 42-539
> raise.

By the time the bodies were located on the 4200 level, two bodies had been reported discovered on the 5000 level and 17 on the 5200 level. The 5200 level was the last hope of finding men alive. The rescue crews surrendered to the fact they would find no more survivors. Second searches resulted in finding three bodies on the 4200 level and four on the 5200 level. The four men on the 5200 level had attempted to build a crude bulkhead to shield them from the toxic smoke, but died before it could be finished. The Bureau tallied the number of bodies at 91, the total number of missing, and stopped recording the gory details.

Next was the grim job of removing the bodies from the mine. Those assigned the gruesome task treated the remains of their fellow miners with respect as they gently laid them in body bags. It was harder on the Sunshine miners who recognized friends they had shared a cup of coffee and a joke with ten days ago. At least they didn't have to tell the wife or mother of the death of their husband or son.

The News

Wednesday, the rain stopped and the morning sun brightened the dreary mine yard and the relatives and friends waiting for news. Yesterday's rescue of two men had raised their hopes. But depression set in when members of the clergy began to circulate through the crowd and notify families of the deaths of 17 miners whose bodies had been brought to the surface and identified. Even the ministers had difficulty holding back their emotions at the number, aware there were still 15 more bodies to be identified and 40 men missing. It is always difficult to explain God's ways, and the list they were handed were all in the prime of life.

Howard Fleshman, 38, left a wife and three children; Gregory Dionne, 23, who had volunteered to act as a cager rather than escape, left a wife and baby daughter; Richard Lynch, 24, left a wife and child; Donald K. Firkins, 37, left a wife and three children; William T. Follette, 23, left a wife; Robert W. Goff, 35, left a wife and five children; Wayne L. Johnson, 43, left a wife and five children; Joe Naccarrato, 40, left a wife; Delbert J. McNutt, 48; Casey Pena, 52, left a wife; Virgil Bebb, 53, left a wife and child after the shifter stayed to make sure his men got out; Gene F. Salyer, 51, left a wife; Robert B. Scanlan, 38, left a wife after sacrificing his life to raise the men from the lower levels; Norman S. Fee, 27; Joe Armijo, 38, left a wife and three children; Glen R. Rossiter, 37, left a wife and child; John R. Rawson, 27, left a wife a two children; and Louis W. "The Cat" Goos, 51, left a wife. Years earlier, the Cat had survived being trapped alone in a Montana mine for seven days.[16]

The wives and children weren't the only ones grieving. Mothers and fathers also felt the loss. Harvey Dionne, the foreman who narrowly escaped death after attempting to rescue fellow miners, and Robert Follette, a miner on the 5000 level who escaped, both heard they lost sons that day.

The crowd thinned as ministers and friends led the weeping families to the parking lot. Those who waited heard more heartbreaking news at 10:00 p.m. Four more bodies were discovered on the 3400 level. The families did not have to wait for their bodies to be identified. The wives and children of Delbert C. "Dusty" Rhoads, the 57-year-old lead mechanic, and Arnold E. Anderson, the 48-year-old lead electrician, knew the dedicated miners had volunteered to go to the 3400 level to turn off the exhaust fans. And the families of 59-year-old Custer L. Keough and 29-year-old William R. Walty had been told they were the only two men working on the level.

---

16 The number of children was taken from the Bureau's records only listed dependents and did not include children living away from home.

Thursday, the tenth day of their sentence in purgatory, the families' only real hope was for the miners on the 5200 level. The first announcement that 14 more bodies were found was tempered by Chase not divulging where the bodies were discovered. The bodies on the 3700 level included men who had been hoisted from other levels.

At 6:20 p.m., an emotionally exhausted Chase appeared and told the families in a quivering voice that 17 bodies had been discovered on the 5200 level and two on the 5000 level. He told them to go home and the company would notify them if there were any new developments. Crews were still searching for the last seven missing men. The mine yard erupted in tears and screams. Chase couldn't face their anguish. He knew most of the men and he had to maintain his composure when making the heartbreaking announcement a second time to the press.

The reporters knew the news was bad when they saw a crowd walking towards their cars weeping without shame and lashing out at anyone near about the unfairness of life. They accepted Chase's words, aware the end was near and the mine manager was an emotional cripple from grief.

Two hours later, the Bureau's Lewis Helm and Chase divided the terrible chore. Helm handled their last press conference in the parking lot and Chase met with the dozen or so family members and friends who refused to surrender to the inevitable at the Jewell portal. The last seven bodies had been found, four on the 5200 level and three on the 4200 level.

For the first time, the press didn't ask for details or an analysis of what occurred. It would be up to them to write of the futility of the race to build bulkheads and get down the shaft to the lower levels. They took up a collection and presented the money to Chase as a donation to a fund for the survivors, then left to write their stories in their campers and vans parked in a Sunshine parking lot. Tomorrow, the national reporters would be gone. Upon the discovery of the last body, the volunteer rescue crews left. There would be few local press stories about the Sunshine and Bureau crews still erecting bulkheads to put out the fire and bringing bodies to the surface.

Jarrett noted in his report that the Bureau's moral was low and the bodies were in a "very bad state of decomposition." Even his offer of a case of whiskey didn't entice the crews to have all of the bodies out by 11:00 p.m. on May 12. But rumors were that the crews drank far more than a case the following day when they were done with the morbid assignment.

The minor news that almost went unnoticed was Osborn's announcement that all mines in the Coeur d'Alene Mining District would be inspected in cooperation with the United Steelworkers of America to ensure the public that the local mines were safe and show that the Bureau was serious about its safety responsibilities. He also approved Jarrett's selection of Roland V. Wilson, Robert E. Riley, and E. Levi Brake as members of his investigating committee into the cause of the disaster.

The next national story would take place in Washington on Monday, May 15, at a congressional hearing into the disaster under Democrat Dominick Daniels of New Jersey. To make sure he made the headlines, Daniels had announced the hearing on May 9 while the rescue crews were still searching for missing miners. Chase had objected to Daniels's callous timing of the May 9 announcement for a hearing while Sunshine was still attempting to rescue its miners and the mine was still on fire.

Dr. Elburt Osborn, the Bureau's director, left on May 10 to prepare his testimony, which he never gave and left to his subordinates to take the heat.

Marvin Chase, the beleaguered mine manager, went home under the protection of eight National Guardsmen. Two deputy sheriffs took over guarding his house because of telephone threats on his life.

THE LAST WORD?

The Shoshone County Coroner, Dr. Albert M. Peterson, announced there were to be no autopsies. All the men died of carbon monoxide poisoning. He stated that all the men were dead within 40 to 60 seconds after the poisoned air reached them. It wasn't true. Possibly, he felt it would ease the relatives' concern whether the men suffered.

Dr. Peterson was quoted: "Blood tests we ran on the first 11 men brought out of the mine indicated the air was between 70 and 80 percent carbon monoxide." That could be a press misquote. Such amounts of carbon monoxide in the air is impossible. However, the amount of carboxyhemoglobin in the victims' bloodstreams was probably at a lethal level between 70 to 80 percent.

PART THREE

_____ THE AFTERSHOCK

CHAPTER 18

PUBLIC HEARINGS

Mine Disasters and Politics

The Sunshine Mine disaster was the second worst non-coal mine disaster in United States history. Only the 1917 Granite Mountain Copper Mine fire in Butte, Montana, killing 163 men, resulted in more non-coal mine deaths. "Mine disasters," a cold government statistic classifying five or more mine deaths in a single accident, are one of the worst blights on the industrial era and mining history. MSHA statistics list 725 United States mine disasters since records were kept in the early 1800s.

In 1891, Congress passed the first coal mine safety legislation, the Territorial Mine Inspection Act, which only applied to the territories because of the powerful influence of Eastern and Midwestern coal and steel companies. The law was primarily noted for banning the hiring of children under the age of twelve. It wasn't until 1910, a year that saw 19 coal and 6 non-coal mine disasters and the public still remembered the 1907 Monongah, West Virginia, methane explosion that killed 362 coal miners in the nation's worst coal mine disaster, and the 1909 Cherry Mine fire in Cherry, Illinois, that ended with 259 coal miners dying, did Congress create the Bureau of Mines and charge it with conducting mining research. During the first decade of the twentieth century, over 2,000 coal miners lost their lives every year. Nevertheless, the 1910 law denied the Bureau the authority to inspect coal mines. In 1913, after the Stag Canyon Mine No. 2 methane explosion in Dawson, New Mexico, claimed the lives of 263 coal miners, Congress permitted the Bureau to extend its research into mine health and safety.

In 1941, Congress allowed Bureau inspectors in the coal mines, but the toothless law only granted the authority to make recommendations. After President Truman's threatened takeover of the coal mines and his battle with John L. Lewis, president of the United Mine Workers of America (UMWA), the Bureau and UMWA drafted a health and safety code in 1946 as part of the settlement. However, the code lacked real enforcement authority and only applied to coal mines on federal lands and covered under the Walsh-Healey Act in connection with government contracts.

After the 1951 West Frankfort, Illinois, disaster took the lives of 119 coal miners, Congress passed the Coal Mine Safety and Health Act of 1952 (1952 Coal Act), which delegated enforcement responsibilities to the states and exempted mines with less than 15 employees. Poor enforcement by the majority of the coal producing states, often a result of coal industry political influence, made a mockery of the 1952 Coal Act.

A coal dust explosion in Farmington, West Virginia, in 1968 entombed 78 coal miners at the time Congress was debating revising the 1952 Coal Act. There was no stopping the enactment of the pervasive 1969 Coal Act requiring four annual inspections of all underground coal mines, mandatory fines, and granting inspectors the power to close the mine in cases of imminent danger. Not trusting the Bureau to promulgate strict standards, with the aid of the UMWA and Bureau employees, Congress incorporated statutory standards. In several instances where they lacked criteria for regulations, they adopted British standards. [17]

---

17 In 1974, I visited the United Kingdom in my capacity as MESA Administrator. During a tour of an underground coal mine, I learned that the methane gas was in excess of 2.5%. The methane was far in excess of the 1% maximum requiring work be stopped in the mine area and the 1.5% requiring the miners be withdrawn from the affected area (often the entire mine) under the British law that Congress had adopted. The chief British mine inspector advised me he would have to close down 90% of the coal mines if he enforced the law and furnished me with an internal government report proving the noncompliance when I expressed my disbelief.

A week later, I advised Sir Joseph Gormley, the head of the British Coal Miners Union, of my experience. He gleefully said he would tell the National Coal Board that U.S. Mines were meeting the standard and gave me a gory print of a British coal mine disaster. Later, I presented the print to one of my successors to hang in MSHA. As the regulation was controversial in America, I never publicly mentioned the revelation after I arrived home.

The history of coal mine safety legislation is tied to the public's awareness of the tragedy of mine disasters. After the Sunshine Mine disaster, many on Capitol Hill and the United Steelworkers of America saw their silver opportunity to amend the weak 1966 MNM Act and infuse it with the enforcement powers of the 1969 Coal Act. And they had the memory of the 1968 Farmington coal mine disaster to help. On May 12, the day the press emblazoned headlines that 91 miners had perished in the Sunshine Mine, many carried the grim story that five bodies had been removed from the Farmington mine, bringing the total to 21 bodies that had been recovered. The mine had been sealed after explosions rocked the surface for several weeks, but was still burning after three years and 57 bodies had not been recovered.

As expected, the metal and nonmetal mining industry geared up to fight any change in the law. J. Allen Overton, president of the American Mining Congress, announced a mining industry study that "placed emphasis on technology, individual training, and individual responsibility." According to Overton, "Safety legislation can stultify our quest for new mineral resources if you aren't careful."

No Whitewash

In 1972, as director of the Interior Department's Office of Hearings and Appeals (OHA), I served as an ex officio member of four appellate boards having jurisdiction over government contracts, public lands (including oil and gas leasing and mining claims), Indians, and mine health and safety. For a brief period, I was also chairman of the Oil Import Appeals Board, an inter-agency board with members from the Departments of Justice and Commerce. Including two dozen administrative law judges, the OHA had 100 lawyers to handle over 3,000 cases per year. The OHA case docket was growing because of the 1969 Coal Act and the oil crisis, which demanded I spend most Saturdays and Sundays in the office. I wasn't alone in the office on weekends. Many of the board members were also working, dispelling the belief, including mine, that all government employees were clock-watchers.

The last thing I needed was a case involving extended time away from the office and having to write a lengthy and complex decision. My duties included sitting on two understaffed boards

(Indians and coal mine health and safety, which only had two members and required me to cast tie-breaking votes) and to participate in public land appeals cases with political implications. On June 13, 1972, John "Jack" B. Rigg, Sr., the Deputy Assistant Secretary for Minerals, called and asked me to come to the Assistant Secretary for Mineral's office.

The Assistant Secretary for Mineral Resources, Hollis M. Dole, was an Oregon geologist with a voice as smooth as silk or gravel, depending on his mood. He told be to pack my bags and go to Kellogg, Idaho, and conduct a public hearing into the Sunshine Mine disaster. I tried to explain my heavy schedule and suggested I assign an administrative law judge, but Dole and Rigg wouldn't hear of it, claiming the hearing was not on legal issues and required political finesse.

Dole added firmly, "Damn it, I don't want the Bureau of Mines to whitewash the investigation!"

I told them the mine was still on fire and it would be impossible to determine the cause of the fire and the Bureau had not completed its investigation.

"I know it," Dole said, as if I was an idiot. "Tell them what you want in their final report and finish the hearings after the fire is extinguished."

"Can Jarrett be trusted?" I asked.

"No. Why the hell do you think I'm sending you? The three mining engineers on the investigating team are good men and will do all the work, but Jarrett is their boss. You write a final report and say what you think."

"Even if it hurts the Department?" I asked.

Dole squinted at me as he mulled over instances I had criticized the Nixon administration on price and wage freezes and controls and the Mandatory Oil Import Program policies in private meetings. Neither were smart for a political appointee to do. Also, I had ranted about the Bureau's inept civil penalty system under the 1969 Coal Act. In Dole's presence, I had told the Under Secretary, Fred Russell, that the Department's lawyers were incompetent and would lose the first criminal case they were prosecuting under the 1969 Coal Act. Fortunately, Dole agreed with my views and the criminal case was thrown out of court.

"Do what you think is right," Dole said, "but don't blame some

miner who has been in the mines since he was seventeen for screw-
ing up and be diplomatic when you kick the Bureau's ass. And
another thing, don't listen to some mining industry big shot when he
claims safety precautions cost too much."

Dole had been at the Sunshine Mine when they discovered the
bodies on the 5200 level and the hard-nosed geologist had been
shaken by the number of deaths. He had no faith in Osborn and Jarrett and did not want the Department of the Interior to lose jurisdiction over mine health and safety to the Department of Labor. Dole
never received credit for creating the separate research and health
and safety divisions in the Bureau two years earlier. It was the first
step to eliminate the Bureau's glaring conflict of interest between
mining industry promotion and research versus mine health and
safety enforcement.

That afternoon I dictated a *Federal Register* announcement of
the hearing and told Francis Patton, a lawyer and one of my legal
assistants, to edit it and rush the publication as soon as my secretary,
Marian Russ, found a hearing location in Kellogg. I never worried
about the legality of any procedure Mrs. Patton approved; and effi-
cient Mrs. Russ guaranteed the most convenient and largest place for
a hearing was the Kellogg Junior High School cafeteria.

I asked Thomas Mascolino, another legal assistant, to locate
the Bureau's depositions I had read about in the newspaper so I
could get a handle on what I was facing. Tom had an astute and
practical legal mind. His responsibilities included preventing me
going off half-cocked when I thought something was a miscarriage
of justice and calming me down when I went on a tirade. He shook
his head as he lugged two boxes into my office containing photo
copies of 67 depositions, several of which were barely legible. Few
depositions had the exhibits attached and the Department's attorneys
didn't know where the exhibits were. That was the cause of my first
diatribe. My next harangue started when I began reading the depositions.

After reflection on forty years of practicing law, they are still
the most incompetently conducted depositions I ever read. Few, if
any, of the government attorneys had experience taking depositions.
Richard V. Backley, an Interior Department trial lawyer experienced
in prosecuting cases under the 1969 Coal Act, a former Assistant
U.S. Attorney, and later Chairman of the Federal Mine Health and

Safety Review Commission, was sent from Washington to manage the attorneys taking the depositions. Backley and Bureau engineers drafted more than adequate pro forma questions for the three teams of two Interior Department lawyers taking depositions at three different locations. But for the most part, Backley's instructions were not followed. There were virtually no follow-up questions in crucial areas, leaving huge gaps in the testimony, and the witnesses were allowed to ramble on in irrelevant areas. With three separate teams not coordinating their findings, there were few questions asked about conflicting testimony. That the government attorneys lacked experience in mining and interpreting mine safety standards was not their fault, but their arrogance in not allowing the Bureau's experienced engineers furnished to assist them question witnesses was inexcusable. Many of the attorney's questions showed their ignorance in mining and the safety standards.

Being government lawyers, they had to take a boondoggle to Canada to depose four Canadian rescue crew members. They learned nothing. One deposition lasted 15 minutes and consisted of 19 pages, five of which were the formalities of attorney's names and objections. A second deposition contained 22 pages, with five and one-half pages of formalities, that lasted 25 minutes.

The questions posed by the Steelworkers' lawyers were no better. Miners were a small part of the union's membership and, like the government lawyers, the union's lawyers knowledge of mining was nil. Fortunately, they quickly learned to allow two capable former miners on the union's staff, Marco Vestich and J.P. Mooney, to ask questions and assist them in preparing questions. Idaho's Deputy Attorneys General were also inexperienced in mining and mine safety law, but they permitted the Idaho inspectors, all former miners, to ask questions.

The Sunshine Mining Company's attorneys outclassed the other lawyers in mining knowledge and every attorney's duty —they came prepared. They also had two major advantages. They were skilled trial lawyers and had discussed possible questions with many of the miners and all the mine foremen and officials in advance.

The Interior Department lawyers faced another disadvantage conducting the depositions that I had to contend with at the hearing. The 1966 MNM Act did not grant the government subpoena power. I had to rely on miners and company officials voluntary testimony, and admit to several nights dreaming of banging my gavel to open the hearing in a junior high school cafeteria without witnesses. Although requested, Albert Walkup, the Sunshine Mine superintendent, didn't volunteer to testify. Nevertheless, to avoid adverse publicity, if Sunshine did not appear cooperative, and with the sword hanging over their head that they needed to obtain the Bureau's approval to reopen the mine, Sunshine put on a well-orchestrated dog and pony show at the hearing that proved highly informative, albeit one-sided.

The Hearing

To avoid meeting attorneys and witnesses in a Kellogg motel, I reserved a hotel room in Coeur d'Alene, 45 miles from Kellogg. Upon arriving the day before the hearing, I thought I was attending an American Bar Association convention. A half-dozen trial attorneys representing the widows and children of the dead miners introduced themselves as I sat by the swimming pool reading the depositions of witnesses scheduled to testify. One evening two widows asked me to join them for a drink in the hotel bar and introduced me to their lawyer. Before I could finish my Scotch and escape, the attorney asked me if I was interested in joining him as co-counsel in the suit against the Sunshine Mining Company and the Bureau. I respectfully declined and excused myself a few minutes later, never to return to the hotel bar.

The first morning I met with the attorneys for the Bureau, Sunshine, Steelworkers, and Idaho Inspector of Mines at a pre-hearing conference to set the rules for the hearing, which no one liked. I spent the afternoon editing questions I planned to ask witnesses and reading the transcript of the May 15 and 16 hearings before the Select Subcommittee of Labor of the House of Representatives. The most salient point in the transcript was that Representative Dominick Daniels planned to finish his hearings on July 31, two weeks after my hearings began, and the Steelworkers were planning a second appearance with the same witnesses. It was obvious the union was going to take the opportunity to criticize the Bureau's and Sunshine's statements at the Interior Department's hearing and scream it was an attempt to whitewash the investigation before a friendly congressional panel without fear of rebuttal.

The hearing started with the television cameras on James McClure, Congressman from Idaho, and Bureau Director Dr. Elburt Osborn. Osborn wasted the taxpayer's money by traveling a great distance to say nothing. After their speeches, I barred television cameras and photographers from the hearing room. There were the usual cries of "freedom of the press," but I banned photos and video cameras focused on a mother's or widow's face when hearing how their son or husband died.

Idaho Deputy Attorney General, Warren Felton, representing the Idaho Inspector of Mines, objected to holding a public hearing, obviously irate that I had denied him national television coverage. He claimed there was no authority under the 1966 MNM Act to conduct hearings; it was too early to conduct a hearing because the fire had not been extinguished; the Bureau had not determined the cause of the fire; and I refused to allow cross-examination of the witnesses. After the Bureau's testimony, the Steelworkers joined the State's motion.

I ruled there was ample authority under the Department's statutory grant to conduct investigations in any form it chose. Felton was aware I had advised at the prehearing conference that the hearing would be recessed until the fire was extinguished and the Bureau completed its investigation and my position that a hearing now would be more productive while the disaster was fresh in the minds of the miners. He had no answer to my comment that the Congress had started its hearings two months earlier and planned to reconvene them in two weeks. I refused to allow open cross-examination on the basis that it was generally not allowed in fact-finding or rule-making hearings and would have turned the hearing into an adversary proceeding. In the spirit of compromise, I agreed to allow the attorneys to submit questions to me in writing that I would ask, if pertinent.

The State of Idaho and the Steelworkers were not anxious to follow the Bureau's professional testimony by its engineers and inspectors under Richard Backley's questioning. They also knew that Sunshine's able attorneys, Carl Burke and Leo J. Driscoll, were prepared to present lengthy testimony and evidence that would make the State and union appear inconsequential.

Felton advised that Carl Griner, the State Inspector of Mines, declined to testify, however, I said I had questions for Mr. Griner.

During the next recess, I hinted that if they refused to cooperate at the hearing, I might rule they had no right to submit questions or participate in the hearing. In fear of embarrassment, Griner agreed to answer questions the following day, but he contributed nothing of value. Griner was aware his organization was pathetically weak compared to the Bureau and lacked competency. His position rankled the citizens and several newspapers criticized the State's action. The *Washington Post* quoted my last line in connection with the State Inspector of Mine's position verbatim: "One cannot help but be amazed that a representative of the State of Idaho, with a duty to protect its citizens and to determine the cause of such disasters so that they can be prevented in the future, would take such a position."

The Steelworkers' witnesses provided little constructive testimony, except for Frank McKee, Director of the Western District. McKee offered worthwhile safety recommendations, but lessened the value by his occasional rhetoric. Lavern Melton, a shaft miner and president of Steelworkers Local 5089, lost his credibility as a witness when he refused to disclose the source who gave Sunshine management advance notice of Bureau inspections after testifying Sunshine was given advance notice. He lost more credibility after Marvin Chase, the mine manager, testified it was the State of Idaho inspectors and local Steelworkers officials who gave Sunshine advance notice of the Bureau's inspections.

The Bureau's second witness, Assistant Director for Metal and Nonmetal Mine Health and Safety Stanley Jarrett, read a general statement about the Bureau's participation in the rescue attempts. He contributed nothing and referred all questions in connection with safety standards to the Bureaus' engineers.

During Roland Wilson's testimony regarding his recommendation to use dunnage bags as inflatable stoppings for bulkheads, I reached for the Bureau's Exhibit No. 1, its preliminary report on the disaster. The report bothered me because it contained no conclusions in its 95 pages, including 30-odd pages of exhibits, six of which listed every Bureau employee who appeared at the disaster, to inflate the report. It was obvious in the Bureau's cursory preliminary findings that Sunshine was in violation of a number of advisory and mandatory safety standards.

As I listened to Wilson's testimony, I thumbed through the preliminary report and found another thing that had bothered me — a statement that Jarrett had taken the initiative to obtain the inflatable bags. I said to myself, "Wilson's sticking his neck out by not letting Jarrett get away with taking the credit. I like this witness, but it's not the right time to chastise Jarrett."

Once the Bureau's experienced engineers and inspectors began their testimony the hearing was well worth conducting. To the man, they were honest about the shortfalls in the safety standards and the Bureau's interpretations and enforcement. Several admitted on hindsight that they could have done a better job.

Hearing Interim Report

With the fire still burning and the Bureau yet to complete its investigation, I faced the task of reviewing over 6,000 pages of testimony and depositions and a three-foot stack of exhibits before writing an interim report on the disaster. Pressured to draft *something* in a hurry, allowed me to keep it short and defer a detailed analysis of the disaster and safety standards until the Bureau completed its investigation and I concluded the hearing. The crux of my preliminary conclusions was summed up on page 9, which the *Wall Street Journal* quoted almost verbatim:

> ". . . it is evident that a large number of deaths and the magnitude of the disaster are a direct result of inadequate safety standards, industry-wide poor safety practices, the lack of training of the miners in the event of a disaster, and the fact that no one expected that a disaster of such size or extent could occur. Further, not only are some standards inadequate, but they have been diluted and rendered ineffective by interpretation . . . others have been voided by the label 'advisory'."

My principal preliminary findings included that the mandatory standard requiring two separate escapeways was inadequate because it did not require both contain hoists and had been narrowly interpreted during the claimed development on the 5400 and 5600 levels. There was no doubt this was a contributing cause of the deaths of the men below the 3700 level. The violation of the advisory standard requiring underground main fans be provided with remote controls was the direct cause of the deaths of two heroic miners, Delbert "Dusty" Rhoads and Arnold Anderson. Most important, there was no standard requiring that all men be issued personal self-rescuers and be trained in their use, as required under the 1969 Coal Act, which was the direct cause of countless needless deaths. Although self-rescuers were not required under the 1966 MNM Act, the failure to furnish them on the 5400, 5600, and 5800 levels was a gross dereliction of duty by the current and former safety engineers.

As Assistant Secretary Dole advised, I set out the subjects the Bureau was required to include in its final report, including the lack of up-to-date technology, and devoted two pages to the inadequacy of the Bureau's McCaa self-contained breathing apparatus. One piece of evidence was personal and I left it out, but later told Dole about. After being trained on a McCaa for three hours in an abbreviated 20-hour course, I appeared at the mine to obtain a McCaa before entering the mine while it was still on fire. A Bureau Education and Training Division instructor told me to take a Draeger and that the McCaa was "as worthless as teats on a bull."

A stern-looking Dole sat silent for a few seconds when we met to discuss my report before telling me Secretary Morton had also read the report. Then he burst into a grin and repeated what Morton had told him: "Day was the only innocent SOB in Idaho."

It was after hours and in 1972 one could enjoy an alcoholic libation in a federal building. We discussed the report and the demands of the Steelworkers and several members of Congress that mine health and safety to be removed from the Interior Department and transferred to the Labor Department and our lack of faith in the Bureau's leadership. I pointed out my belief that the Bureau's inspectors and engineers were dedicated and competent. Dole and Rigg agreed.

What Dole, Rigg, and I didn't agree was who first thought of the idea to create a separate agency within the Interior Department with jurisdiction over mine health and safety. Rigg had the edge on us when he came up with the name for the new agency, the Mine Enforcement and Safety Administration with its acronym MESA. Rigg joked that he was from Mesa County, Colorado. However, Rigg, a master at bureaucratic and congressional politics, had a practical reason for not calling it the Mine Safety and Health Administration or MSHA. The name was too similar to the Occupational

Safety and Health Administration or OSHA, established by Congress in 1970 under the Department of Labor. In addition, Congress had debated coal surface mining legislation to halt the degradation of the lands through erosion, acid drainage, water quality deterioration, and disruption of fish and wildlife habitat caused by coal mining. Under MESA, the Interior Department would have an agency ready to step in with mining engineers and inspectors and argue that its inspectors could combine their safety and environmental inspections and avoid requiring inspectors from two agencies with conflicting responsibilities and standards.[18]

---

18 President Gerald Ford twice vetoed the surface mine act, arguing there was a shortage of coal and it would escalate the price of coal during the oil crisis of the 1970s. The Interior Department stood ready with MESA's plan to take jurisdiction, but was never used. Nor did the Department release the Bureau's study claiming the 1969 Coal Act increased coal mining costs 24.5%. MESA objected to the study on the grounds it conflicted with improving safety. Seven months after taking office, President Carter signed the Surface Mining Control and Reclamation Act of 1977, based on the ostensible principals of federalism that gave the states power to enforce surface mining reclamation under the Interior Department's supervisory jurisdiction. The Congress did not learn from the so-called federalism concept that was a failure under the 1952 Coal Act, and the Surface Mining Act remains irregularly and poorly enforced.

CHAPTER 19

SWITCHING POSITIONS

Proposed Mandatory Safety Standards

On December 9, 1972, the Bureau issued proposed mandatory safety standards requiring miners be provided and trained in the use of self-rescuers, mines contain two escapeways with mechanical hoists, and mine operators develop evacuation plans and conduct evacuation drills. As expected, Advisory Committee industry members appointed under the 1966 MNM Act were antagonistic and their votes nullified the standards being mandatory. The mining industry, led by the American Mining Congress (AMC), objected to any standards that increased mining costs.

Every mine in the Silver Valley and most major hard rock mines in the nation were already furnishing self-rescuers and offering training as a result of the Sunshine Mine disaster. In spite of their widespread use, the lack of unanimous Advisory Committee approval allowed the AMC and its members to demand a public hearing under a lengthy rule-making process requiring an administrative law judge to issue a recommended decision and the Secretary of the Interior to ratify and publish the regulations. The mandatory standard requiring self-rescuers did not become effective until September 9, 1974, and self-rescuer training provisions were delayed until October 19, 1974, almost two years after the Bureau proposed the regulations.

The cost of self-rescuers was relatively minor and in many cases the Bureau provided the training or trained and certified mine personnel to train the miners. On the other end of the spectrum, the cost of sinking a shaft to provide a second escapeway with a hoist could run into the millions and force small and marginally profitable mines to close. This caused an even more protracted delay in promulgating the mandatory standard.

The practice of the AMC, the spokesman and lobbying arm for the major mining companies, was to protest the inability of small mining companies to afford the safety costs before Congress and MSHA. The AMC's successor, the National Mining Association, continues to do so today. Often the argument is based on the economic feasibility of a standard and flies in the face of the legislative history of the 1969 Coal Act and 1977 Mine Act. While weight may be given to costs, a formal cost-benefit analysis is not a required component of rulemaking. Standards can be imposed even if "they are financially burdensome and affect profit margins adversely." [19] In other words, there cannot be a required cost-benefit analysis made on a miner's life, health or safety, which are an integral part of the cost and price of coal or silver.

Bureau Final Report

The "Final Report of the Major Mine Fire Disaster-Sunshine Mine, Sunshine Mining Company, Kellogg, Shoshone County, Idaho, May 2, 1972" (Bureau Final Report) was issued on February 18, 1973. It was the effort of Roland Wilson, Robert Riley, and Levi Brake, with little or no assistance from Stanley Jarrett, and involved the trio spending 40 days in the mine before and after the fire was extinguished plus hundreds of hours of research and interviewing miners and inspectors. Jarrett, the Assistant Director for Metal and Nonmetal Mine Health and Safety, had been bumped up to Acting Deputy Assistant Director for Mine Health and Safety. In the Bureau's titled bureaucracy, the report was reviewed and approved by Jarrett's successor, the Deputy Director, and the Director before release.

---

19 Sen. Rep. No. 181, 95th Cong., 1st Sess. 21-22 (1977), citing two Occupational Safety and Health Administration cases adopting the congressional intent: *AFL-CIO v. Brennan,* 530 F.2d 109 (3d Cir. 1975); and *Society of Plastics Industry v. OSHA,* 509 F.2d 1301 (2d Cir.), cert. denied, 427 U.S. 992 (1975).

Few newspapers gave Bureau Director Osborn's bland press release announcing the Bureau Final Report's issuance much space and fewer read the 175-page report. The press release ended by advising that any party "wishing to request further OHA review, the OHA will consider reopening its hearings." It was the Bureau's last futile attempt to avoid a public hearing and challenges to the report.

I hurriedly scheduled the hearing for May 15, 1973. The timing resulted in an unintended slap at the Bureau. In the interim, Secretary of the Interior Morton issued an order creating the MESA and transferring all health and safety functions to the new agency effective July 16, 1973. But the expedited timing was necessary. I had resigned as OHA Director in January to be effective in early July. "Resigned" is euphemistic, I was being forced out because of my independence. To my surprise, I was presented with the Department of the Interior's Outstanding Service Award, a two-ounce gold medallion rarely awarded and worth a few hundred dollars in a pawn shop. After the hearing, the Civil Service Commission (now the Office of Management and Budget) determined my replacement was not qualified. He was not only inexperienced in mineral and public land law, he had never practiced law. The Secretary asked me to stay on, giving me the opportunity to say in effect: "No thanks, there is a demand for petroleum and mining lawyers and I can make big bucks. I have a daughter about to enter a very expensive college, but I'll stay until I finish my report." I thought it would give me ample time to complete my report free from political suasion within the Interior Department, but I was to be proven wrong.

The Bureau Final Report's findings and recommendations were excellent as far as they went. Written at the staff engineer's level and constrained by requiring the approval of the Bureau's hierarchy and Departmental politics, it failed to evaluate the Bureau's overall enforcement record, weaknesses in the 1966 MNM Act, and inherent conflicts in the Advisory Committee structure that allowed the mining industry to veto mandatory safety standards. The report ably documented the need for the Bureau's proposed mandatory standards without bureaucratic gobbledegook and went as far as it could go to improve metal and nonmetal and safety in light of the tragedy of the Sunshine Mine disaster, which was the primary purpose of the report.

May 1973 Hearing—Spontaneous Combustion

As expected, Sunshine's able attorneys, Carl Burke and Leo Driscoll, attacked the Bureau Final Report from the opening of the hearing. The Steelworkers and Idaho Inspector of Mines offered neither witnesses nor evidence. The hearing was cut short the first morning to allow the attorneys for Steelworkers and Idaho to attend a pretrial conference in a civil case brought by the estates of the miners killed in the disaster. Under Idaho law, victims' dependents receiving workmen's compensation benefits could not sue their employers, in effect protecting employers from any liability for their negligence and malfeasance. Although Sunshine was not a party to the suit, the company had interests to protect through its insurance companies and planned to sue the United States, claiming *inter alia* that the Bureau was negligent in its inspection of the mine. The miners' estates were also suing the United States for damages caused by alleged inadequate inspections. The flurry of lawsuits added an army of trial lawyers to the three hundred-odd spectators in the audience.

Sunshine opened the hearing with its employee-witnesses testifying that the company did not violate any safety standards, even the advisory standards that were not required, but were considered good safety practices. Its principal focus was denying the Bureau Final Report's conclusion that the "probable cause of the fire" was the spontaneous combustion of paper, oily rags, garbage, and explosives abandoned near timbers in the mined-out areas before the mining industry began sand-filling the cavities two decades earlier. As Marvin Chase, Sunshine vice president and the mine manager, had told the press the fire was caused by spontaneous combustion during the rescue attempts, it was a 180 degree reversal in Sunshine's position and a surprise to the many reporters who covered the disaster and hearing. Sunshine also attempted to prove that the fire did not start in the vicinity behind the 09 bulkheads on the 3400 level (or within a radius of 200 feet) claimed by the Bureau and that fire increased in intensity because of the polyurethane foam recommended by the Bureau and used on the bulkheads.

Sunshine's lawyers and experts inferred arson was involved, which meant that an employee deliberately set the fire. Who else

other than an employee was in the mine? Only an experienced
Sunshine miner could have found his way through the confusing
drifts and raises leading to the 3550 level, where they claimed the
fire started. Sunshine withheld naming an employee, and the Bureau
had not advised me of suspected arson or a criminal investigation at
the time of the hearing.

Upon my return to Washington, I obtained a copy of the
Bureau's confidential file on the investigation, including FBI
reports. The file revealed that a few weeks after the fire, the wife
of a miner killed in the fire reported her bizarre conversation with
an apparently mentally unbalanced widow of another miner to
Sunshine management. The widow claimed her husband was not
killed in the fire, but was in Mexico, and his cousin, who looked
identical to her husband, set the fire and was killed before he could
escape. She said that her husband and his cousin had planned to
set the fire and tested an incendiary device in her basement furnace
a few days before the fire. Warned by the widow, if she told anyone about the conversation, that she would be killed, Sunshine officials notified the sheriff.

The Shoshone County Sheriff and Prosecuting Attorney investigated the story and sent fire residue samples from the widow's
furnace and furnace pipe to the FBI laboratory in Washington,
D.C., which reported no residue of incendiary compositions were
present. Samples from the pipe were also analyzed by J.M.
Knisely Engineering Corporation, one of Sunshine's experts.
Knisely's report stated that ammonium compounds and traces of
nitrates were found, but withheld comment as to whether they
were characteristic of residues resulting from incendiarism. The
FBI's and Bureau's laboratory experts discounted Knisely's findings on the basis that such materials were expected to be found in
mines. On December 8, 1972, Marvin Chase sent a telegram to
Jack Rigg stating: "Sunshine Mining Company has not uncovered
any evidence which would establish arson as a cause for the Sunshine fire." Two weeks later, the Shoshone County Prosecuting
Attorney advised the Interior Department Solicitor that there was
no evidence of arson. The conclusion reached by the Shoshone
County law enforcement officials was that the widow was mentally unbalanced and her tale a figment of her imagination. If the file

had been available to me at the hearing, Sunshine's spurious contentions and the credibility of Sunshine's lawyers and experts would have been open to serious questioning.

Sunshine's expert witnesses were John M. Knisely, a chemical engineer with vast experience as an industrial safety consultant in fires and explosions, and Dr. Bernard Lewis, a consultant chemical engineer and former Chief of the Bureau's Explosives and Physical Science Branch. Sunshine also called on the Chief of the Idaho State Forensic Laboratory, a chemist, who added little and offered no concrete conclusions. Sunshine's experts dwelled on the theory for proving the fire was not ignited by spontaneous combustion on the basis that the temperature was not at least 250 degrees Fahrenheit required for materials to spontaneously ignite. Their testimony made mountains out of ant hills that confused the reporters and public. However, Sunshine's experts didn't dazzle the trial attorneys in the audience experienced at finding experts willing to testify black is white. In the end, the hired guns, as lawyers call expert witnesses, could not establish it was arson, but swore the fire was man-made. Both experts admitted they had never investigated a mine fire.

The Bureau's mining engineers, Wilson, Riley, and Brake, proved calm and formidable under questioning. They testified as to the facts, ably discussed spontaneous combustion theories, and listed several mines in which spontaneous combustion was determined as the cause of a fire in a hard rock mine. They admitted spontaneous combustion was the "probable cause of the fire," but could not definitely rule out that the fire was caused by man. Nonetheless, they pointed out that the location where they and Sunshine's experts believed the fire started was almost impossible to reach because of bulkheads, raises filled with waste rock, and caved-in drifts in the mined-out old workings.

Wilson produced the Bureau's Exhibit No. 19, a charred piece of polyurethane foam and wood from the 09 bulkhead on the 3400 level, showing it had burned from inside the sealed wooden bulkhead outward through the polyurethane foam towards the drift. I accepted the exhibit, which was over seven feet long, one foot at its widest point, and up to five inches thick, on the condition that Wilson cut the choicest eight inches so I could carry it on the plane back to Washington, D.C. During a break in the hearing, I offered samples cut from the exhibit to the trial attorneys in the audience, who ripped it apart like sharks in a feeding frenzy. [20]

Dr. Michael G. Zabetakis, the Bureau's principal expert witness, was a chemist and physicist specializing in fires and the combustibility of materials. Dr. Zabetakis had personally conducted thousands of spontaneous combustion experiments and supervised tens of thousands during his twenty-three years with the agency. He had investigated hundreds of mine fires and was familiar with every combustible substance found in mines and the effect oxidation had in lowering the temperatures required to permit spontaneous combustion. With his practical and scientific knowledge of mines and spontaneous combustion, he decimated Sunshine's experts' theoretical testimony. The most remarkable feature of his straight-forward testimony was that he did not come prepared to testify. Richard Backley, the Bureau's attorney, did not get wind that Sunshine was going to dispute the Bureau's spontaneous combustion theory until the previous week and did not advise Dr. Zabetakis he would have to testify until the Friday before the Monday hearing. His only preparation was to read the Bureau Final Report and listen to Sunshine's experts. Dr. Zabetakis was supported by Dr. Lawrence Hofer of the Bureau of Mines, whose duties were to analyze everything the Bureau permitted in mines that are capable of combustion or oxidizing.

One of the unexpected and ancillary results of the hearings was my personal confirmation that the Bureau had a cadre of extremely competent engineers, inspectors, and scientists, dispelling my belief when I joined the Department of the Interior that the Bureau was staffed only by bureaucrats.

After my return to Washington, I waited thirty days to allow Sunshine to submit a brief and the Idaho Inspector of Mines' report on the disaster before drafting my report. The Idaho report made no recommendations in connection with new safety standards to prevent

---

20 Bureau Exhibit No. 19 gathered dust on my credenza and served as a marvelous conversation piece until April 1976. The Department of Justice asked me to surrender it for use as an exhibit in the case involving Sunshine and the miners' estates suing the United States government. The Justice Department attorney complained that every party had a piece of the exhibit except the United States.

similar disasters and provided no definite conclusions as to the cause of the fire. However, the Idaho Inspector of Mines agreed with the Bureau that spontaneous combustion was possible.

The cause of the fire, being the most contentious and difficult issue, drew me to face it up front. The most obvious obstacle was the lack of evidence left in the general area everyone agreed the fire started. The fire had burned through large parts of the 08 and 09 vein from the 3100 level through the 3250, 3400, and 3550 levels to the 3700 level, destroying the evidence and making the area too hazardous to examine. Similar to the Bureau and Sunshine experts, I found it relatively easy to eliminate the other possible causes. Smoking on the 3400 level was prohibited and almost impossible in air velocities of 1,000 to 2,000 feet per minute. An ignition caused by the use of an oxygen-acetylene torch on the 3400 level would have been noticed by the employees and the work took place downwind of the area where the fire started. As there were no energized electrical wires or equipment in the area except for the 3400 fans, which were found in operating condition after the fire, electrical fires were impossible. Blasting on the 3400 level the previous day as a cause of the ignition would have been noticed and was downwind. Yet, it could have contributed to spontaneous combustion. Vibrations from blasting might have loosened the bulkheads and permitted an air leakage. A change in ventilation always precedes spontaneous combustion in an underground mine. [21]

Eliminating the obvious was easy and left me with determining whether it was spontaneous combustion or incendiarism. An accidental man-made ignition was discounted. The fire ignited in an area that was bulkheaded off and miners had no reason to be in the area. It would have taken considerable time and effort to reach the area and leave unnoticed. After studying hundreds of pages of testimony and exhibits, I was forced to discredit the Sunshine expert testimony that spontaneous combustion was impossible. There were dozens of cases in which spontaneous combustion had been found to be the cause of underground hard rock mine fires. Weighing all the facts I concluded spontaneous combustion was the probable cause of the fire and incendiarism was possible, but highly improbable.

---

21 "Symposium on the Prevention of Spontaneous Combustion." Institute of Mining Engineers, London, (November 3, 1970).

MESA

In June 1973 Jack Rigg called and asked me to drop by his office. Assistant Secretary Dole had resigned and Jack was running the office, much to the consternation of the new assistant secretary. Rigg had been asked by Secretary Morton to find a Director of the Bureau of Mines to replace Dr. Osborn, who had resigned, and the first MESA Administrator.

Finding an acceptable MESA Administrator was tantamount to finding a shark that didn't bite. The Democrat-controlled Senate, led by Chairman of the Senate Labor Committee Senator Harrison Williams of New Jersey, insisted a labor-affiliated appointment be made.[22] The Republican White House wanted a mining industry official, even though Rigg's Democrat contacts in the Senate told him it was like nominating the proverbial fox to guard the chicken coop. Rigg told me what a great job I had done at the Sunshine Mine hearings and devising the Bureau's civil penalty assessment system. Also, the Board of Mine Operations Appeals in OHA on which I sat had obtained a reputation for strictly enforcing the 1969 Coal Act ... I was the ideal candidate for MESA Administrator.

I knew that Rigg was giving me a snow job. I had not finished the Sunshine Mine report and the Bureau's penalty assessment procedures were still in disarray because of the lack of funding and were being challenged in the courts. If the court knew that the Bureau's new 1969 Coal Act civil penalty assessment regulations were created over one weekend by three lawyers, my secretary, my administrative officer, and a bottle of Scotch, it could have a bearing on the outcome of the case and become an embarrassment to the Department. When the penalty system was first challenged in court, I told Rigg that I could devise a fair and legal penalty system in two days. That weekend I gathered three extremely bright men in my office to draft the assessment regulations. Tom Mascolino, my top legal assistant and right arm, and I drafted the methodology; Newton Frishberg, Chairman of the Interior Board of Land Appeals and an expert on administrative law, handled the due process; and Gilbert Lockwood, OHA deputy for administration, cranked out the numbers on a computer to ensure

---

22 In 1980 Senator Williams was found guilty of bribery in the ABSCAM sting, in which FBI agents posing as sheiks offered bribes to six representatives and Williams if they would introduce legislation.

fairness and that they added up. Marian Russ, my secretary, typed our drafts (before word processing) until her fingers were numb.

In essence, the concept was simple. We broke down the statutory five criteria required to be considered into a point system having a dollar value for each point up to 100. In considering the size of the mine and company, we allocated points for the annual tonnage of coal mined at the mine plus that of the parent company. The history of previous violations was based on the number of violations per the number of days the mine was inspected. Negligence caused vociferous legal arguments. We had to use such non-legal terms as "low," and "high" negligence and define them. Gravity was broken down to the degrees of likelihood of an injury occurring, severity (no lost work time up to a fatality), and the number of persons effected. The operator's demonstrated good faith in abating the violation was a percentage deduction. The sixth criteria, the effect of the penalty on the coal mine operator's ability to continue in business, was presumed unless the operator submitted information contesting the presumption. The maximum number of penalty points was 100 and equaled the maximum civil penalty of $10,000 under the 1969 Coal Act at the time. In cases involving fatalities and egregious violations, the Bureau was authorized to assess what it believed was warranted under the criteria. The regulations also had the effect of a *de nova* appeal to an administrative law judge and a final administrative appeal to the Board of Mine Operations Appeals, who had the power to *increase* the penalty. The system was rushed to publication in the *Federal Register* two days later. Based on an inspector's check list, the Bureau could rapidly assess the over 70,000 civil penalties it was issuing annually and eliminate its backlog of 80,000.[23]

As in any discussion regarding a political appointment, I had to consider the pluses and minuses. I would have to dig into my dwindling savings to remain on a government salary. Being a Republican was a minus when an appointment involves labor during a Democrat-controlled Senate. On the other hand, there was a stalemate

---

23 The Bureau's civil penalty assessment program was upheld by the Supreme Court in *National Independent Coal Operators v. Kleppe,* 423 U.S. 288 (1976). The civil penalty assessment regulations are found in 30 Code of Federal Regulations at Part 100 and, although amended, remain in their basic form.

between the Senate and the White House and I had received favorable press for my interim report on the Sunshine Mine disaster. Also, the vast majority of the cases decided by the OHA's Board of Mine Operations Appeals had been favorable to the coal miners.

Being a lawyer and not having mining experience wasn't a drawback as far as Rigg was concerned. He said my legal experience under the 1969 Coal Act was a plus. I was thankful no one asked about my private law practice experience. I had represented several small mining companies, although the cases did not involve mine health and safety. It was also a relief no one asked if I had mining experience. I would have been embarrassed. After being discharged from the Army in 1952, I toured the country to see old Army buddies and enjoy myself before returning to college. On my way back from the West Coast I found myself broke in Cripple Creek, Colorado, and took a job as a miner to raise the money to get home. The mine was merely an adit driven 400 feet into the side of a mountain to reach a believed gold vein. During my first night in the mine, the shifter asked if I knew anything about explosives. After I told him I had demolition experience in the U.S. Army Rangers, I was promoted to "shot firer" and given a 15 cents an hour raise. I was glad to leave after three weeks before I killed myself and six other miners on the night shift. I never saw any gold ore or learned if the mine hit the vein of gold.

There were few, if any, pluses why I should accept the appointment and an ugly two-headed monster to be battled if I did. My independent report on the Sunshine Mine disasters could be tainted and labeled as a whitewash if I wrote it while Administrator of MESA. On the flip side, any criticism of the Bureau would involve employees now in MESA and I could lose their loyalty and cooperation, which could make the job difficult, if not impossible, for an outsider. It was decided to delay issuing my report until a propitious time. But not only was the reorganizing and managing MESA a full-time task, there was never a good time to issue the report until after I left MESA.[24]

---

24 In the winter of 1975, I was ordered by my doctors to take two weeks medical leave to exercise and swim 25 laps twice a day because of two deteriorated disks. I had the Sunshine files shipped to a Phoenix, Arizona, motel and started writing, but was unable to complete the 171 - page report in the brief time frame.

THE COURT'S VERDICT

As usual, the courts have the last word. Chief Judge Ray McNichols of the U.S. District Court for the District of Idaho consolidated six cases in the case of *Helen House, et al. v. Mine Safety Appliances, et al,* under CA 1-73-50 (October 19, 1978). In addition to MSA, the estates of the deceased miners and the Sunshine Mining Co. brought actions against six chemical companies for the negligent manufacture and installation of polyurethane, alleging it caused the deaths of the miners and damage to the Sunshine Mining Co. The U.S. was sued for [the Bureau] negligently permitting the use of polyurethane foam in the mine, negligence in conducting the ventilation survey, and negligently conducting inspections, all of which allegedly contributed to the deaths of the miners and damage to the Sunshine Mining Co.

Of interest, the plaintiff's now agreed that the fire originated in the area of the 3400 level 09 bulkhead and the court determined "the evidence supports the view that spontaneous combustion occurred," which agreed with the Bureau Final Report and author's findings.

The judge ruled that polyurethane foam was not the "proximate cause of any damage" and the plaintiffs failed to prove negligence on the part of the companies and the Bureau.[25]

---

25 The District Court's decision was not the last word. In 1997, Robert Launhardt, Sunshine's safety director, wrote *The Sunshine Mine Fire Disaster: A View From the Inside* "to correct the record for the sake of history." His article is available on web site of the United States Mine Rescue Association at *www.usmra.com.* Launhardt challenged the Bureau's and Court's findings with scientific ignorance, bias, and untruths in an belated attempt to absolve Sunshine's misfeasance. Its lack of value is admitted by Launhardt's caveat: "Documents in my possession, in combination with my own observations, leave a gaping hole in the story of May 2, 1972. I also acknowledge that some of my information may be incorrect."

CHAPTER 20

POST-MORTEM

Causes of Death

The Shoshone County Coroner determined the cause of all deaths was carbon monoxide poisoning. His findings were accepted without question by the Bureau, Sunshine, and the relatives of the 91 miners killed in the nation's second-worst hard rock mine disaster. Nevertheless, the reasons for the individual deaths had to be examined case-by-case in my report. There was no single reason, but a combination of numerous factors that contributed to their succumbing to carbon monoxide. The Bureau Final Report listed 17 factors it believed contributed to the severity of the disaster and set out recommendations for new safety standards to prevent similar disasters in the future, which was the primary purpose of the Bureau's and author's reports. *(Figure No. 3 lists the Bureau Final Report factors verbatim.)*

Figure No. 3.

BUREAU FINAL REPORT LIST OF CONTRIBUTING FACTORS TO THE SUNSHINE MINE DISASTER

1. Ineffectiveness of stench warning system.

2. Delay in beginning mine evacuation.

3. Ineffectiveness of the mine communication system.

4. Inadequacy of the emergency escapeway system.

5. Inadequacy of the emergency fire plan.

6. Use of a series ventilation system.

7. Failure to seal abandoned areas of the mine.

8. Failure to monitor the mine atmosphere.

9. Failure to construct incombustible ventilation bulkheads.

10. Lack of remote controls on major underground fans.

11. Failure to maintain self-rescuers in useable condition.

12. Failure to train underground employees in use of self-rescuers.

13. Failure to instruct miners survival training.

14. Failure to designate anyone as being in charge of the entire operation in the absence of top mine officials.

15. Inability to use the No. 10 shaft chippy hoist.

16. Death of the No. 10 hoistman.

17. Failure to use both cages on the No. 10 shaft double-drum hoist.

The Bureau's and author's reports failed to mention the actions of individuals that might have contributed to the deaths or the quick thinking and heroic actions of the miners who saved lives. History demands such omissions be remedied and that the memories of the men who died or risked their lives to save others warrants a record, if for no one but their families and descendants. The author disagrees with the Bureau Final Report in several instances, which must be expected. Reasonable men may disagree, especially if viewed from different perspectives. The major cause of differences I attribute to my years of mine safety experience and the modern technological advantage of being able to set out the events and timing on a computer. For whatever reason, it also changed my findings and analysis from my official report.

Evacuation Orders

The Bureau concluded there was a delay by the foreman ordering the evacuation while they searched for the fire and they were reluctant to order the evacuation on their own volition because management officials were attending the annual stockholders meeting in Coeur d'Alene. The Bureau stated: "Smoke was discovered emanating from the bottom of the 910 raise on the 3700 level about 11:40 a.m." It then deduced: "[T]he evacuation was delayed at least 20 minutes while an investigation was conducted. Undoubtedly many more men could have been hoisted to the 3100 level and could have been traveled to safety, had it not been for the 20 minute delay in evacuation."

The Bureau's findings cannot be substantiated. There was testimony by three men riding the man train that there was no sign of smoke when it left the 3700 level No. 10 station between 11:35 and 11:40 a.m. and passed directly under the 910 raise several minutes later. Mechanics and cagers present around the No. 10 station a few minutes afterwards did not notice smoke. Smoke was first sighted by Gary Beckes, an electrician. Beckes checked the clock in the electric shop at 11:45, then put on his belt and walked outside, where he witnessed a haze drifting towards him turn into billowing smoke. Thus, the smoke was first detected and reported *after 11:45; possibly as late as 11:47 a.m.* (Dusty Rhoads and the others stranded on the 4400 level probably discovered smoke a few minutes earlier, could not communicate with any foreman at the time.) Beckes immediately told Arnold Anderson, who yelled to the foremen in the blue room that there was smoke in the drift.

Foremen Harvey Dionne and Gene Johnson responded instantaneously by running into the smoke and following it to the 910 raise, a distance of approximately 900 feet. Around the same time, several men listening on the phone heard Don Beehner call the blue room from the pipe shop and tell foreman Bob Bush that smoke was pouring from a bulkhead to the old workings between the pipe shop and 08 machine shop. The listeners heard Bob tell Don and the pipe fitters to go to the No. 10 station, *the first order in preparation for evacuation*, then call Pete Bennett in the 08 shop and tell him to check the area for a fire. Bob left the blue room with his brother and foreman, Jim Bush, on a Mancha motor to locate the fire. When they arrived at the 910 raise, Harvey was climbing down from his attempt to look up the raise. Under Gene's leadership, the four foremen immediately decided the fire was above the 3700 level and possibly on the 3400 level and to evacuate the mine from the 3100 level. Considering the distance between the blue room and the 910 raise, the foremen's *decision* to evacuate was made no later than seven or eight minutes after the smoke was detected. But Bob Bush's telephone order was instantaneous.

Bob ran back to the No. 10 station with Gene to assist in the evacuation. Harvey and Jim left on the Mancha motor to close the air door in an attempt to divert the smoke from being routed towards the No. 10 shaft and down it to the lower levels. Gene telephoned the surface maintenance shop and asked maintenance foreman Thomas Harrah to order Robert Launhardt, the safety engineer, to activate the stench warning and bring the McCaa self-contained breathing apparatus to the 3100 No. 10 station. Launhardt received Harrah's call between *12:01 and 12:02 p.m.* Gene then called the double-drum hoistman, Ira Sliger, who was hoisting the south cage loaded with muck. Sliger continued to raise the south cage to the 3100 level and dumped the muck at *12:03* in preparation to hoist the men. The sequence of events confirms the necessary *telephone* orders to evacuate were made at no more than between 14 to 16 minutes after the smoke was first detected. However, it is clear that the foremen's decision to evacuate the mine was made without hesitation earlier at the 910 raise.

Although Sunshine's posted "Procedure to Follow in Case of a Mine Fire" was outdated and its methods and strategies incomplete, it contained the following basic rule: "Send first available shift boss to ascertain the exact condition of the fire, by the safest available route. Have him report immediately, either by phone or in person." No supervisor should order an evacuation until he has determined the safest route. The foremen realized the men had to be evacuated on the 3100 level because of the heavy smoke and possible carbon monoxide on the 3700. The fact that Gary Beckes followed the foremen as far as the Strand substation and believed the smoke was too thick to walk to the Jewell shaft, supports their decision. The near death of Hap Fowler, the only man to walk out the 3700 level from the No. 10 station, and the deaths of Bob Bush, Pat Hobson, and Wayne Blalack substantiate that the 3700 level was inundated by carbon monoxide before the 3100 level. Also, the mechanics, electricians, and others hoisted from the 3700 level to the 3100 level, testified that the smoke was not as thick on the 3100 level. That it took 14 to 16 minutes to order the hoistman to begin the evacuation was necessary to determine the source of the smoke and the safest route.

No doubt, if Gene Johnson and the other foreman ordered an evacuation at the first sign of smoke, more men could have been hoisted in a 14 to 16-minute period. But whether they would have been evacuated to the 3100 level is conjecture. The 3700 level was the normal evacuation level and no one, even the Bureau's experts, expected the speed in which the smoke and carbon monoxide inundated the mine. It has never been witnessed before, nor since. If the foremen had not investigated the source of the smoke and determined the safest route was the 3100 level, dozens more men would have perished if evacuated on the 3700 level. It was a sound judgment call that may be debated for many years, but it was a judgment only the foremen on the scene could have made under the conditions they were aware of at the time.

The No. 10 Double-drum Hoist

The No. 10 chippy hoist, with a four-deck cage normally capable of carrying 48 men, could only hoist to the 3700 level. The No. 10 double drum-hoist, limited to a single nine-man cage hung below each of its two skips, was a poor substitute during a fire, but the only means to hoist to the 3100 level. Testimony by several witnesses was that Gene Johnson instructed Ira Sliger to only use one cage. Sliger testified it was too dangerous to hoist men with tons of muck in the skip overhead, although that morning he had twice hoisted men to the 3400 level when loaded with muck.

Several foremen testified that the use of only one double-drum cage was a proper decision. Again, reasonable men may differ in matters of judgment, but there were also unmentioned factors. The hoisting by Sliger, a sixty-one-year-old with silicosis and one lung, was erratic. Gene Johnson ordered him to escape because of his health as Sliger was lowering the south cage to the 5000 level the first time.

After being told there was a fire and to get his cager, Sliger dumped the muck from the south cage on the 3100 level at 12:03 p.m. then dropped it to around the 4400 level at 12:05 and held it there while he raised the north cage to the 4400 level at 12:07.

Meanwhile, he lowered the south cage from the 4400 level at 12:06 to pick up Byron Schulz, his cager, who had signaled for him to pick up Elmer Kitchen, a miner acting as a second cager above him. The cage stopped slightly above the 5600 pocket a few seconds before 12:08, then was immediately raised above the 5600 level and instantly dropped to above the pocket, where he picked up Schulz a few seconds before 12:10. Sliger did not pick up Kitchen and took over seven minutes to pick up Schulz *after being told of the fire.*

Sliger's raising of the north cage from the 4400 level a few seconds after 12:17 to the 3700 level cannot be explained. The cage had been parked there for ten minutes and men on the 4400 level had been signaling for a cage for one-half hour. The cage arrived on the 3700 level at 12:18:30. He raised the cage from the 3700 level at 12:22 to around the 3250 level, where it remained until 12:27 before being lowered it to the 4200 level at 12:28. Tragically, nine men were on the north cage and got off on the 3700 level. It was the level they traveled every day and they had every reason to believe they were being evacuated. Instead they succumbed to the carbon monoxide and perished on the level that had been evacuated two minutes earlier. [26]

The Bureau determined that the death of Robert "Bob" Scanlan, the No. 10 double-drum second hoistman contributed to the number of deaths. It postulated, if Bob survived and raised all 21 men on the 5200 level, they could have walked to the Jewell. According to the Bureau, there were 24 self-rescuers stored on 5200 level, yet it could not say if any of the victims on the 5200 used self-rescuers, nor, if used, how long the one-half-hour duration devices were worn by men not trained in their use. Most, if not all, had been exposed to the carbon monoxide for at least one-half hour and up to an hour by the time the 5000 level was evacuated. If they were hoisted to 3100 level, they would have encountered dead and dying men around the shaft station and in a drift they were not familiar with, and would have had to walk over 2,000 feet to fresh air. It is problematic that few, if any, could have survived unless they were

---

26 The fact that the carbon monoxide overcame the experienced miners familiar with the level is evidence that the smoke and toxic gas were far worse on the 3700 level that the 3100 level and further supports the foremen's judgement and decision to evacuate the mine from the 3100 level.

young, healthy, and capable of enduring abnormally high concentrations of carboxyhemoglobin. But it was a possibility, however slight.

It was not determined if Sliger had an annual medical examination to determine if he was physically fit to operate a hoist pursuant to advisory standard 57.19-58 (later made mandatory). It is axiomatic that a sixty-one-year-old man with silicosis would be more susceptible to carbon monoxide than a healthy individual and its exposure would affect his ability to perform as a hoistman. It also explains why Gene Johnson relieved him of his duties and asked Bob Scanlan to take over. Unfortunately, Scanlan had been exposed to lethal concentrations of carbon monoxide while Sliger was operating the hoist, and he succumbed soon afterwards, but not before he valiantly stayed at the hoist until the men from the 5000, 5400, 5600, and 5800 levels had been raised. Bob Scanlan was one of the true heroes of the disaster.

After battling through the 1966 MNM Act's prolonged rule-making process, on June 1, 1979, MSHA promulgated MESA's proposed mandatory standard 57.11-59, requiring independent respirable atmospheres and a two-hour self-contained breathing apparatus for escape during evacuations be provided hoist operators.

The Bureau listed the failure to utilize both the north and south cages and the lack of an "adequate number of qualified cagers" were contributing factors to the severity of the disaster. Several foremen testified that the use of one cage was sound judgment, but they were not questioned whether their rationale would have been different if Bob Scanlan had been the hoist operator. Sliger testified he only had one cager, although he had two, Byron Schulz and Elmer Kitchen, and Greg Dionne acted as a cager. Thus, the Bureau's and foremen's conclusions are debatable.

The Bureau's recommendation that key personnel be trained as cagers is valid, although most key personnel act as cagers on a regular basis. There was no shortage of men capable of acting as cagers. Twenty-one-year-old Byron Schulz was an experienced cager, as was fifty-four-year-old shaft miner Elmer Kitchen. The chippy hoist cagers, twenty-one-year-old Randy Peterson and nineteen-year-old Roger Findley were also available. Gene said the chippy cagers were not needed and should walk to the Jewell. However, Roger insisted he help the foreman count the men getting off the cages on the 3100 level. Roger stayed at the 3100 level station until Gene collapsed and Roger was the second last man to walk out. He barely made it to fresh air with the help of James Zingler and others.

Possibly, Gene Johnson requested Greg Dionne, a pipe fitter, to act as cager because he was slightly older and more experienced than Byron and Randy and Gene had more confidence in Greg during an emergency, although Byron served as a second cager with Greg. Every foreman and shifter and many other miners were qualified to act as cagers. Gene Johnson and Doug Wiederrick acted as cagers. Charles Casteel and Virgil Bebb, experienced shifters, assisted Gene on the 3100 level during the hoisting and were capable of acting as cagers. Greg Dionne and Byron Schulz risked their lives to save their fellow miners. Greg died in the effort. Byron was the last man to escape and had to be rescued before reaching fresh air. The above points out that cagers and key personnel cannot rely on self-rescuers and that cagers should be provided self-contained breathing apparatuses during a fire emergency.

Lack of Supervision

In my report I disagreed with the Bureau Final Report finding that the attendance of Sunshine's top management officials at the annual stockholders meeting caused the foremen to delay ordering the evacuation. I also said it was not a violation of advisory standard 57.18-9: "A competent person should be in charge at all times when men are working." My brief comments were that the concept had merit, but the standard was vague and unenforceable, and I limited my findings to the foremen's actions in connection with ordering the evacuation. As a result, I failed to analyze the other consequences of the lack of management supervision.

The Bureau correctly pointed out that the individual foremen were reluctant to decide whether the exhaust fans on the 3400 level should be cut off to stop the contaminated air from recirculating over the fire and coursing it into the fresh air on the 3100 and 3700 levels. The decision to change the ventilation during a fire is always dangerous, as miners may be depending on the known airflows to seek refuge. Sunshine's "Fire Protection and Escape Plan" emphasized:

IT IS OF UTMOST IMPORTANCE IN A MINE
FIRE THAT THE VENTILATION IS NOT
ALTERED AT RANDOM BY ANYONE. NEVER
LEAVE A DRAFT DOOR OPEN OR TAMPER
WITH A FAN DURING A FIRE. If changes in the
ventilation will be of benefit to the men, the decision must be made by responsible management personnel who are thoroughly familiar with the
ventilation system.

With no responsible management personnel at the mine, Delbert "Dusty" Rhoads and Arnold Anderson, both experienced lead
men, volunteered to risk their lives by going to the 3400 to turn off
the exhaust air fans in an effort to stop the smoke and carbon monoxide from recirculating into the fresh air. Both were overcome by carbon monoxide while waiting for authorization. Regardless of
whether the fans should have been cut off, Dusty Rhoads and Arnold
Anderson, who bravely volunteered to help their fellow miners, died
because no management personnel were at the mine to give them
instructions.

The lack of management at the mine was a major contributing factor to the failure of Robert Launhardt to deliver the McCaa self-contained breathing apparatuses to the 3100 No. 10 station. Sunshine's
outdated mine fire procedures called for first notifying the Jewell
chippy hoistman to dump the stench in the compressed air line and
notify the mine superintendent. Neither was done because the
stench system had been removed from the hoist room a year earlier
and the mine superintendent was not at the mine. In addition, as stated by the Bureau, the emergency fire plan was inadequate.[27] The
safety engineer and his predecessor, whose task was to prepare the
plan, failed to keep it current.

---

27 There was no standard specifically requiring the posting of fire emergency
    plans, although most mines posted plans. Advisory standard 57.4-32 mere-
    ly required that employees be instructed in the applicable procedures. The
    Bureau proposed mandatory standard 57.11 -53 on December 9, 1972,
    requiring detailed escape plans, which was finally adopted on March 13,
    1974, after objections and the usual protracted rulemaking process.

Launhardt was ill-prepared to deliver the life-saving equipment and there were no management personnel on the surface to direct and assist him in the effort, except for maintenance foreman, Tom Harrah. After activating the stench warning, Launhardt: (1) wasted time on the surface returning to his office to obtain carbon monoxide detector; (2) wasted precious minutes making phone calls when others were available in his office to call; (3) waited for a cage to take him to the 3100 level because no one was told to hold the cage for him; (4) had no management personnel to arrange transportation to the No. 10 station; (5) had no one to assemble a full crew to assist him; and (6) had to walk back 400 feet when the train returned from the No. 10 station.

Why Harrah did not tell Launhardt there was a mine fire and Gene Johnson needed the McCaa apparatus underground when he telephoned was not explained. It could have saved Launhardt from returning to his office on one occasion and Launhardt could have obtained assistance in getting the apparatus to the Jewell top station faster. No doubt, time was wasted because of the lack of organization and foresight.

By the time Launhardt left the 3100 Jewell station, the last survivors from the 5000 level had walked to the Jewell and the men on the No. 10 station were dead or dying, except for Roger Findley and Byron Schulz. Schulz, the last to make it out alive, left the hoist room after Bob Scanlon hoisted the men from the 5400, 5600, and 5800 levels at 1:01 p.m., returned to the hoist room with Doug Wiederrick, then went to the station to wet his shirt, before he ran out the drift approximately 1,300 feet and was rescued by Launhardt and the others.

Larry Hawkins, James Zingler, and Donald Beehner volunteered to assist Launhardt to deliver the McCaas to Gene Johnson. Although the three were trained in the use of self-contained breathing apparatuses, Hawkins and Zingler were not technically qualified because of weight and medical reasons and Beehner had recently walked from the No. 10 station and been exposed to carbon monoxide for over one-half hour. Nor was Launhardt technically qualified to wear an apparatus in a contaminated atmosphere because he had not taken a refresher course in over five years. The safety engineer, as the leader, failed to assure than Beehner and Zingler had their McCaas on after determining the carbon monoxide level was lethal.

After running into Roger Findley and sending Zingler to take him to fresh air, Byron Schulz was discovered in distress. Beehner risked his life by giving Schulz oxygen from his McCaa and within seconds was overcome and died. Hawkins, unaware he had torn a hole in his inhalation hose, was forced to run approximately 500 feet to fresh air, leaving Launhardt alone with Schulz. After Schulz told his rescuers that everyone on the No. 10 station was dead, Launhardt's mission to deliver the McCaas to Gene Johnson was aborted.

The chaotic attempt to deliver the McCaas to the No. 10 station was flawed from the beginning because of the lack of planning and management officials not on the scene. From the time Launhardt claims he was called to activate the stench and told to deliver the McCaas to the 3100 No. 10 station at 12:01 or 12:02 p.m. until he ran into Schulz, over one hour elapsed. Launhardt admitted during his deposition, "[B]y the time the motor came out [it was] close to one o'clock."

No one can guess how many men could have been saved if the attempt was organized and managed with a sense of urgency. Launhardt testified at the July 21, 1972, hearing that when he arrived on the surface afterwards, "I realized then that we had a much more serious condition in the mine than what I had anticipated, and that we would need [a] much better organized rescue attempt." During an interview for *Critical Rescue* aired over the Discovery Channel on June 5, 2003, he said the sight of the smoke coming out the exhaust tunnel when he emerged from his office, "Sent a chill up his spine." His statements are conflicting.

The fact that there was no management personnel in charge of the mine was a contributing cause to the deaths of Dusty Rhoads and Arnold Anderson and others because of the failure to deliver of the breathing apparatuses to Gene Johnson at the 3100 No. 10 shaft station in a timely manner. It was violation of the vague advisory standard 57.18-9, later strengthened by MSHA to require "a competent person designated by the mine operator shall be in attendance to take charge in case of an emergency." Sunshine had no competent person in charge at the time of the disaster and the failure contributed to the confusion and deaths.

Conjecture and the word "if" always loom after a disaster. One could speculate, if the ten McCaa self-contained breathing apparatuses Gene ordered had arrived at the 3100 level within a reasonable time, more lives could have been saved. Only heroes like Gene Johnson, Charles Casteel, Virgil Bebb, and Bob Scanlan knew whether the timely arrival of the McCaas would have helped more men survive. But they cannot tell us. If the author was forced to speculate, I would venture that they would be alive to tell us if the McCaas had been delivered within a reasonable time.

Self-Rescuers

Sunshine took pride that it provided self-rescuers when they were not required under the 1966 MNM Act or Bureau regulations. However, its boasting was tarnished by its failure to instruct the men in the use of the devices and the company's storage and maintenance practices. No doubt providing self-rescuers saved lives, but the lack of an adequate training program resulted in deaths. Sunshine submitted conflicting data that it stored either 184 or 228 self-rescuers at shaft stations on the active levels and 3700 safety room. The Bureau Final Report stated there were only 156. Neither claim could be confirmed after the fire. During the evacuation the devices were discarded near the Jewell shaft and on the surface, and several miners took theirs home as souvenirs of the device that saved their life.

The failure to provide the devices on the 5400 and 5600 levels and 5800 shaft area was inexcusable and contributed to the number of deaths. There was no evidence that a miner could not obtain a self-rescuer on the levels they were furnished. However, the 1969 Coal Act and current regulations require every miner be provided with a self-rescuer and carry or wear it is for a good reason. The storage of the life-saving devices at various locations did not make them readily available to miners working several thousand feet away. It appears that 31 men were working on the 3700 level, but only 24 devices were stored on the level. Pat Hobson, a mechanic stationed in the 08 shop over 1,000 feet from where they were stored, died when walking out the 3700 level. No self-rescuers were stored in the Jewell Shaft area. While self-rescuers should only be used as a means of escape during a fire, one cannot but wonder if Roberto Diaz and Paul Johnson, who left the safety of the Jewell shaft area and lost their lives while attempting save three fellow miners, might have survived if they had self-rescuers.

According to the Bureau Final Report, 80 men did not use self-rescuers. (The Bureau could not state with certainty if the 22 men on the 5200 level used them.) *(See Figure No. 4.)*

Figure No. 4
SELF-RESCUER USE

Survivors:

Used	43
Did not use	<u>37</u>
	80

Died:

Used	26
Did not use	43
Unknown (5200 level)	<u>22</u>
	91
Rescued-Used	<u>2</u>
Total men in mine	173

The record is replete with testimony of men who did not know how to activate the devices and were not familiar with their operation because of the lack of training. Without training, which would not have involved more than one hour instruction, resulted in their mis-use. A number of men complained the self-rescuers became hot and removed them under the mistaken belief that they were not working properly. Training would have told them that the greater the concentration of carbon monoxide, the self-rescuer's oxidation process generated higher temperatures. It also created the impression they were breathing smoke or other contaminants because the air passing through the devices made their mouths and throats dry and caused them to remove them from their mouths. Removing the devices in the lethal atmosphere for even minutes could result in death.

No one can state with certainty if any men died because they could not activate their self-rescuers, which was a relatively simple process of breaking a seal and attaching nose clips on the pre-1969 B-1447 model. But attempting it for the first time during a fire is not the proper time to learn. There were also numerous instances where miners had never handled or seen a self-rescuer, no doubt adding to their confusion and anxiety. Most hit the button with their wrenches if they could not depress it with their thumbs. The self-rescuers were stored on the stations in padlocked cabinets to prevent tampering with the devices that could be rendered useless by exposure to air, but the cabinets were opened easily by a swipe with a miner's wrench. Ironically, the devices were sometimes opened and their usefulness destroyed by curious miners desiring to examine them, which would have been cured by training.

Launhardt, as safety engineer, testified that he periodically inspected the self rescuers, but did not maintain a record of the inspections. Two miners testified that when they opened the cartons they discovered they were rusty. According to Sunshine's records, the self-rescuers were the pre-1969 B-1447 models except for 36 newer B-14F76 models. The Bureau sent 31 pre-1969 models found in the mine on the 4200, 4400, 4600, 4800, and 5000 levels after the fire to its Technical Support Center laboratory for testing that revealed disquieting and surprising results.[28] Of the 31 shipped, the seal on one was broken and was not tested, one was kept for later testing, and 20 were rusted due to their exposure to the air and humidity in the mine and could not be tested. Of the nine tested, all passed the carbon monoxide test, even though eight exceeded manufacturer's, Mine Safety Appliances Company (MSA), recommended five-year shelf life. (The two oldest were 15 and 20 years old.)

The only deterioration noted on those tested was that the gasket on the cover appeared "vulcanized," which the Bureau reported made them difficult to open and many miners said they forced them open by hitting them with a ten-inch wrench. MSA experts testified that the gasket was needed to keep the hopcalite cartridge sealed in a vacuum and the seal could be expected to deteriorate after storage in the high heat and humidity of a mine for many years. Yet the

---

28 On May 20, 1972, the Bureau also sent eight pre-1969 self-rescuers to its Pittsburgh Technical Support Center for testing. Unfortunately, they were not properly sealed for shipment and the results were withdrawn from the Bureau Final Report at the May hearing. Of the eight, two were rusted and could not be tested. Three were deemed not suitable for use and three were found in working order. The most remarkable find was that two were determined useable were manufactured in 1952, fifteen years in excess of the manufacturer's five-year recommended shelf life.

Bureau's lab technicians reported that of the nine buttons tested to break the seal, six opened easily, two required the pressure of both thumbs, and one had to tapped with the handle of a screwdriver. Again, training would have mitigated the confusion. But it doesn't explain why life-saving self-rescuers were discovered rusted, if Sunshine routinely inspected them, as Launhardt claimed. Nor does it justify why they were kept in use many years after the manufacture's recommended shelf life.

Stench Warning

The Bureau Final Report stated that the stench-warning system was not effective, a violation of mandatory standard 57.4-51 and a factor in the cause of deaths, which Sunshine denied. A Bureau test of the system after the fire with the same quantity of ethyl mercaptan used by Sunshine, revealed the stench was detected within 15 minutes after activation in all locations of the mine except the West Syndicate lateral drift, but dissipated within three to four minutes. Utilizing a 1920 Bureau technical paper, the Bureau determined the amount of ethyl mercaptan was only about 20 percent of the necessary amount. (That the Bureau and mine operators had to rely on a technical paper over fifty years old is inexcusable.) A review of the miners' depositions reveals not a single miner swore he smelled the stench. But is understandable. The miners had never been exposed to the stench and most had no idea what it smelled like, nor had Sunshine tested the system.

With the exception of John Davis, Orlin Nelson, and Paul Russell, miners on the 4200 level 1,500 feet from the No. 10 station, all the men underground were made aware of the fire by the smoke or verbally told. As the three men died in the stope and were the only men working on the 4200 level, it is probable they never smelled the stench or did not know what the odor was. If they had, they would have gone to the No. 10 station. (The south cage stopped at the 4200 level at 12:20, but left 15 seconds later empty.)

The Bureau commented that the delayed activation of the stench and the density of the smoke might have been factors in its ineffectiveness in reference to its claimed delay in ordering the evacuation. But other than three men on the 4200 level, it is unlikely that effectiveness of the stench system or the delay in being activated

212 ••• James M. Day

was a factor in any deaths. All the other men died attempting to escape, including waiting for a hoist. The Bureau's implication that a delay in ordering the stench activated was in effect a delay in ordering the evacuation is misplaced. The actual orders to start the evacuation were given to the No. 10 double-drum hoistman by Gene Johnson and to the miners by phone by Bob Bush and Jim Salyer.

Nevertheless, the Bureau properly recommended that the stench be tested every six months during evacuation drills and regulations were adopted requiring drills when the miners would be exposed to the stench.

Mine Communications

There is no doubt that the single-circuit telephone system was ineffective during the disaster, but there is no clear evidence it was a factor in the deaths of any men. For reasons never explained, the emergency line to the surface was not used to notify the safety engineer. If the emergency telephone line been used to contact the safety engineer, Robert Launhardt, it is possible he would have been able to reach the 3100 No. 10 station with the McCaa self-contained breathing apparatus and his ad hoc rescue crew could have saved the lives of Gene Johnson, the hoistman, and others. But such is speculation.

Lack of Remote Controls on Fans

The Bureau found that the lack of remote controls was a factor causing the severity of the disaster and a violation of advisory standard 57.5-21. Notwithstanding whether or not Dusty Rhoads and Arnold Anderson were correct in going to the 3400 level to turn off the exhaust fans, they would not have traveled to the level if the fans had been provided with remote controls *on the surface*. Today, remote controls are required; however, current standard 57.8519 requires only that the "controls be placed at a suitable protected location and *preferably* on the surface." *(Emphasis added.)* As history has sadly often proven, will it take a fire that cuts off the "protected location" and the death of miners to promulgate a standard requiring remote controls on the surface?

Series Ventilation System and Sealing of Bulkheads

The Bureau Final Report broadly stated: "The mine ventilation system was not designed to reduce hazards by a mine fire." This included the failure to seal abandoned areas and construct incombustible bulkheads, which the Bureau required before the mine was permitted to reopen. The Bureau also required Sunshine to install carbon monoxide detectors at locations throughout the mine before reopening. Today incombustible bulkheads are not required in hard rock mines.

Sunshine's suit against the government, based in part on the alleged negligence of the Bureau's engineers reporting and conducting the ventilation survey, was dismissed by the U.S. District Court because Sunshine failed to prove negligence. Nevertheless, Kenneth Russell, the Bureau's Subdistrict Manager and an experienced mining engineer, pointed out during the hearing on July 18, 1972, that the series ventilation system could be expected cause a rapid build up of smoke and carbon monoxide if there is a short circuit in the system feeding the contaminated air from the exhaust air flow into intake air flow, which was specifically found as a cause in the Bureau Final Report. Although a short circuit in a series ventilation system is not prohibited in the current regulations, standard 57.8520 requires that a mine ventilation plan be submitted to the MSHA District Manager for review.

One of the reasons the court determined that the Bureau was not negligent was its finding: "The [ventilation] survey was properly carried out. It was not the function nor the purpose of this survey to enforce any safety standards." The court's ruling is contrary to a memorandum to the Bureau's Western District Manager, Allen Look, and Subdistrict manager, Kenneth Russell, from Roland Wilson dated April 7, 1972, after Wilson read the ventilation survey (25 days before the disaster). Wilson stated that he found no fault with the technical content of the report, but that it failed to consider health and safety and listed numerous items that were not considered. Although the series ventilation system was not specifically mentioned in the brief memorandum, he concluded: "When it comes to the subject of ventilation, especially where we have our weakest standards, their [Technical Support] participation should be given to the overall Bureau safety program." Hopefully, standard 57.8520 will prevent similar failures.

Failure to Monitor the Mine Atmosphere

The Bureau Final Report found that the fire smoldered for a considerable time before it broke through the bulkhead and Sunshine failed to make tests of the mine atmosphere in violation of former advisory standard 57.5-26, which read:

> Instruments should be provided to test the mine atmosphere quantitatively for carbon monoxide, nitrogen oxide, and other gases that occur in the mine. Test should be conducted as frequently as necessary to assure that the required quality of air is maintained.

While Sunshine did not perform the tests on a regular or daily basis, the safety engineer claimed he periodically tested the atmosphere at various locations in the mine for carbon monoxide. The Bureau believed it was uncertain whether the carbon monoxide could have been detected in the intake air until one of the bulkheads broke through and short-circuited into the intake air. At the time, Sunshine's tests were made by hand-held detectors because detection equipment was not commercially available to continuously monitor for carbon monoxide in the high humidity of the exhaust airways.

Advisory standards were eliminated under the 1977 Mine Act. Congress required MSHA and a special advisory committee containing three members from industry, three member from labor, and seven members having no economic industry in the mining industry to review all advisory standards with a view to upgrade them and make them mandatory. MSHA and the special advisory committee revoked advisory standard 57.5-26. Their flawed review six years after the Sunshine disaster was that the standard fell under Subpart D — Air Quality and applied to miners exposure to airborne contaminants, a health standard, without considering safety. Carbon monoxide is not only a health hazard, it should be monitored for safety reasons, as it indicates a fire that could otherwise go undetected, especially in abandoned areas of the mine. The periodic testing for carbon monoxide as an airborne contaminant is no substitute for the continuous monitoring for safety to detect a fire.

Continuous carbon monoxide detectors capable of operating at underground locations and in the high humidity of exhaust air have been commercially available and widely used in deep hard rock mines for two decades. On two occasions, such monitors detected underground fires in the Homestake Mine in the mid 1980s. MSHA's coal mine standard 75.351 requires the continuous monitoring for carbon monoxide at underground locations from the surface capable of detecting five parts per million above the ambient air at particular locations. It is long past time for MSHA to reassess the need for the continuous monitoring for carbon monoxide and issue the necessary regulations.

In conclusion, the author's findings were based on an exhaustive study of the records and experience. It disagrees with the Bureau Final Report in several instances. No doubt, others may hold different opinions. What cannot be denied is the fact that the Sunshine Mine, the Bureau, and our government could have done more to insure mine safety and, if they had, more miners would have survived the horrible disaster.

HEROES

For fear of leaving a single miner out of any honor roll of heroes, the author leaves it to the reader to determine those men who risked their lives to save their fellow miners. Further, I cannot sum up the actions of the foremen and shifters better than Gordon Osterberg, 4600 level motorman, when asked during his May 9, 1972, deposition while the rescue attempt was continuing, if the foremen and shifters performed their responsibilities:

Well, there was an awful lot of shifters not coming out from under there. They stayed there where they belonged. I would say they done good.

CHAPTER 21

MESA

The Bureaucracy

My appointment a MESA Administrator was well-received in the press. Drew Von Bergen's complimentary UPI article, "Miners Gaining a Voice," appeared in dozens of newspapers throughout the country. Even Ward Sinclair of the Louisville *Courier*-Journal, from the Democrat left, was non-committal. Sinclair's worst criticism was I had worked on Senator Barry Goldwater's 1964 presidential campaign.

Von Bergen and Sinclair reported that one of my major problems was my preordained deputy, Donald P. Schlick, the Bureau's Deputy Director for Health and Safety. Schlick, a macho former college football lineman, had ruled health and safety with a velvet glove shielding an iron fist and had appointed my inherited bureaucracy. He had been accused of accepting perks, such as rides in a mining company jet, and publicly remarked, "It was safer to work in a mine than drive a car." The UMWA opposed Schlick holding any position of authority, as if I could fire a career civil servant without cause. I did not know Don Schlick except by reputation and he accepted an invitation to tour Soviet Union coal mines when I took over, paving the way for me to reorganize MESA during the interval.

John "Jack" W. Crawford, deputy for coal mine health and safety, and Arthur "Art" P. Nelson, his recently appointed metal and nonmetal mine counterpart to replace Stanley Jarrett, were excellent administrators as well as capable mining engineers. It was a simple bureaucratic maneuver to eliminate Schlick's deputy position, authorize Jack and Art to report directly to me as assistant administrators, and name Don as Assistant Administrator for Technical Support. Don kept his grade and Jack and Art moved up a notch. It proved to be a good move. Don was a hard-driving problem solver who got things done without bureaucratic delay, and his development of Technical Support with its cadre of extremely skilled engineers greatly increased MSHA's technical capabilities. I never had any regrets about the reorganization, even when I had to get a spittoon in my office for tobacco-chewing Jack Crawford and Herschel H. Potter, his exceptionally competent and dedicated deputy for coal mine safety.

The idea to transfer Don came from Gilbert O. Lockwood, my assistant for administration at the OHA, a bureaucratic genius who joined me as Assistant Administrator for Administration at MSHA. The meat-cleaver approach severing the Bureau's health and safety functions had left MESA with scant administrative support personnel, which had to be organized. As I had no faith in the Interior Department's Solicitor's Office for legal advice, except for a handful of capable administrative trial attorneys, I asked Tom Mascolino, my top legal assistant at the OHA, to join MESA as my legal advisor and hire a small staff of lawyers.

To my surprise, the reorganization headed by a lawyer instead of a mining engineer was welcomed. Most high-level staff were skeptical of political appointees from either labor or industry, fearing they would have an institutional bias. After I told them that I saw my task of administrator as organizing the agency, obtaining the necessary congressional budget, and supporting MESA's experts in their enforcement of the law we became an excellent team. The budget proved easy. Congress could not deny funding an appropriation for one hundred additional inspectors to meet the mandated minimum four annual inspections of underground coal mines and two annual inspections of surface coal mines under the 1969 Coal Act. After the Sunshine disaster, Congress accepted our budget request for sufficient metal and nonmetal mine inspectors to inspect the underground mines twice annually, even though the 1966 MNM Act only required one annual inspection.

The collection of the civil penalties was a major enforcement problem. After only six weeks on the job, I was called before the House Government Operations Subcommittee and chastised for mishandling the penalty-collection program as if had been on the job for years. During the first four years of the 1969 Coal Act, only $4.7 million had been collected out of $25.4 million assessed. There was also an admitted backlog of 60,000 violations that had not been assessed, although no one really knew the actual number, and 15,000 civil penalty cases involving 70,000 violations pending before administrative law judges. At the time, the Bureau was issuing 75,000 notices of violation annually. The collection process required not only adding manpower, but publicizing and proving tough enforcement.

Good fortune arrived my first week on the job in the form of two vice presidents from a major coal company paying a courtesy call on the new administrator to give him a free advice how to run MESA. Before their arrival, I requested a report on the company's safety record and violations. Herschel Potter knew I would be interested in a newspaper article quoting one of my visitors bragging that the company had not paid a single assessment out of a total of almost $1 million. After listening to their advice, I advised them I had no objection to their appealing improperly issued violations and excessive assessments, but that bragging about flaunting the system was part of a conspiracy to cripple the penalty system and unacceptable. I recommended their company install a bed in each of its fifty-odd coal mines because I was assigning an inspector to live at each mine until they "straightened out their act." Two weeks later, the company paid almost $400,000 in assessments and one month later an additional $200,000 arrived in the mail. After MESA obtained additional inspectors, we developed an inspection program to increase the number of inspections of the twenty-five coal mines with a highest number of violations and injuries. Word of the "hit list" and that flooding the penalty system with scurrilous appeals spread, and would not be tolerated, reduced injuries and lessened frivolous appeals.

Training mine inspectors as enforcement officers was crucial. Not to denigrate the inspectors, required to have a minimum of five years working in the mines under the 1969 Coal Act, few had more than a high school education. They had to be trained to document violations, much like a policeman reporting a crime, and to testify at hearings. Experienced inspectors and mining engineers were trained to investigate accidents and gather evidence similar to crime scene investigators. Help came in the form of the National Mine Health and Safety Academy in Beckley, West Virginia, MESA staff jokingly called

"Byrdland" after Senator Robert C. Byrd, Democrat from West Virginia. The academy was established to train inspectors in their basic duties, the uniform interpretation of the regulations, and such specialties as electricity, roof control, and other major causes of fatalities. Senator Byrd thought specialization training was a good idea, especially if it was money spent in West Virginia. He added $9 million to MESA's appropriation the Interior Department and the Office of Management and Budget (OMB) had eliminated from MESA's budget request. I was accused of going behind the Republican administration's back during a budget crunch when most federal agency appropriations were being slashed, which was untrue.

During my House of Representatives budget hearing several weeks later, a Republican and Democrat member of appropriations committee from Pennsylvania complained that I gave money to West Virginia, but nothing was earmarked for Pennsylvania. Off the record, I was told to supply them with a statement of $5 million in programs to be added to the budget they could announce was going into the economy of Pennsylvania. Of course, I had to advise the Interior Department budget number crunchers, who forever branded me as a "big spender."

Issuing new health and safety standards was a cross to bear, especially the so-called "Sunshine" standards the Bureau had proposed that were trapped in the rulemaking quagmire. The problem of an advisory committee under the 1966 MNM Act was partially solved after I recommended to Secretary Morton that he appoint a new slate of members who I selected because they were more safety conscious. As expected, politics prevented a clean sweep.

One afternoon I flew into a tirade about the delay in issuing the Sunshine and several important coal standards. Herschel Potter, the deputy assistant administrator for coal mine safety who took the brunt of my harangue, told me it was impossible to release any standard in less than nine months and that it took over a one year if they were controversial. I insisted he prove it. Several weeks later he gave me a detailed report listing every bureaucratic step required. Regulations under the 1969 Coal Act required a minimum of 260 days, if there were no adverse comments or a hearing, and 600 days, if there were adverse comments. Under the 1966 MNM Act, the minimum was 395 days without hearing and 712 days if a hearing was required. Not only was Interior's vast bureaucracy involved, but the OMB, Environmental Protection Agency, Department of Justice, Department of Commerce, and Department of Health, Education and Welfare were required to comment on everything from legal issues, inflationary impact, excess paperwork, environmental impact to international trade. As expected, the Bureau of Mines commented on the regulation's effect on mining. When I presented the findings at Secretary Morton's weekly meeting of assistant secretaries and bureau heads, everyone denied they were the cause, but Herschel stood like a rock and listed their records during the past two years. In the end we were fighting the entire federal bureaucracy, and only managed to get the time reduced 45 to 90 days.

Labor Relations

One of my first appointments was to create an assistant for labor liaison to maintain day-to-day contact with the UMWA, Steelworkers, Operating Engineers, and other unions representing miners. Wayne M. Grames, a crusty, cigar-chewing mining engineer and Chief of Training Operations, fit the bill because of his experience in organizing mine safety training programs and dealing with union officials. His first priority was to arrange a meeting with the new UMWA President, Arnold Miller, and his staff, which could have posed as poster models for the young radicals of the 1960s. Miller was a quiet, soft-spoken former miner with black lung from his years in the coal mines who still smoked despite the debilitating disease. From the outset I liked Miller. He was honest and dedicated to creating better working conditions for the nation's 190,000 coal miners. Miller was also a far cry from the corrupt UMWA leaders of recent years. The former UMWA president, W.A. "Tony" Boyle, was convicted of murdering his defeated challenger to the union's presidency, Joseph A. "Jock" Yablonski, and the Department of Labor took control of the union after the disputed rigged election.

Miller had been elected to replace Boyle and he distrusted the UMWA's organization hierarchy. He installed the young Miners for Democracy militants in the union's headquarters who had helped elect them and relied on their advice. After my cordial meeting with Miller, he told the press he was impressed with my plans and looked forward to working with me. But, like all meetings with Miller, he was accompanied by no less that three of his Young Turks and seldom by a former coal miner or engineer. Miller's entourage wouldn't let him out of their sight and it soon became apparent that they wanted to use health and safety as a lever in their collective bargaining and dealings with the coal companies.

Within months, I made several decisions the UMWA opposed, which was expected. No one can satisfy both labor and industry. Secretary Morton laughed and quipped: "I have a stack of complaints six inches high from the UMWA complaining that you're a bastard and stack six inches high from the mining industry saying your a son-of-a-bitch. You must be doing something right." Relations hit a nadir at a reception Miller gave for Sir Joseph "Sir Joe" Gormley, the head of the British coal miners union. One of Miller's young shadow aides accused me of being "on the take from the mining industry." I told him: "If he repeated the accusation outside in the alley and he would loose his teeth." Sir Joe laughed and told me he would rather deal with me rather than Britain's stuffy National Coal Board and invited me to visit him in London. But it ended possible cordial relations with the UMWA.

The UMWA tried to oust me from the job. My appointment did not require I be confirmed by the Senate because I was grandfathered under an appointment before the legislation requiring confirmation. However, the White House sent my name for confirmation after I had offended the UMWA and mining industry with hard decisions. A cartoon by Morrie Brickman in the *Washington Star* said it all: "He's a perfect man for the job. He has nerves of steel, is a top-notch administrator . . . and nobody likes him." The UMWA sent 1,500 miners to picket the Interior Department for my ouster while they were in Washington for a meeting. I responded to a *Washington Star* reporter: "Frankly, they better hurry up because I'm only going to stay in this job another year." (He omitted my use of "damn job.")

the small society   **by Brickman**

FOR JAMES M. DAY — WITH ALL THE BEST —
MORRIE BRICKMAN

Democrat Senator Harrison Williams of New Jersey, Chairman of the Senate Labor Committee, claimed he had the votes to bottle up my nomination in the committee. Fortunately, I had friends in the Operating Engineers, battling the UMWA for representation in the open pit coal mines in the West. The Operating Engineers advised Senator Williams that there were no coal mines in New Jersey, but there were 15,000 operating engineers who liked Jim Day. Two days later Senator Williams said my appointment was grandfathered and I did not require Senate confirmation.[29]

The End

Personally, the task of MESA Administrator was a lose-lose job, regardless of results. By the end of the 1974, the number of violation citations was up 15%, closure orders for imminent dangers had increased 50%, and extensions to correct violations were down 30% — all indicative of stronger enforcement. And the true test, mine fatalities, were the lowest in history. After two years, I was tired of the job, Although I had excellent relations with the Steelworkers and Operating Engineers safety professionals, the petty and incompetence of the UMWA was wearing thin. On the home front, I needed money for my children's college education.

My final tirade came one afternoon in the office of Jack W. Carlson, Assistant Secretary for Mineral Resources. He refused to approve my directive to open a small two-inspector office in Senator Byrd's home town that he had requested. Yes, it was a waste of money, but Byrd shoveled money at MESA faster that it could be spent. Carlson didn't understand Washington politics. I resigned invective on the spot and told Jack Crawford to establish the office anyway. Then my staff and I went out and got drunk.

---

29 Western cheaper low-sulfur surface coal mines are continuing to replace expensive Eastern underground coal. Wyoming is now the largest coal-producing state. Three-quarters of the coal mines in the U.S. in 1975 have closed and the number of coal miners has dropped from 230,000 to 76,000 during the period. The once powerful UMWA now represents a mere 20,000 miners, who produce less than 20 percent of the nation's coal.

Secretary Morton asked me to stay on until he found a replacement. It took five months. No one wanted the job. I had to convince Robert Barrett, one of MESA's career civil servant coal district managers, to take the job. I left for the private practice of law and later lobbied for the 1977 Mine Act. I never represented a coal company in connection with health and safety issues as a lawyer except for several small coal companies with less than a dozen employees. Most of the major coal companies thought I was an [expletive deleted]; and I believed they had an 1800s-robber baron mentality. I did represent Western hard rock mining companies, which I found to be more progressive and safety conscious.

My two years at MESA was rewarded with many victories that improved mine safety and health and the privilege of working with a group of dedicated MESA employees I could call friends. Those criticizing MESA then and MSHA today should limit their remarks to the political appointees. The caliber of the career employees over the decades cannot be matched for their dedication to the thankless task of making America's mines safe.

I admit to shedding a tear at my going away party after being presented with my portrait and a swivel chair I used in my law office for many years.

EPILOGUE

Sunshine's Sunset

The demise of the Sunshine Mining Company was slow and tortuous after the May 1972 disaster, except during the bizarre manipulated soar of silver prices between 1976 and 1983.

The mine remained closed until mid-December of 1972, seven and one-half months after the fire. Sunshine spent $3 million in repairs and to upgrade safety and meet the Bureau's demands required before it could open and was nearing 80 percent of its normal production when the miners went on strike in March 1973. While the days pay men obtained satisfactory raises of 24 cents per hour and 16 ½ cents in the second and third years, the gypo contract miners paid by the number of feet mined per shift received no increase. As the price of silver had doubled since the fire, Sunshine's position was difficult for the employees to understand. The local Steelworkers union vote of 295 to 5 in favor of a strike that lasted six months.

In 1974 Irwin P. Underweiser was ousted as president at the insistence of the Hecla Mining Co. and the Silver Dollar Mining Co., respectively owners of 33 and 10 percent of the Sunshine Mine. Their dissatisfaction was not only with Underweiser's management of the mine, but the activities of Underweiser and two "New York" board members who were part of the 1969 takeover of the company. The board's vice chairman, Karl J. Schwartzbaum, was indicted and later convicted of making payoffs to officers of a New York furriers union in violation of the Taft-Hartley Act. Francis J. Renkowicz was accused of the misuse of funds for his personal benefit of the Underwriters Bank & Trust Co., of which Underweiser was vice chairman. In 1970, Underweiser and the two had been accused of using corporate funds to finance their personal takeover of Underwriters Bank & Trust. Underweiser and the directors of the Citizens Casualty Co. were also under investigation by the New York State Insurance Department for fraudulently wasting the insurance company's assets. Underweiser was demoted to vice president, but continued to receive a sizeable salary because of the block of stock he controlled. This also allowed his New York law firm to earn five and six figure legal fees from Sunshine.

The price of silver took off, averaging $4.35 in 1976, $4.62 in 1977, and $5.40 in 1978, over tripled the average 1972. The continuing skyrocketing price was in great part thanks to Nelson Bunker Hunt and William Herbert Hunt and their oil-rich Saudi friends. The Hunt brothers used the billions inherited from their legendary Texas oil-man father, H.L. Hunt, in an attempt to corner the silver market. Through their sugar company, Great Western United Corp. (renamed Hunt International Resources Corp.), they sought control of the Sunshine Mining Co. in a nasty proxy fight in 1977 that netted them 28 percent of the stock at a cost of $19.5 million and an agreement to acquire the balance for $15.00 a share totaling $60 million.

It mattered little that the Sunshine Mine had been closed during a year-long strike and the company's net assets were only $27.7 million, nor that its Anchor Post subsidiary's fence manufacturing sales regularly produced over twice the revenue as its mining operations. The Hunts ordered a prompt settlement of the strike and boasted they controlled the nation's largest silver producer. Although they denied it, the brothers were really after Sunshine's most important intangible asset. The Hunts were now qualified as commercial producers and users of silver and thus exempt from trading restrictions applicable to silver futures market speculators.

With their bloc of stock, the Hunts removed the entire board of directors and replaced it with three Hunt International Resources officers and named G. Michael Boswell President, Chairman of the Board, and Chief Executive Officer. The "Texas Boys with their tailor-made suits and blow-dried hair" were different and far better liked than the "New Yorkers" by the employees and shareholders. The entire Silver Valley appreciated the Hunts driving up the price of silver that reached $7.50 in April 1979, when the company held its annual shareholders meeting and released its 1978 annual report. It was the company's first annual report issued in full color and depicted miners underground, including an attractive female — another first. (Upon close inspection her mining clothes did not contain a speck of dirt, she was wearing lipstick, and her fingernails were manicured. She also was probably the only underground miner not wearing a cap lamp when the photo was taken.)

Boswell moved the corporate headquarters to Dallas, Texas, the headquarters of the Hunt Oil Co. where they think big, and literally reinvented the Sunshine Mine. In a brochure sent with the 1978 annual report, he bragged that the Sunshine Mine was the largest silver producer in world history and was actually discovered in 1878, rather than 1884, making it the oldest mine in the Silver Valley and giving it reason to celebrate Sunshine's "One Hundredth Discovery Year." The boast was based on the correspondence of A.J. Prichard, who wrote that he had discovered the "Evolution Lead" claim in 1878, but didn't get around to staking it until 1882 or recording the claim in 1884. [30]

As dubious as Boswell's histrionics were, Prichard's Evolution Lead claim played a major part in Sunshine's history. It was one of the many nearby mining claims purchased by the Sunshine Mining Co. after it was organized in 1918 for the purchase of the Blake brothers' Sunshine Mine. In 1931, 1700 feet below the surface under the Evolution Lead, Sunshine hit a bonanza, a vein of high grade galena-silver up to 23 feet wide. Although the price of silver was regulated at $1.39 an ounce during the Great Depression, it drove Sunshine's stock from 2 ½ cents a share to over $25.00; and the Sunshine Mine was on its way to becoming the nation's largest silver producer.

The Hunt brothers decided to exercise their option to purchase Sunshine's remaining shares in 1979. To their chagrin, they were faced with the treason of Boswell and his two former Hunt International Resources associates on personal and financial grounds. The

---

30 The Evolution Lead was not a "rich body of gold and silver," as claimed by Boswell in the brochure. It was galena, a lead ore consisting primarily of lead sulfide, as Prichard's claim name implies, containing silver and other metals. In addition to silver, the Sunshine Mine produced antimony, copper, zinc, and lead.

traitors were making too much money running the company. The three rallied the shareholders and defeated the tender for the stock and subsequent litigation. The Hunts sold their shares and continued to buy silver futures and silver in the open market, which helped boost the price to an average of $11.11 in 1979 and $20.66 in 1980, when it reached the astronomical high of $48.70 an ounce during a brief buying frenzy. Eventually, the Hunts failed in their asinine attempt to control the world's silver market that cost them an estimated $2 billion.

The price of silver averaged around $10.00 an ounce for three years before dropping to $8.16 an ounce in 1984. Then the price steadily declined, ranging between $4.00 or $5.00, and at times dropping below $4.00 through 2001. Sunshine's losses grew by tens of millions year after year, reaching an annual loss of $115 million in 1990 alone. The company sold its subsidiaries, including the profitable Anchor Post, and Boswell and the other Texans departed the scene. In addition to silver prices that failed to keep up with inflation, mining costs increased drastically. Sunshine also faced untold millions of environmental clean up costs under the Comprehensive Environmental Response, Compensation and Liability Act of 1980 (the "Superfund") and a $43 million bond debt it could not pay. When its stock fell below $1.00 per share, it was delisted by the New York Stock Exchange in March 2000.

The Sunshine Mining Company filed for bankruptcy in August 2000 and closed the Sunshine Mine in February 2001. Its legacy remains that it produced 350 million ounces of silver, more than any other mine in history. In June 2003 the Sterling Mining Company leased the mine in an attempt to raise the silver phoenix from its ashes of despair. It has been a slow progress cutting tunnels to the new vein and installing a secondary escape route, and Sterling hopes to be producing in early 2008.

In March 2006, the price of silver reached a 22-year high of over $10.00 an ounce, which is what life in the silver mines is about — *the price of silver.*

GLOSSARY

Definitions were taken from *A Dictionary of Mining, Mineral, and Related Terms,* compiled and edited by Paul W. Thrush and the Staff of the United States Bureau of Mines. U.S. Government Printing Office (1968). Most definitions contained in the dictionary are extensive, thus only those parts applicable to the text were included.

adit. A horizontal entrance to a mine. The portal.

air door. A door to close the passage of air or direct the air flow by closing part of the air circulation.

back. The roof or upper part of an underground mining cavity.

cap. A plank or timber placed on top of a prop, stull or post. The horizontal roof or top piece of a three-piece timber set used for tunnel support.

country rock. The rock traversed by or adjacent to an ore deposit. The common rock of the region.

crosscut. A tunnel driven through country rock to connect with a vein, lode or drift.

diamond drill. Drill with a hollow diamond-studded bit that cuts a circular channel around a core to provide a continuous and complete columnar sample of the rock penetrated. Diamond drilling is a common method of prospecting for minerals and locating an ore vein.

double-drum hoist. A hoisting device having two cable spools or drums rotating in opposite directions that can be driven in tandem or separately.

drift. A horizontal underground passage. A tunnel. A drift follows a vein, as distinguished from a crosscut, which intersects a vein or a drift.

gob. Waste rock (muck) or rubbish and timbers left in or returned to a mine cavity to support the ground. Also a verb. From the Welsh *goaf.*

grizzly. Steel bars or rails crisscrossed over a chute to prevent oversized rocks from entering the chute and clogging up the chute or a hoist bucket (skip).

grizzly man. A worker who breaks the rocks with a sledge hammer until they are sufficiently small to pass through the grizzly's grid.

headframe. Frame or support at the top of a shaft containing the sheave or pulley for the hoist rope.

jumbo. Self-propelled drill or multiple drills mounted on tires or rails and propelled and powered by compressed air, electric, hydraulic or diesel motors. Sunshine principally used jumbos to mine drifts and crosscuts.

lagging. Wooden planks, sheathing or small timbers placed over caps or behind the posts of the timbering, not to carry the main weight, but to form a ceiling or a wall to prevent rock fragments from falling. Any wooden plank.

level. A main underground roadway or passage driven horizontally to afford access to the stopes or workings and to provide ventilation and haulageways for the removal of ore or waste. Mine workings that are approximately at the same underground elevation.

man car; man train. Mine cars or locomotives fitted with seats for the transport of miners.

muck. Waste rock. Useless material; earth or rock which may or may not be mixed with minerals. Rubbish; soft useless material. (Scot.) Refuse from a mine; to remove such refuse. Miners often refer to any rock blasted down as muck.

nipper. A worker who does odd jobs such as cleaning up and disposing of waste materials and trash.

pocket. A bin or compartment off the shaft with a capacity equal to the size of the skip used to facilitate quick and accurate skip loading. Also a rich deposit of ore as distinguished from a vein of ore.

raise. A vertical or inclined opening driven upward from a level to connect with the level above. Also called a rise. Raises are inclined slightly to follow the dip of the ore vein. Between Sunshine's 200-foot levels, the ladder climb is often 230 or 240 feet in length.

raise climber. Sunshine used Alimak raise climbers, which are essentially platform elevators used to transport miners and equipment up the face of a raise. They are driven by a compressed-air motor on guides bolted to the wall of the raise.

rib. The side of a pillar or the wall.

rockbolt. A steel bar inserted into a drilled hole in the back or rib for the purpose of ground control. They are anchored by expansion, grouting or a wedge to hold in place steel plates or mats to support the rock in place. Also called a roof bolt. Sunshine's rockbolts were four and six feet in length and ¾ inch in diameter.

sand fill. Granulated mine tailings conveyed underground hydraulically to fill and support cavities left after the extraction of ore.

sheave. A wheel with a grooved circumference that guides and supports a cable or rope between the hoist drum and skip.

shifter; shift boss. A foreman in charge of miners on a shift. In metal mining, a foreman in charge of a specific part on the mine. In the Coeur d'Alene Mining District and many other regions, a shifter is boss over a level and reports to a foreman over the production levels.

shoe. Part of a braking mechanism made of wood or steel that contacts the brake flange on a wheel or hoist drum. Also a piece of steel fastened to a mine cage and formed to fit over the guides to guide the cage when it is in motion.

skip. A guided steel hoppit (bucket), usually rectangular, used in vertical or inclined shafts for hoisting ore and waste.

sill. A piece of wood or steel beneath upright timber or steel props to prevent or reduce squeezing. Also the floor of a mine.

slusher. A mechanical dragshovel or scraper loader. A mobile drag scraper capable of elevating the bucket to the dump point.

station. The excavation adjoining the shaft at the different levels. A station often houses first aid supplies, telephone, tools, and the shifter's work bench.

stope. An excavation in which ore is mined in a series of steps in highly inclined or vertical veins. To excavate ore in a vein by driving a series of workings horizontally, one immediately over the other. Each horizontal working is called a stope because when a number of them are in progress they assume the shape of a flight of stairs. The stopes in Sunshine were 100 feet long along the strike of the vein between level intervals of 150 feet on and above the 4000 level and 200 feet long below the 4000. *(Stopes are diagramed in Appendix C.)*

stub drift. A short drift not connected to other workings; a dead end.

stull. A timber prop set between the walls (ribs) of a stope or drift. The top piece of a set of mine timbers.

swamper. A rear brakeman on a train. A laborer who assists in hauling ore and muck by loading and unloading, coupling and uncoupling cars, and throwing switches.

APPENDIX A

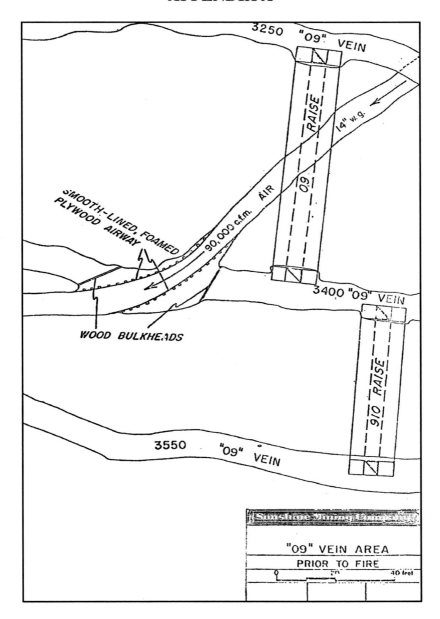

APPENDIX B-1

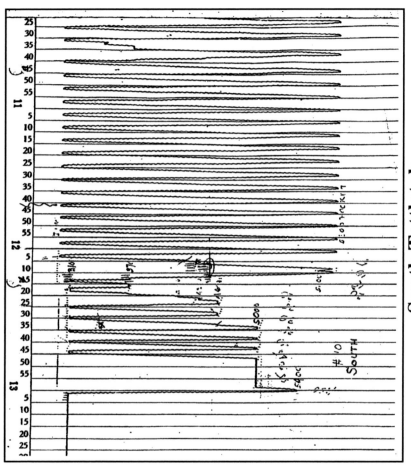

South Tattletale

APPENDIX B-2

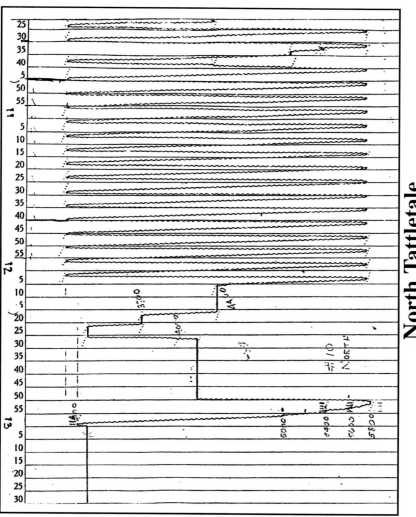

APPENDIX C

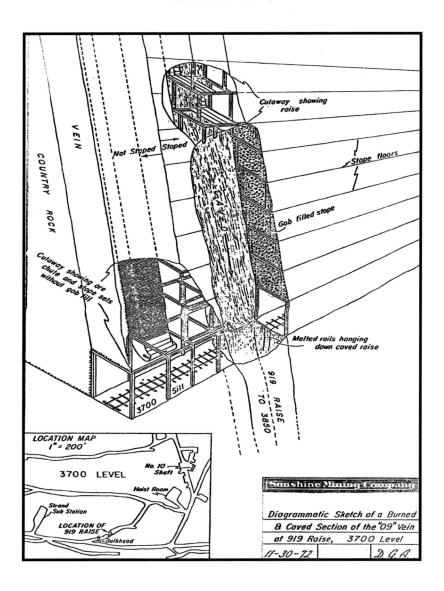

Cutaway showing raise

VEIN

COUNTRY ROCK

Not Stoped   Stoped

Stope floors

Gob filled stope

Cutaway showing ore chute and stope sets without gob fill

Melted rails hanging down caved raise

919 RAISE TO 3850

3700   Sill

LOCATION MAP
1" = 200'

3700 LEVEL

No. 10 Shaft

Hoist Room

Strand Sub Station

LOCATION OF 919 RAISE

Bulkhead

Sunshine Mining Company

Diagrammatic Sketch of a Burned & Caved Section of the "09" Vein at 919 Raise,   3700 Level

11-30-72   D.G.A.

APPENDIX D
BOREHOLE RESCUE TEAM VOLUNTEERS*

Bureau of Mines

Baker, Jack	Tennessee
Brake, E. Levi	Arizona
Castor, Thomas J.	Tennessee
Delimba, Frank	Indiana
Donley, William H.	Utah
Fraser, James A.	Missouri
Grbowski, John	Pennsylvania
Gottschalk, Horst S.	Colorado
Hawkins, John V.	Tennessee
Kanack, Wayne D.	Missouri
Morris, Donald K.	Indiana
Munoz, Michael	Nevada
Murphy, John	Pennsylvania
Pitts, James D.	Arkansas
Povondra, Raymond R.	California
Riley, Robert E.	Utah
Schlagel, John G.	Washington
Weberg, Larry O.	Nevada
Wilson, Roland V.	Washington
Wofford, Charles B.	Missouri
Yenter, Warren M.	Idaho

Sunshine Mining Company

Barton, Thomas	Kellogg, Idaho
Becker, Wilfred	Osburn, Idaho
Klabouch, Milo	Kellogg, Idaho
Nickelby, Richard	Wallace, Idaho
Tiedman, Donald W.	Kellogg, Idaho

Corporations

Campbell, Robert	Westinghouse Electric Co. Baltimore, Maryland
Kravitz, Jeffrey	Westinghouse Electric Co. Baltimore, Maryland
George, David	Westinghouse Georesearch Laboratory Boulder. Boulder, Colorado
Solaegoi, Frank	Reynolds Electric and Engineering Co. Las Vegas, Nevada

---

*Includes support personnel.

APPENDIX E
SUNSHINE MINE DISASTER SURVIVORS

Name	Occupation	Location/Escape Route*
Anderson, Darol A.	Raise Miner	5000 Hoisted to 3100
Baillie, Ernest F.	Drift Miner	5000 Hoisted to 3100
Beare, Jasper W.	Motorman	3700 drift
Beckes, Gary W.	Electrician	3700 Motored and walked
Bennett, Peter L.	Mechanic	3700 08 shop-walked
Bennett, William L.	Mechanic	3700 Hoisted to 3100
Benson, Homer G.	Mechanic	3700 Hoisted to 3100
Bourgard, Leonard R.	Stope Miner	5000 Hoisted to 3100
Breazeal, Richard D.	Mechanic	4400/4500 Hoisted to 3100
Bruhn, Wilber C.	Raise Miner	5000 Hoisted to 3100
Bush, James E.	Prod. Foreman	3700 Walked out— on 3700 rescue attempt
Clapp, Dennis	Stope Miner	4800 Hoisted from 4600 to 3100
Davis, Edward O.	Repairman	3700 drift
Dionne, Harvey	Proj. Foreman	3700 Motored out— on 3700 rescue attempt
Dunlap, Clyde L.	Cager	Jewell shaft
Fenner, James D.	Raise Miner	5000 Hoisted to 3100
Findley, Roger V.	Cager	4400/4500 Hoisted to 3100—aided in the evacuation
Fister, Wayne	Stope Miner	4800 Hoisted from 4600 to 3100
Flory, Ronald R.	Stope Miner	4800 Rescued up #12 borehole
Follette, Robert S.	Stope Miner	5000 Hoisted to 3100

Fowler, Harvelle E.	Warehouseman	3700 Warehouse-walked
Fox, Edward	Grizzlyman	4600 Hoisted to 3100
Gardner, John H.	Mechanic	3700 Hoisted to 3100
Gonzales, Edward R.	Stope Miner	4600 Hoisted from 4400 to 3100
Hansen, Larry E.	Stope Miner	4000 Climbed to 3700 Jewell
Harris, Wilber	Mechanic	4400/4500 Hoisted to 3100
Hawkins, Larry	Sampler	3700 Jewell—on 3100 rescue crew
Henry, John	Grizzlyman	4800 Hoisted from 4600 to 3100
Jerome, Terrance M.	Raise Miner	4600 Hoisted to 3100
Kienholz, Ernie E.	Stope Miner	4800 Hoisted from 4600 to 3100
Kitchen, Delmar J.	Raise Miner	5000 Hoisted to 3100
Koisti, Roger	Raise Miner	4600 Hoisted to 3100
Lamphere, James A.	Oiler	3700 Hoisted to 3100
Lovesee, Jasper C.	Drift Miner	5000 Hoisted to 3100
Macartney, Robert M.	Raise Miner	5000 Hoisted to 3100
Markve, Howard J.	Stope Miner	5000 Hoisted to 3100
Mathews, Robert L.	Motorman	3700 drift
McCoy, Robert F.	Grizzlyman	5000 Hoisted to 3100
McDaniel, Remos P.	Drift Miner	4800 Hoisted from 4600 to 3100
McGillivary, Charles W.	Stope Miner	5000 Hoisted to 3100
McKeen, William F.	Motorman	3700 Hoisted to 3100
McKinney, Richard F.	Repairman	Jewell shaft topside
Mendy, Harold	Motorman	4600 Hoisted to 3100
Mendy, Reuben	Motorman	4600 Hoisted to 3100
Mitchell, William	Stope Miner	4400 Hoisted to 3100

Morris, Robert E.	Stope Miner	4800 Hoisted from 4600 to 3100
Mossburgh, Leslie M.	Mechanic	3700 Hoisted to 3100
Napier, Clyde	Mechanic	3700 Hoisted to 3100
Nickelby, Richard L.	Repairman	3700 Walked— on 3700 rescue attempt
Norris, Frank D.	Raise Miner	4600 Hoisted to 3100
Olson, Henry G.L.	Repairman	2300 Jewell shaft
Oman, Birdeen	Repairman	Jewell shaft
Osterberg, Gordon M.	Motorman	4600 Hoisted to 3100
Ostoj, Robert L.	Raise Miner	4600 Hoisted to 3100
Pederson, Einer	Repairman	2300 Jewell shaft
Perkins, Robert L.	Mechanic	3100 Jewell shaft. Hoisted from 1900 to surface
Peterson, Clifford R.	Repairman	Jewell shaft topside
Peterson, George R.	Cager	4400 Hoisted to 3100
Reardon, John F.	Mechanic	3700 Jewell shaft
Rihtarshik, Lando	Motorman	5000 Hoisted to 3100
Riley, Kenneth A.	Stope Miner	5000 Hoisted to 3100
Robles, Gilbert**	Motorman	3100 Assisted motorman during the evacuation
Ross, Kenneth B.	Geologist	3700 Jewell shaft
Sabala, Tony J.	Pipe fitter	3700 Hoisted to 3100
Seagraves, Jack M.	Stope Miner	4000 Climbed to 3700 Jewell
Sheppard, James E.	Stope Miner	4800 Hoisted from 4600 to 3100
Schulz, Byron L.	Cager	5600 Hoisted to 3100–acted as cager during evacuation
Sliger, Ira F.	Hoistman	3100 Hoist room–rode
Smith, Alfred E.	Motorman	3100 Ran train during evacuation

Stanley, Clarence B.	Mechanic	3700 Hoisted to 3100
Stansbury, Ronald H.	Motorman	3700 drift–on 3700 rescue attempt
Stevenson, Isaac D.	Stope Miner	5000 Hoisted to 3100
Story, Marcellus E.	Mechanic	3700 Hoisted to 3100
Strand, Floyd W.	Elect. Foreman	3700 Jewell shaft
Tucker, Kenneth W.	Mechanic	3700 08 shop-walked
Ulrich, Norman R.	Electrician	3700 Rode out–on 3700 rescue attempt
Watts, Thomas D.	Drift Miner	5000 Hoisted to 3100
Wells, Gary D.	Cager	Jewell shaft
Wilber, Kenneth B.	Cager	Jewell shaft–on 3700 rescue attempt
Wilkinson. Thomas R.	Stope Miner	4800 Rescued up #12 borehole
Williams, John L.	Electrician	3700 Hoisted to 3100
Zingler, James D.	Repairman	Jewell shaft topside–on 3100 rescue crew

---

*Location when fire discovered. Accurate records of whether the survivors walked or rode the muck train to the 3100 Jewell shaft station are not available.

**Robles not listed in Bureau Final Report.

APPENDIX F
SUNSHINE MINE DISASTER VICTIMS

Name	Age	Occupation	Location/ Traveled
Alexander, Robert H.	50	Stope Miner	5200
Allen, Billy W.	24	Raise Miner	5200
Allen, Wayne L.	39	Drift Miner	5600 Hoisted to 3100
Allison, Richard M.	37	Drift Miner	4800
Anderson, Arnold E.	48	Lead Electrician	3700 Hoisted to 3400 to turn off fans
Anderson, Robert, L.	37	Shift Boss	5000
Armijo, Joe E.	38	Stope Miner	5000 Hoisted to 3100
Barber, Benjamin S.	31	Shaft Repairman	4400 Hoisted to 3700
Barker, Robert E.	42	Shaft Repairman	4400 Hoisted to 3700
Bebb, Virgil F.	53	Shift Boss	4600 Hoisted to 3100 to help evacuation
Beehner, Donald G.	38	Nipper	3700 Hoisted to 3100–on rescue try
Bewley, Richard D.	40	Motorman	4800
Birchett, George W.	40	Stope Miner	4600 Hoisted from 4400 to 3700
Blalack, Wayne	35	Electrician	3700 Walked out drift to help evacuation
Bush, Robert A.	47	Production Foreman	3700 Walked out drift to help evacuation
Byington, Floyd L.	35	Stope Miner	4600 Hoisted from 4400 to 3700

Case, Clarence L.	55	Shift Boss	5200
Casteel, Charles L.	30	Shift Boss	4600 Hoisted to 3100 to help evacuation
Croker, Kevin A.	29	Repairman	4800 Climbed to 4400
Crow, Duwain D.	39	Drift Miner	5600 Hoisted to 3100
Davenport, Roderick	35	Stope Miner	4600 Hoisted from 4400 to 3700
Davis, John W.	28	Diamond Driller	4200
Delbridge, Richard L.	24	Stope Miner	5200
Delbridge, William R.	55	Stope Miner	5200
Diaz, Roberto	55	Motorman	3700 Attempted to rescue fallen miners
Dionne, Gregory G.	23	Pipe Fitter	3700 Hoisted to 3100–cager during evacuation
Don Carlos, Carter M.	47	Repairman	5200
Fee, Norman S.	27	Motorman Helper	5000 Hoisted to 3100
Findley, Lyle M.	30	Repairman	5200
Firkins, Donald K.	37	Drift Miner	5400 Hoisted to 3100
Fleshman, Howard L.	28	Stope Miner	5000 Hoisted to 3100
Follette, William L.	23	Raise Miner	5400 Hoisted to 3100
Garcia, Richard	56	Stope Miner	5200
George, Richard G.	20	Motorman Helper	5200
Goff, Robert W.	35	Stope Miner	5000 Hoisted to 3100

Goos, Louis W.	51	Raise Miner	5400 Hoisted to 3100
Guertner, John P.	54	Repairman	5200
Hanna, William F.	47	Pump Man	5600 Hoisted to 3100
Harrison, Howard	34	Drift Miner	4400
Hobson, Patrick M.	57	Mechanic	3700 Walked out drift to help evacuation
House, Melvin L.	41	Repairman	5200
Hudson, Merle E.	47	Stope Miner	5000
Ivers, Jack B.	44	Stope Miner	4600 Hoisted from 4400 to 3700
Johnson Fred E. (Gene)	45	Shaft Foreman	3700 Hoisted to 3100–led the evacuation
Johnson, Paul E.	47	Shift Boss	3700 Attempted to rescue fallen miners
Johnson, Wayne L.	43	Repairman	5000 Hoisted to 3100
Johnston, James M.	20	Motorman Helper	5200
Keough, Custer L.	59	Repairman	3400
Kester, Sherman C.	60	Trackman	5200
Kitchen, Dewellyn E.	31	Stope Miner	5000 Hoisted to 3100
Kitchen, Elmer E.	54	Shaft Miner	5600 Hoisted to 3100
La Voie, Kenneth C.	29	Repairman	5200
Lynch, Richard M.	24	Motorman	5000 Hoisted to 3100
McLachlan, Donald J.	23	Motorman	5200
McNutt, Delbert J.	48	Motorman	5600 Hoisted to 3100

Moore, James C.	29	Repairman	5200
Mullin, David J.	34	Stope Miner	4800
Naccarato, Joe R.	40	Raise Miner	5400 Hoisted to 3100
Nelson, Orlin W.	32	Stope Miner	4200
Norris, Richard D.	24	Raise Miner	5200
Orr, Donald R.	50	Stope Miner	5200
Patrick, Hubert B.	45	Drift Miner	4800
Pena, Casey	52	Shaft Miner	5600 Hoisted to 3100
Peterson, John W.	57	Motorman	4400
Phillips, Francis W.	42	Repairman	5200
Puckett, Irvan L.	51	Shaft Repairman	4400
Rais, Floyd A.	61	Pump Man	5800 Hoisted to 3100*
Rathbun, Leonard D.	29	Stope Miner	4600 Hoisted from 4400 to 3700
Rawson, John R.	27	Drift Miner	5400 Hoisted to 3100
Reichert, Jack L.	45	Hoistman	4400 Hoisted to 3700
Rhoads, Delbert C.	57	Lead Mechanic	4400 Hoisted to 3700 then 3400 to turn off fans
Rossiter, Glen R.	37	Motorman	5400 Hoisted to 3100
Russell, Paul M.	37	Stope Miner	4200
Salyer, Gene F.	54	Repairman	5800 Hoisted to 3100*
Salyer, James P.	51	Drift Foreman	3700
Sargent, Allen L.	38	Drift Miner	4400
Scanlan, Robert B.	38	Hoistman	3100 In hoist room

Serano, John	37	Stope Miner	5200
Sharette, Nick D.	48	Shaft Miner	5800 Hoisted to 3100
Sisk, Frankie R.	31	Stope Miner	4600 Climbed to 4400
Stephens, Darrell E.	20	Motorman Helper	4800
Thor, Gustav G.	38	Stope Miner	4600 Hoisted from 4400 to 3700
Truelock, Grady D.	40	Raise Miner	5400 Hoisted to 3100
Waldvogel, Robert E.	50	Stope Miner	4400
Walty, William R.	29	Repairman	3400
Whatcott, Gordon	37	Stope Miner	4800
Wiederrick, Douglas L.	37	Shaft Miner	5800 Hoisted to 3100
Wilson, Ronald L.	41	Drift Miner	4800
Wilson, William E.	28	Hoistman	5800 Hoisted to 3100*
Wolff, John D.	49	Stope Miner	5200
Wood, Don B.	53	Hoistman	3700

---

* The Bureau and Sunshine records are confusing and contradictory as to where the shaft crew was working in the shaft and there are no surviving witnesses, although it is known that Wiederrick and others were on the 5800 shaft level when hoisted.

END NOTES

General

The principal source for *The Price of Silver* is a four-drawer file cabinet containing copies of the Department of the Interior's official and non-official records of the Sunshine Mine disaster that has been waiting for me in my study for over thirty years. Included are depositions of Sunshine miners, rescue crews, and Sunshine's management taken after the fire broke out; transcripts of public hearings conducted in Kellogg, Idaho, between July 18 and 26, 1972, and in Coeur d'Alene, Idaho, during May 14 through 16, 1973; and thousands pages of exhibits, photographs, mine maps, and Bureau of Mines and Sunshine Mine Company memoranda. The Mine Safety Appliances Company and Westinghouse Electric Corporation official's testimony and data were also invaluable. Unofficial sources included Bureau internal reports and memoranda, personal log of Bureau Director Dr. Elburt F. Osborn, daily reports of Bureau Assistant Director for Metal and Nonmetal Mine Health and Safety Stanley M. Jarrett, and personal records of Deputy Assistant Secretary for Mineral Resources John B. Rigg, Sr.

Extensive references were made to the Bureau's "Final Report of Major Mine Fire Disaster Sunshine Mine, Sunshine Mining Company, Kellogg, Shoshone County, Idaho, May 2, 1972," released February 14, 1973; the Bureau's "Preliminary Report-" dated June 19, 1972; and the author's "Report on the Sunshine Mine Disaster of May 2, 1972" issued by the Office of Hearing and Appeals, Department of the Interior, dated March 22, 1976.

Background and personal information on the miners were taken from depositions, testimony at the hearing, and the author's personal conversations, as distinguished from formal interviews.

Distances expressed in feet and descriptions of the mine shops and levels are from personal observation and mine maps. References to cubic feet per minute air flows were taken from the "Ventilation Survey)Sunshine Mine" by Bureau mining engineers, Ralph K. Foster and J. Warren Andrews, performed September 14 through October 4, 1971.

Numerous insights into press relations were taken from Helm, Lewis M. *Informing the Public: A Public Affairs Handbook.* New York: Longman, 1981, pgs. 218-227. Helm devoted a chapter titled: "Sunshine Mine: Handling the Media in a Disaster."

Repetitive footnotes and end note references to the depositions, hearing transcripts, and the Bureau's and author's reports were eliminated in depicting the fire and evacuation to make Chapters 2 through 17 more readable and conserve space.

Chapter 1 Gold's Poor Stepsister

Gold and silver prices are Englehard industrial bullion quotes from the *Wall Street Journal,* March 24, 2006. In *United States v. Gear,* 42 U.S. (3 How.) 120 (1945), the Supreme Court ruled that prospectors and miners were trespassers on public lands. The General Mining Law of 1872 quote on extralateral rights was from 30 U.S.C. § 26. References to lode and placer claims are from 30 U.S.C. §§ 23, 35, and 36. The history of silver, Coeur d'Alene mining region, mining, and coinage were derived from the following:

Lenon, Robert. *Western Mining.* Norman: Univ. of Oklahoma Press, 1970, pgs. 141-142

Mall, Loren L. *Public Land and Mining Law* 3rd ed. Seattle: Butterworth (Legal Publishers), 1981, pgs. 174-179.

Rickard, Thomas A. *A History of American Mining.* New York: McGraw-Hill, 1932, pgs. 318-322.

Ridgeway, James. *Who Owns the Earth.* New York: Macmillan, 1980, pgs. 133-135.

Wallace, Robert. *The Miners.* New York: Time-Life Books, 1976, pgs. 32-37.

Watkins, T. H. *Gold and Silver in the West.* New York: Crown Publishers, 1981, pgs. 87-90.

Yeoman, R.S. *1997 Handbook of United States Coins* 54th ed. Racine: Golden Books Publishing, 1997, pgs. 112-121.

Sunshine Mine history and financial figures were taken from the Sunshine Mining Co. Annual Reports of 1971 and 1978; *Wall*

Street Journal, Apr. 18, 1974; and Scott, Rachel. *Muscle and Blood.* New York: E.P. Dutton, 1974, pgs. 216-217.

Chapter 2 Tuesday, May 2, 1972

On June 5, 2003, the Discovery Channel aired "Critical Rescue" depicting the Sunshine Mine disaster. It concentrated on the rescue of Ron Flory and Tom Wilkinson and its factual accounts were dubious when compared to the evidence. Nevertheless, two interviews were useful. In his deposition, Ben Sheppard stated that he smelled smoke and passed it off as someone smoking the night before the fire was discovered. In his TV interview thirty-two years later, he said that Ray Rudd, his shifter, had just lit a cigarette, which explains why the miner did not report the smoke. In characterizing the thoughts of Robert Launhardt, Sunshine safety engineer, when he saw smoke coming from the exhaust air tunnel, I quoted his interview that it "sent a chill up his spine."

Time is of the Essence was based on the author's personal experience in the Sunshine Mine on July 22, 1972.

Chapter 3 Evacuation

Ira Sliger's background was taken in part from Scott's *Muscle and Blood,* pg. 205.

Self Rescuers was based on the testimony of Dr. Frank W. Smith, Harry N. Cotabish, and Robert Merkle of the Mine Safety Appliances Company (MSA), who volunteered to explain the proper use of self-rescuers and the consequences of improper use and lack of training. Their candid testimony shocked and held the audience in awe. Data was also taken from MSA instruction booklets.

Carbon Monoxide was based on the following:
Joseph V. Rodricks. *Calculated Risks: The Toxicity and Human Health Risks of Chemicals in Our Human Environment.* Cambridge, England: Cambridge University Press, 1992, pgs. 86-89. John Harte, Cheryl Holden, Richard Schneider, and Christine Shirley. *Toxics A to Z: A Guide to Everyday Pollution Hazards.* Berkeley: Univ. of California Press, 1992, pgs. 257-259. Bernard Knight. *Simpson's Forensic Medicine* 11th Ed. New York: Oxford Univ. Press, 1997, pgs. 199-201.

Chapter 10 Wednesday, May 3, 1972

The Bureau's penalty assessment fiasco was based on the author's experience. Records of the Bureau and Mining Enforcement and Safety Administration (MESA), which took over the Bureau's mine health and safety functions in 1973, were consulted.

Material on W. Carl Griner and the State of Idaho was based on the transcripts of his testimony before the House of Representative's Select Subcommittee on Labor, Committee on Education and Labor on July 31, 1972; Bureau and MESA records; and the *Spokesman-Review* (Spokane, Washington), May 5, 1972.

Newspaper sources were: *Spokane Daily Chronicle* (AP and UPI credits), Bill Morlin "Hope Said 'Good,'" May 3, 1972, and Dean Lokken and Wafford Conrad, "Fate of Miners Is Still Unknown," May 4, 1972. Leverett Richards, "Interior Chief Morton, Idaho Governor at Mine Disaster Scene," *The Oregonian*, May 4, 1972. Tom Burnett, "Search Continues for Trapped Miners," *Spokesman-Review* (AP credit), May 4, 1972. Felix Belair, Jr. "Mine in Idaho Got Safety Warnings," *New York Times* (AP credit), May 4, 1972. Leroy F. Aarons, "24 Dead, 58 Trapped In Idaho Mine," *Washington Post* (AP credit), May 4, 1972. "24 Dead, 58 Trapped In Sunshine Mine Fire," *The Wallace Miner,* May 4,1972.

Chapter 11 Thursday, May 4, 1972

Spokesman-Review articles dated May 5, 1972, included: Kent Swigard, "Miners Review Safety Plans," Stefanie Pettit and Tom Burnett, "Death Toll is 32; 50 Still Trapped;" Jerry Wigen, "Nader Criticizes Mining Safety Act;" and Launhardt quote by Staff Writer. *Northern Idaho Press* (Wallace, Idaho), (Underweiser quotes), May 5, 1972. Chuck Rehberg and Bill Morlin, "Mine Toll at 32; 50 Still Missing," *Spokane Chronicle,* May 5, 1972. Leroy F. Adams, "8 More Bodies Found in Idaho Mine," *Washington Post,* May 5, 1972. Steven V. Roberts, "Death Toll Is Now 32 in Silver Mine Fire," *New York Times,* May 5, 1972.

Chapter 12 Friday, May 5, 1972

Igor Davis, London Express Service, "Diary of a Miner's Survival," *Washington Daily News,* May 12, 1972. Tom Burnett, "Mine Toll Reaches 35, 3 More Bodies Found," *Spokesman-Review,* May 6, 1972. Jack Roberts, "Depression was Enemy of Survivors,"

Spokesman-Review, May 10, 1972. Carole Barnes, "Mood Somber," *Spokane Daily Chronicle,* May 6, 1972. Jan Davis, "Vigil Maintained," *Spokane Daily Chronicle,* May 6, 1972. Doug Floyd, "Rescue Crews Near Key Shaft in Mine," *Spokane Daily Chronicle,* May 6, 1972. *Northern Idaho Press* (Staff and UPI), "Crews Hope to Reach Miners Sunday Morning," May 6, 1972.

Chapter 13 Saturday, May 6, 1972

Tom Burnett and Stefanie Pettit, "TV Probe Begun by Rescue Crews," *Spokesman-Review,* May 7, 1972. Goodyear Tire & Rubber, *Spokesman-Review* (AP), May 7,1972. Rick Zaher, "Miner Tells of Escaping, Raps Safety," *Spokesman-Review,* May 7, 1972. Chuck Rehberg, "Two Rescued Miners Recount Ordeal," *Spokane Daily Chronicle,* May 10, 1972. Tom Burnett, "Mine Hunt Goes On for 40 Missing Men," *Spokesman-Review,* May 11, 1972. Helm, *Informing the People,* pg. 225.

Chapter 14 Sunday, May 7, 1972

Kent Swigard, "Power Fails, Mine Rescue Plans Stall," *Spokesman-Review,* May 8, 1972. Jack Mayne (AP), "Increased Smoke Hits 3700 Level" and "Sunshine Chief Sees About 2 Months Close," *Kellogg Evening News,* May 8, 1972. Carole Barnes (AP), "Bad Luck Dogs Rescue Workers At Sunshine," *Kellogg Evening News,* May 8, 1972. Steven V. Roberts, "Danger of Flash Fire Ruled Out Before 35 Die in Silver Mine," *New York Times,* May 8, 1972. "Disaster Could Jolt Area Economy" and "Union Will Seek Probe of Disaster," *Spokesman-Review,* May 8, 1972. "Nader Aide Asks for Investigation" and "Lack of Union Role Cited in Disaster," *Spokane Daily Chronicle,* May 8, 1972. Mathis Chaznov (UPI), "58 Now Reported Missing in Mine," *Washington Star,* May 8, 1972. "Mine Tragedy May Result in Increased Silver Price," *Spokesman-Review,* May 9, 1972. "Sunshine Stock Takes Beating," *North Idaho Press,* May 10, 1972. "Critical Rescue," Discovery Channel, (mine rescue crewman cried), June 5, 2003. Helm, *Informing the People,* pg. 224.

Chapter 15 Monday, May 8, 1972

Chuck Rehberg and Doug Floyd, "Rescue Crews Pushing Effort," *Spokane Daily Chronicle,* May 9, 1972. Chuck Rehberg, Bill Morgan and Doug Floyd, "Hope Fading at Mine; Blaze said Intensifying,"

Spokane Daily Chronicle, May 9, 1972. Jerry McGinn (UPI), "Reporter Poses as Red Cross Worker," *Northern Idaho Press,* May 9, 1972. "Price of Silver Continues to Rise," *Northern Idaho Press,* May 9, 1972. Leroy F. Aarons, "Rescue Hopes Dim; Count of Missing Miners Rises to 58," *Washington Post,* May 9, 1972.

Chapter 16 Tuesday, May 9, 1972

Chuck Rehberg, "Two Rescued Miners Account Ordeal," *Spokane Daily Chronicle,* May 10, 1972. Chuck Rehberg and Doug Floyd, "Fate of 44 Remains in Doubt After Rescue of 2 Miners," *Spokane Daily Chronicle,* May 10, 1972. "Hospital Activates Plan," *Spokane Daily Chronicle,* May 10, 1972. Jack Roberts, "Depression was Enemy of Survivors," *Spokesman-Review,* May 10, 1972. Kent Swigard, "Relatives, Friends Joyous as Rescued Men Emerge," *Spokesman-Review,* May 10, 1972. Stefanie Pettit, "Overjoyed Families Greet men After Week's Ordeal," *Spokesman-Review,* May 10, 1972.

Chapter 17 Wednesday and Thursday, 10 and 11, 1972

"Andrus Joins Vigil for Miners," Northern Idaho Press," May 10, 1972. "Mine Hearing Ahead," *Spokesman-Review,* May 10, 1972. Tom Burnett, "Mine Hunt Goes On for 40 Missing Men," *Spokesman-Review,* May 11, 1972. "Mines' Inspection Planned," *Spokesman-Review,* May 11, 1972. Chuck Rehberg and Doug Floyd, "14 Added to Toll at Mine," *Spokane Daily Chronicle,* May 11, 1972. Dean Lokken and Wafford Conrad, "Bodies in Mine, Removal Grim Job," *Spokane Daily Chronicle,* May 12, 1972. Ken Connaughton, "Last 40 Bodies Found, Final Mine Toll is 91," *Washington Post,* May 12, 1972. Tom Burnett and Stefanie Pettit, "Mine Toll Reaches 91, Search Ends," *Spokesman-Review,* May 12, 1972. Richard Charnock, "Fate Catches Up to Veteran Miner," *Spokane Daily Chronicle,* May 12, 1972.

The Last Word. Tom Burnett, "Battle Against Mine Fire May Last Many Weeks," *Spokesman-Review,* May 14, 1972.

Chapter 18 Public Hearings

Mine Disasters and Politics was derived from MSHA Web site www.msha.gov/MSHAINFO "History of Mine Safety and Health

Legislation" and "Historical Data on Mine Disasters in the United States," June 8, 2003; and Fox, William F. *Federal Regulation of Energy,* Colorado Springs: Shepard's/McGraw-Hill, 1993, pgs. 665-667. Barry Newman, "Silver Mine Disaster Prompts Fight on Laws Tightening Safety Rules, *Wall Street Journal,* October 26, 1972. "Five More Bodies Found in West Virginia Mine," *Washington Post* (UPI), May 12, 1972.

The Hearing sources included the hearing transcripts and newspaper articles: Carole Barns, "Mine inspector says Kellogg warning system out of date," *Kellogg Evening News* (AP), July 19, 1972. Chuck Rehberg, "Official Defends Mine-Death Quiz," *Spokane Daily Chronicle,* July 20, 1972. Stefanie Pettit, "U.S. Mine Inspectors Testify," *Spokesman-Review,* July 19, 1972. Stefanie Pettit, "Union Chief Hits Safety Practices," *Spokesman-Review,* July 26, 1972.

Interim Report was taken from the author's "Interim Report of the Sunshine Mine Disaster of May 2, 1972," dated October 27, 1972, and newspaper articles: Stan Benjamin, "Hazardous Mines Rapped by Official," *Washington Post,* November 11, 1972. "Poor Industry, Federal Safety Practice Cited in Sunshine Mine Disaster Fatal to 91," *Wall Street Journal,* November 13, 1972.

Chapter 19　Switching Positions

Bureau Final Report included rulemaking notice published in the *Federal Register* at 37 Fed. Reg. 26,379-26,380 (December 9, 1972).

May 1973 Hearing was taken from the hearing transcript, the author's notes taken at the hearing, interview with Richard V. Backley, and the following newspaper articles: Bill Morlin, "Mine Explanation Challenged," *Spokane Daily Chronicle,* May 14, 1973. Bill Morlin, "Mine Fire Seen as "Man-Caused," *Spokane Daily Chronicle,* May 15, 1973. "Sunshine Mine Fire Cause, Death Toll Said Not Related," *Spokesman-Review,* May 15, 1973. Kent Swigard, "Spontaneous Combustion Theory Hit," *Spokesman-Review,* May 16, 1973. "Long-Smoldering Mine Fire Theory," *Coeur d'Alene Press,* May 16, 1973. Bill Morlin, "Mine Fire Cause Argued at Inquiry," *Spokane Daily Chronicle,* May 16, 1973. Kent Swigard, "U.S. Holds to Sunshine Mine View," *Spokesman- Review,* May 16, 1973. Kent Swigard, "Mine Rules Before Fire Are Target," *Spokesman-Review,* May 17, 1973.

The Court's Verdict: *Helen House v. Mine Safety Appliances,* CA 1-73-50 (October 19. 1978). [Not reported.]

Chapter 20 Post Mortem

Failure to Monitor the Mine Atmosphere: 43 Fed Reg. 40,766 and 40,789 (1978); 44 Fed. Reg. 48,490- 48,509 (1979).

Chapter 21 MESA

Jim Moran, "U.S. Seeks Control of Miners' Union," *Washington Post,* May 9, 1972. Don Stillman, "James Day to Head MESA; Schlick No. 2." *United Mine Workers Journal,* August 15-31, 1973. Drew Von Bergen of UPI, "Miners Gaining Voice," *Lexington Herald,* August 17, 1973. Ward Sinclair, "Nixon names his choice for Mines Bureau Chief," *Louisville Courier-Journal,* August 19, 1973. Ward Sinclair, "New U.S. mine-safety-chief calls enforcement 'a mess'," *Louisville Courier-Journal,* September 13, 1972. "Mine Job Hanging," *Washington Star,* May 20, 1974. Nicholas P. Chironis, "Jim Day's MESA . . . A Dynamic organization expanding its functions in health and safety," *Coal Age,* November 1974. James M. Day, "Status of Federal Mine Health and Safety Programs," *Mining Congress Journal*, February 1975.

Labor Relations. Freese, Barbara. *Coal: A Human History.* Cambridge: Perseus, 2003, pgs. 179-180.

Epilogue–Sunshine's Sunset

"Sunshine Silver Mine Ready To Resume Operations," *Mining Record* (Denver), December 20, 1972. "Sunshine Expects Full Output Soon," *Wallace Miner,* January 18, 1973. "Sunshine Strikers Plan To Hold Out on Issues," *Mining Record,* April 4, 1973. "Sunshine Omits 3 Directors For Reelection) Investigating 2," *Mining Record,* April 5, 1973. "Operations At Sunshine Mine Halted By Strike," *Wallace Miner,* May 15, 1973. "Strike Vote Due," *Spokesman-Review,* May 15, 1973. "$3 Million Improvements Give Sunshine 'Safest' Tag," *Spokesman-Review,* August 14, 1973. "Sunshine Mining Co. Ex-Officer Convicted In Fur Payoff," *Wall Street Journal,* April 5, 1974. "Sunshine Mining Co. Names C.E. Nelson Its New President," *Wall Street Journal,* April 18, 1974.

Other sources included: Harry Hurt III. *Texas Rich: The Hunt Dynasty from the Early Oil Days through the Silver Crash,* New

York: W.W. Norton, 1987, pgs. 363, 396-397. Sunshine Mining Co. Annual Reports: 1971, 1972, 1973, 1977, 1978, 1990, 1999, and 2000. Sunshine Mining Co. Securities and Exchange Commission Form 10 K (April 26, 2000), Form 10 Q (September 30, 2001), and Form 8K (February 14, 2003.) Sterling Mining Co. Press Release (June 11, 2003).

Silver prices were obtained from The Silver Institute, Comex Spot Settlement, *www.silverinstitute.org/price*, and *Wall Street Journal,* March 24, 2006 (Silver hits a 22-year high).

Ron Flory being led out of the mine by a doctor and paramedic after being trapped for nine days 4,800 feet underground.

Thomas Wilkinson emerging from the cage on the 3,700 foot level that raised him 1,100 feet up a four-foot borehold after being trapped underground for nine days.

Entrance to the Electrical Shop on the 3,700 level where smoke was first detected.

Rescue crews of Sunshine miners preparing to enter mine.

Double drum hoist room on the 3,100 foot level.

Stench Warning System.

Sunshine miners and Bureau of Mines inspector in the surface machine shop issuing self-contained breathing apparatus to rescue crews.

The author after coming out of the Sunshine Mine.

Photo credit:
Pages 258-263
Gene Rapp,
Mine Safety and
Health Administration

Families and friends waiting for news of the missing miners in the mine yard.

Sunshine Mine. On the right is the Jewell shaft headframe and sheave wheel.

Other books by James M. Day

The Black Giant

Trade Paper 146 pages
Isbn: 1-893157-01-6
$14.95

The discovery of the Black Giant in 1930 was the largest oil strike in the United States. Its gushers changed the race of the oil industry. A conman found to much oil. During the depression, tens of thousands streamed into east Texas engendering the biggest oil boom in history, cutthroat wars between big oil and small independent oilman. This book reveals the history of the H.L. Hunt, the first oil billionaire and the oil industry shenanigans. Based on documented history this book will expose the oil industry workings. A "must" read for every Texan and those who love or hate the "Big Oil."

TO ORDER
CALL 800-729-4131
OR VISIT
www.nohoax.com

What Every American Should Know about the Mid East and Oil

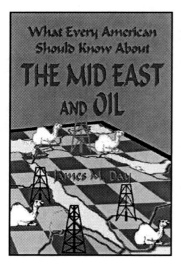

Trade Paper 304 pages
Isbn: 096401047X
$16.95

This guide to the mysterious history and politics of the Middle East will help Americans decipher the latest diplomatic delusions of their President, Congress and the U.S. State Department, untangle the rationale for Palestinian terrorists bombs in the West Bank and Israeli jets strafing civilians in Lebanon, it explains why your sons and daughters are still in the Middle East so you can have oil.

The Western colonial powers created the boundaries in the Middle East, without regard to the religion, culture or ethnic background of the people, for selfish reasons after World War I – power and oil. America has failed to wield its influence in the region because of its political leaders myopic support of Israel and failure to understand and/or refusal to admit to the complex regional issues. As a result, America is now part of the problem rather than offering an equitable solution and is in danger of losing its superpower leverage.

Saddam Hussein scoffs at Americas impotent threats, Iran sneers at the Great Satans sanctions and Saudi Arabia has no faith in our promises. A recent Israeli newspaper reported that Binyamin Netanyahu owns the U.S. Congress. Will tiny Palestine and oil be Americas downfall?

Machiavellian perceptive, irreverently witty and an enjoyable read, this book provides invaluable insights into the volatile Mid East and world oil for the serious student as well as the host or hostess at their next cocktail party including why gasoline cost over $3.00 a gallon.

TO ORDER
CALL 800-729-4131
OR VISIT
www.nohoax.com

To order a catalog
call 800-729-4131
or visit
www.nohoax.com

Printed in the United States
81719LV00002B/223-300